Meeting the Standards in Primary English

4 wk
2 std left

This straightforward guide to the professional standards and requirements for primary teachers illustrates the best ways of developing knowledge and how to acquire the skills needed to achieve QTS.

Meeting the Standards in Primary English will:

- help you to understand the Standards relating to English teaching;
- link the theory associated with the teaching of English to the practical application;
- look in detail at the teaching of reading, fiction, writing, speaking and listening, ICT in literacy and drama;
- assist you with your understanding of grammar and language study;
- consider issues of continuing professional development.

This practical guide to meeting the Standards is invaluable for students on primary training courses, lecturers and mentors supporting trainees in English education programmes, and newly qualified teachers (NQTs).

Eve English is a lecturer in English and Course Leader of the PGCE Primary Course in the School of Education at Durham University. **John Williamson** is Senior Lecturer in English and Director of ITT in the School of Education at Newcastle University.

Meeting the Standards Series

Series Editor:
Lynn D. Newton, School of Education, University of Durham, Leazes Road, Durham, DH1 1TA

Meeting the Standards in Primary English
Eve English and John Williamson

Meeting the Standards in Primary Mathematics
Tony Brown

Meeting the Standards in Primary Science
Lynn D. Newton

Meeting the Standards in Primary ICT
Steve Higgins and Nick Packard

Meeting the Standards in Secondary English
Michael Fleming, Frank Hardman, David Stevens and John Williamson

Meeting the Standards in Secondary Maths
Howard Tanner and Sonia Jones

Meeting the Standards in Secondary Science
Lynn D. Newton

Meeting the Standards for Using ICT for Secondary Teaching
Steve Kennewell

Meeting the Standards in Primary English

A Guide to the ITT NC

Eve English and John Williamson

With contributions from Sue Beverton, James Crinson, George English, Frank Hardman, Steve Higgins and Nick Packard

 RoutledgeFalmer
Taylor & Francis Group

LONDON AND NEW YORK

First published 2005 by RoutledgeFalmer
2 Park Square, Milton Park, Abingdon, Oxon, OX14 4RN

Simultaneously published in the USA and Canada
by RoutledgeFalmer
270 Madison Ave, New York, NY 10016

RoutledgeFalmer is an imprint of the Taylor & Francis Group

© 2005 Eve English and John Williamson selection and editorial matter;
individual chapters © the contributors

Typeset in Bembo by Graphicraft Limited, Hong Kong
Printed and bound in Great Britain by Bell & Bain Ltd, Glasgow

British Library Cataloguing in Publication Data
A catalogue record for this book is available from the British Library

Library of Congress Cataloging in Publication Data
   Meeting the standards in primary English : a guide to the ITT NC /
[edited by] Eve English & John Williamson.
        p. cm. — (Meeting the standards series)
   includes bibliographical references and index.
   ISBN 0–415–23090–X (pbk. : alk. paper)
   English language—Study and teaching (Elementary)—Standards—
Great Britain language arts (Elementary)—Great Britain—Computer-
assisted instruction.   3. English learners—Training of—Great Britain.
I. English, Eve.   II. Williamson, John.   III. Titles.
LB1576.M44 2004
372.6′0941—dc22
                                                            2004006452

ISBN 0–415–23090–X

Dedicated to the memory of George English 1948–2003

Contents

Illustrations

TABLES

FIGURES

Contributors

Sue Beverton is a lecturer in English and Education Studies in the Education Department at the University of Durham. She has responsibility for the coordination of primary English.

James Crinson is a primary headteacher with a particular interest in the teaching of drama. He has worked on Initial Teacher Training programmes at the University of Newcastle.

Eve English is a lecturer in English and Course Leader of the PGCE Primary Course in the School of Education at the University of Durham.

George English had a varied career as a lecturer in media studies and as a BBC radio broadcaster and programme maker. As a programme maker he produced a regular series on children's literature. He was also co-editor of the Ragdoll publication: *Books for your Children*.

Frank Hardman is a Reader in Education and runs the secondary PGCE course at the University of Newcastle. He has responsibility for the teaching of English.

Steve Higgins is a senior lecturer at the University of Newcastle. He is a specialist in the use of ICT in supporting learning across the curriculum.

Nick Packard is a primary teacher and ICT consultant.

John Williamson is a senior lecturer in English and Director of ITT in the School of Education at the University of Newcastle.

Series Editor's Preface

This book has been prepared for students training to be teachers who face the challenge of meeting the many requirements specified in the government's Circular 02/02, *Qualifying to Teach: Professional Standards for Qualified Teacher Status* (DfES/ TTA). The book forms part of a series of publications that sets out to guide trainees on initial teacher training programmes, both primary and secondary, through the complex package of subject requirements they will be expected to meet before they can be awarded Qualified Teacher Status (QTS).

Why is there a need for such a series? Teaching has always been a demanding profession, requiring of its members enthusiasm, dedication and commitment. In addition, it is common sense that teachers need to know not only what they teach but how to teach it most effectively. Current trends in education highlight the raising of standards (particularly in the areas of literacy and numeracy), the use of new technologies across the curriculum and the development of key skills for lifelong learning. These run alongside the early learning goals, baseline assessment, the requirements of the National Curriculum, the National Literacy and Numeracy Strategies, PSHE and citizenship work, national tests (Standard Assessment Tasks (SATs)), interim tasks, GCSE examinations, post-16 assessment, . . . The list seems endless. Such demands increase the pressure on teachers generally and trainee teachers in particular.

At the primary school level, since the introduction of the National Curriculum there is an even greater emphasis now than ever before on teachers' own subject knowledge and their ability to apply that knowledge in the classroom. Trainees have to become Jacks and Jills of all trades – developing the competence and confidence to plan, manage, monitor and assess all areas of the National Curriculum plus religious education. The increasing complexity of the primary curriculum and ever more demanding societal expectations makes it very difficult for trainees and their mentors (be they tutors in the training institutions or teachers in schools) to cover everything that is necessary in what feels like a very short space of time. Four of the books in this series are aimed specifically at the trainee primary teacher and those who are helping to train them:

- *Meeting the Standards in . . . Primary English*
- *Meeting the Standards in . . . Primary Mathematics*
- *Meeting the Standards in . . . Primary Science*
- *Meeting the Standards in . . . Primary Information and Communications Technology*

For those training to be secondary school teachers, the pressures are just as great. They will probably bring with them knowledge and expertise in their specialist subject, taken to degree level at least. However, content studied to degree level in universities is unlikely to match closely the needs of the National Curriculum. A degree in medieval English, applied mathematics or biochemistry will not be sufficient in itself to enable a secondary trainee to walk into a classroom of 13- or 16-year-olds and teach English, mathematics or science. Each subject at school level is likely to be broader. For example, science must include physics, chemistry, biology, astronomy, and aspects of geology. In addition there is the subject application – the "how to teach it" dimension. Furthermore, secondary school teachers are often expected to be able to offer more than one subject. Thus, four of the books are aimed specifically at the secondary level:

- *Meeting the Standards in . . . Secondary English*
- *Meeting the Standards in . . . Secondary Mathematics*
- *Meeting the Standards in . . . Secondary Science*
- *Meeting the Standards in . . . Secondary Information and Communications Technology*

All of the books deal with the specific issues that underpin the relevant Teacher Training Agency requirements identified in Circular 02/02. The very nature of the subject areas covered and the teaching phases focused upon means that each book will, of necessity, be presented in different ways. However, each will cover the relevant areas of:

- subject knowledge – an overview of what to teach, the key ideas underpinning the relevant subject knowledge that the trainees need to know and understand in order to interpret the National Curriculum requirements for that subject;
- subject application – an overview of how to interpret the subject knowledge so as to design appropriate learning experiences for pupils, organize and manage those experiences and monitor pupils' progress within them.

The former is not presented in the form of a textbook. There are plenty of good quality GCSE and A-level textbooks on the market for those who feel the need to acquire that level of knowledge. Rather, the subject knowledge is related to identifying what is needed for the trainee to take the National Curriculum for the subject and translate it into a meaningful package for teaching and learning. The latter is structured in such a way as to identify the generic skills of planning, organizing, managing, monitoring and assessing the teaching and learning. The content is related to the specific requirements of Circular 02/02. The trainee's continuing professional development needs are also considered.

The purpose of the series is to give practical guidance and support to trainee teachers, in particular focusing on what to do and how to do it. Throughout each book there are suggested tasks and activities that can be completed in the training institution, in school or independently at home. They serve to elicit and support the trainee's development of skills, knowledge and understanding needed to become an effective teacher.

Prof. Lynn Newton
University of Durham
August 2004

1 Introduction: Welcome to Your Teaching Career

JOHN WILLIAMSON

Teaching is without doubt the most important profession; without teaching there would be no other professions. It is also the most rewarding. What role in society can be more crucial than that which shapes children's lives and prepares them for adulthood?

(TTA, 1998, p. 1)

So, you have decided to become a teacher in the Primary phase. As the TTA say in the quotation above, there is no more important profession than teaching; within teaching, we would argue, there is no more important role than that of teaching English. This is true partly because a good command of English is necessary for learning in all other aspects of the curriculum; even in subjects which are not heavily reliant on language there is a need to read for information, to put ideas down in writing with clarity and accuracy and to explore ideas through talking and listening. But even more important than this, language is at the very heart of what it means to be human; we use our language skills to interact with others, to explore and share our own feelings and to develop our understanding of the world in which we live. Your work in English teaching will be varied and challenging but it will never be dull because the demands of the curriculum and the needs of your pupils allow you to create a rich, diverse programme of activities to promote the development of some of the key skills for living.

RECENT DEVELOPMENTS IN ENGLISH TEACHING

As with most things, the teaching profession is constantly buffeted by the winds of change. In particular, the last decade or so has been a time of great change for all involved in secondary education. At the heart of this change has been the Education Reform Act (ERA) of 1988. The Act brought about a number of far-reaching developments, the most significant of which was the creation of a National Curriculum and its related requirements for monitoring and assessment.

Although there have always been guidelines from professional bodies (such as teachers' unions), local authorities and even official government publications, until 1988 teachers generally had freedom to decide for themselves *what* to teach and *how* to teach. Different approaches to curriculum planning and delivery have proved influential at different times. There has been a series of reports over the last quarter of a century which have impacted on the teaching of English in our schools, which largely arose from ongoing concerns in government and other influential circles with the quality of provision in a teaching subject which is seen as being of the highest importance. The Bullock Report (DES, 1975) went into great detail about all aspects of English teaching at both primary and secondary level but, in spite of saying a great deal which is still of value today, its recommendations went largely unheeded because, unlike National Curriculum documents, it did not have statutory force. Concerns about English teaching persisted and HMI produced a booklet *English from 5 to 16* (DES, 1984), which was the first of a series of important publications produced during the 1980s. Although this booklet was not universally welcomed by English teachers, it can be seen as the precursor of the first version of the National Curriculum. Another influence on the National Curriculum was the Kingman Report (DES, 1988) whose focus was 'explicit knowledge of the structure of the language' (p. iii). This has been a persisting theme running through the various forms of the National Curriculum for English. However, the most important work of this period was the Cox Report (DES, 1989) which laid out the framework for the first *English in the National Curriculum* (DES, 1990). This was generally, if cautiously, welcomed by English teachers but did not meet the demands of their political masters who set up a review chaired by Lord Dearing which led to the second *English in the National Curriculum* (DFE, 1995). In 1995, English teachers were assured that there would be no further curriculum changes for five years, an assurance which was adhered to quite punctiliously since 1999 saw the publication of the third version of National Curriculum English, which is the one which you will be implementing in (at least) the early years of your career. This brief narrative has been intended simply to help you place the National Curriculum in something of a historical context; the details will be explored in the following chapters of this book.

The other major initiative in terms of English teaching in recent years has been the National Literacy Strategy; this is seen as a central plank in the government's drive to improve standards and is a policy which the Standards for Qualified Teacher Status require you to become familiar with.

THE STANDARDS DEBATE

Parallel to the changing perspectives on curriculum has been an increasing emphasis on standards. There has, in essence, been a shift in perspective from *equality in education* (as reflected in the post-war legislation of the late 1940s through to the 1970s) to the *quality of education*, the bandwagon of the 1980s and 1990s.

The term 'standard' is emotive and value-laden. According to the *Oxford English Dictionary*, among other descriptors of a standard, it is (i) a weight or measure to which others conform or by which the accuracy of others is judged, and (ii) a degree of excellence required for a particular purpose. Both of these definitions sit well with the educational use of the term, where it translates as acceptable levels of performance by schools and teachers in the eyes of the public and the politicians.

Over the last decade, the media have reported numerous incidents of falling standards and the failure of the educational system to live up to the degree of excellence required for the purpose of educating our young in preparation for future citizenship. We teachers have, purportedly, been measured and found lacking. It was this, in part, which was a major force behind the introduction of the National Curriculum and the National Literacy Strategy.

In 1989, when the National Curriculum was introduced, the Department for Education and Science claimed:

> There is every reason for optimism that in providing a sound, sufficiently
> detailed framework over the next decade, the National Curriculum will
> give children and teachers much needed help in achieving higher standards.
> (DES, 1989, p. 2)

One of the major thrusts underpinning changes over the last decade or so has been the question of how we measure and judge the outcomes of the teaching and learning enterprise. To achieve the appropriately educated citizens of the future, schools of the present must not only achieve universal literacy and numeracy but must be measurably and accountably seen to be doing so, hence the introduction of league tables as performance indicators.

Gillian Shephard, the Secretary of State for Education and Employment, said in 1997:

> Poor standards of literacy and numeracy are unacceptable. If our growing
> economic success is to be maintained we must get the basics right for
> everyone. Countries will only keep investing here at record levels if they
> see that the workforce is up to the job.
> (DfEE, 1997a, p. 2)

While the economic arguments are strong, we need to balance the needs of the economy with the needs of the child. Few teachers are likely to disagree with the need to get the 'basics' right. After all, literacy and numeracy skills underpin much that we do with children in all areas of the curriculum. However, the increased focus on the 'basics' should not be at the expense of these other areas of experience. Children should have access to a broad and balanced curriculum if they are to develop as broad, balanced individuals.

All schools are now ranked each year on the basis of their pupils' performances in standardised tests and external examinations (GCSE and A level). The performances of individual children are conveyed only to parents, although the school's collective results are discussed with school governors and also given to the local education authority (LEA). The latter then informs the DfES (Department for Education and Skills), who publish the national figures on a school/LEA basis. This gives parents the opportunity to compare, judge and choose schools within the LEA in which they live. The figures indicate, for each school within the LEA, the percentage above and below the expected level, that is, the schools which are or are not meeting the standard. This results in inevitable conclusions as to whether standards are rising or falling. Such crude measures as Standardised Assessment Tasks for comparing attainment have been widely criticised, notably by education researchers like Fitz-Gibbon (1996) who criticise the fact that such measures ignore the 'value added elements' – in other words, the factors which influence teaching and learning such as the catchment area of the school, the proportion of pupils for whom English is an additional language, and the quality and quantity of educational enrichment a child receives in the home. Davies (1996) suggests that

> Dissatisfaction [with standards] is expressed spasmodically throughout the year but reaches fever pitch when the annual national test results are published. Whatever the results they are rarely deemed satisfactory and targets are set which expect future cohorts of children to achieve even higher standards than their predecessors.

(Davies, 1996, p. 162)

There are also targets for initial teacher training, to redress the perceived inadequacies in existing course provision. These centre on a set of Standards which all trainees must attain before they can be awarded Qualified Teacher Status (QTS). It follows, therefore, that as a trainee for the teaching profession you must be equipped to deal with these contradictory and sometimes conflicting situations as well as meeting all the required standards. So how will you be prepared for this?

ROUTES INTO A CAREER IN TEACHING

To begin, let us first consider the routes into teaching open to anyone wanting to pursue teaching as a career. Teaching is now an all-graduate profession, although this has not always been the case. Prior to the 1970s it was possible to become a teacher by gaining a teaching certificate from a college of higher education. However, in the late 1960s and early 1970s, following a sequence of government reports, the routes were narrowed to ensure graduate status for all newly qualified teachers.

For many teachers in the United Kingdom this has been via an undergraduate pathway, reading for a degree at a university (or a college associated to a university) which resulted in the award of Bachelor of Education (BEd) with Qualified Teacher Status (QTS). Such a route has usually taken at least three and sometimes four years. More recently, such degrees have become more linked to subject specialisms and some universities offer Bachelor of Arts in Education (BA(Ed)) with QTS and Bachelor of Science in Education (BSc (Ed)) with QTS.

Many other teachers choose to gain their degrees from a university first, and then train to teach through the postgraduate route. This usually takes one year, at the end of which the trainee is awarded a Postgraduate Certificate in Education (PGCE) with QTS. In all cases, the degree or postgraduate certificate is awarded by the training institution but the QTS is awarded by the Department for Education and Employment as a consequence of successful completion of the course and on the recommendation of the training institution.

There are also now a range of training routes which do not involve conventional attendance at a university or college. The Graduate Teacher Programme places trainees (who must be graduates over 24 years of age) directly in a school which employs them and is responsible for helping them meet the Standards. The Overseas Teacher Programme offers an employment-based route into teaching for teachers who trained in other countries.

Whichever route is followed, there are rigorous government requirements which must be met by both the institutions providing the training and the trainees following the training programme, before QTS can be awarded. In the 1970s and early 1980s, teacher training institutions had guidelines produced by a group called the Council for the Accreditation of Teacher Education (CATE). The guidelines identified key requirements which all Initial Teacher Training (ITT) providers should meet to be judged effective in training teachers. Alongside the CATE criteria were systems of monitoring the quality of programmes.

During the late 1980s and early 1990s, there were a number of government documents which moved initial teacher training in the direction of partnership with schools. This has involved school staff taking greater responsibility for the support and assessment of students on placements and a transfer of funds (either as money or as in-service provision) to the schools in payment for this increased responsibility. Along with this responsibility in schools, staff have increasingly become involved in the selection and interviewing of prospective students, the planning and delivery of the courses and the overall quality assurance process.

More recent legislation has culminated in the establishment of the Teacher Training Agency (TTA), a government body which, as its name suggests, now has control over the nature and funding of initial teacher training courses. This legislation is crucially important to you as a trainee teacher, since the associated documentation defines the framework for your preparation for and induction into the teaching profession. So how will the legislation affect you?

REQUIREMENTS ON COURSES OF INITIAL TEACHER TRAINING

In 1997, a government Circular number 10/97 introduced the idea of a national curriculum for initial teacher training (ITT), to parallel that already being used in schools. This was to be a major development in the training of teachers. In the circular there was an emphasis on the development of your professionalism as a teacher. This implies

> . . . more than meeting a series of discrete standards. It is necessary to consider the standards as a whole to appreciate the creativity, commitment, energy and enthusiasm which teaching demands, and the intellectual and managerial skills required of the effective professional.
>
> (DfEE, 1997b, p. 2)

In May 1998, the DfEE issued Circular number 4/98, *Teaching: High Status, High Standards*, in which the Secretary of State's criteria were revised and extended. As well as generic standards for the award of QTS, the new document specified separate national curricula for initial teacher training in English, mathematics and science at both primary and secondary levels, and a national curriculum for the use of Information and Communications Technology (ICT) in subject teaching to be taught to all trainees, regardless of phase focus.

Since then, the format for the Standards set out in the late 1990s has come to be seen as overly prescriptive and we are now working to a set of Standards for Qualified Teacher Status set out in the document *Qualifying To Teach: Professional Standards for Qualified Teacher Status and Requirements for Initial Teacher Training* (TTA 2002).

In *Qualifying to Teach*, the Standards are brought together under three main headings: the first focuses on Professional Values and Practice, these Standards setting out key elements of the teacher's relationship with pupils and with other adults; the second group of Standards is concerned with Knowledge and Understanding and sets out what teachers of children at different age ranges need to know in order to function effectively. The final set of Standards involves teaching and includes issues relating to Planning, expectations and targets (section 3.1), Monitoring and assessment (3.2) and Teaching and class management (3.3).

So how does this affect you as a student teacher? In essence, you must 'meet the Standards' before you can be awarded QTS. As a trainee, you must show that you have done so by the end of your training programme so as to be eligible for the award of QTS. Courses in universities and other higher education institutions are designed to help you to do so, both in schools and in the institution, but the onus is likely to be on you to provide the evidence to show how you have met the requirements. This series of books, is designed to help you with this task. This particular book focuses on those skills and competences you will need to acquire to show that you have met the requirements for primary English.

There is more to teaching English than simply having a good knowledge and understanding of the subject as it is often taught in universities. One of the major tasks ahead of you is to develop your knowledge of the whole range which is covered by the English component of the National Curriculum; this involves a knowledge of the children's literature which school pupils will encounter and of aspects of language development including speaking, listening, writing and reading. Those coming to English via the BA plus PGCE route may be familiar with some of these elements but few will be prepared for all of them. Furthermore, you will need the ability to transform what you know and understand about English into worthwhile teaching and learning experiences for your pupils. You need to develop your *pedagogical skills, knowledge and understanding*. This is as important as your knowledge and understanding of the National Curriculum Order for English. The latter provides you with a framework of *what* to teach in English. The National Literacy Strategy will provide you with a fairly full idea of *how* to teach it. But you yourself must work to develop the skills of planning, organising, managing and assessing the learning of the thirty or so children in your class, each with varied and changing needs. This is left to your own professionalism. This book is designed to help you to make a start on this task.

OVERVIEW OF THIS BOOK

Very few students on initial teacher training programmes begin their courses with all the subject knowledge they will need to teach English effectively. Nor are you likely to have expertise in the teaching and learning process although you will all have experienced it in some shape or form. While such experience and expertise does vary from person to person, you all have one thing in common – *potential*. You have successfully cleared the hurdles of the application form and the interview and have been offered a place on an initial teacher training course. Your tutors have decided that you have the necessary personal qualities which indicate that you are capable of acquiring the skills, knowledge and understanding needed to become effective teachers. In other words, you have shown evidence that you have the *potential* to meet the standards.

This book is designed to help you to do this, but it is only a part of the picture. It will be most useful to you if you read it in conjunction with the other experiences offered to you on your training programme. These will range from theoretical to practical in the following way.

- *directed reading*: reading might be handouts related to lectures, books and articles for assignments or professional newspapers and magazines simply to broaden your own professional base;
- *taught sessions*: these could take the form of formal lectures, informal practical workshops or combinations of either, whether in schools or in the institution;
- *talks/discussions*: again, these could be held in school or in the institution and can range from formal structured seminars with a group to more informal one-to-one discussion, usually with the aim of integrating theory and practice;
- *tutorial advice*: one-to-one sessions with a tutor, mentor or teacher to plan for and reflect upon your practical experiences;
- *observations*: opportunities to watch your mentor and other experienced teachers at work in their classrooms;
- *restricted experience*: opportunities to try out, under the guidance of your mentor or other teachers, limited teaching activities with a small group of children, perhaps building up to a whole-class session;
- *teaching practice*: a block placement where you take responsibility for the planning, teaching and assessment of classes of children, under the guidance of your school mentor and tutor and usually within defined parameters.

What is important about all of these is the amount of effort you put into them. No one else can do the work for you. Your tutors, your mentors in school and other teachers can all offer you advice, guidance and even criticism, but how you respond is up to you. This, once again, is a reflection of your professionalism.

REFERENCES/SUGGESTIONS FOR FURTHER READING

In addition to the references we recommend texts at the end of each chapter which are of specific relevance to the chapter's contents; the following texts will give you an insider's view of some of the processes underlying the development of the National Curriculum for English.

Cox, B. (1991) *Cox on Cox: An English Curriculum for the 1990s*, London: Hodder and Stoughton

Cox, B. (1995) *Cox on the Battle for the English Curriculum*, London: Hodder and Stoughton

Davies, C. (1996) *What is English Teaching?* Buckingham: Open University Press

DES (1975) *A Language for Life* (The Bullock Report), London: HMSO

DES (1984) *English from 5 to 16*, London: HMSO

DES (1988) *Report of the Inquiry into the Teaching of English Language* (The Kingman Report), London: HMSO

DES (1989) *English for Ages 5 to 16* (The Cox Report), London: HMSO

DES (1990) *English in the National Curriculum*, London: HMSO

DFE (1995) *English in the National Curriculum*, London: HMSO

DfEE (1997a) *Shephard Welcomes BBC/Basic Skills Agency Numeracy Campaign* (Circular 6/97), London: HMSO

DfEE (1997b) *Teaching: High Status, High Standards* (Circular 10/97) *Requirements for Courses of Initial Teacher Training*, London: HMSO

DfEE (1998) *Teaching: High Status, High Standards* (Circular 4/98) *Requirements for Courses of Initial Teacher Training*, London: HMSO

Fitz-Gibbon, C. (1996) *Monitoring Education: Indicators, Quality and Effectiveness*, London: Cassell

TTA (1998) *Teaching: A Guide to Becoming a Teacher*, London: Teacher Training Agency

TTA (2002) *Qualifying to Teach: Professional Standards for Qualified Teacher Status and Requirements for Initial Teacher Training*, London: Teacher Training Agency

2 What Do We Mean by Primary English?

SUE BEVERTON

THE HISTORY OF THE DEFINITION AND PURPOSE OF PRIMARY ENGLISH

Prior to the beginning of the twentieth century, understandings of the nature and purpose of English as a primary school subject were influenced by legacies from more classical, traditional concepts of the school curriculum. While nineteenth-century public secondary school curricula were dominated by instruction in Greek and Latin, the majority of the nation's secondary-aged pupils received teaching in the English language and literature because, the view was, of the civilising influence and 'moral wealth' that such instruction would produce (Knight, 1996, p. 34). Also, as the century drew to a close, the subject-based organisation of the secondary curriculum was heavily influenced by the universities. They set the examinations by which entry to universities was determined, thus English literature figured prominently in secondary curricula. However, English as a primary curriculum subject was not examined, explored, questioned or considered. The content of the primary curriculum was defined by its role, which was to instruct pupils in the '3 Rs', and prepare them for their secondary education.

A turning point came soon after the First World War, with the publication of the Newbolt Report (Board of Education, 1921). The Newbolt Committee had been charged with inquiring into the position occupied by English in the educational system of England, and to advise how its study may best be promoted in schools of all types. While the Committee's report did see English language teaching as a means of saving the nation's children from poor speech habits, it also exposed the inappropriateness of teaching grammar using Latin grammar as a template. Most significantly, it distinguished between the use of prescriptive and descriptive grammars of English as textbooks. This can now be seen as an early stage in what has become a lengthy controversy over which approach to English grammar should be adopted in primary schools. Newbolt compromised in seeing the study of language as best being kept simple and basic, but also important. The report spoke of the fundamental role of English (literature and language) in forming cultural knowledge and in realising experience. It emphasised the common cultural heritage embodied in English as a school subject. Thus it provided a role for English and reasons for all teachers to teach English that went far beyond compensatory models of the previous century, reasons that included a way of finding '. . . a bridge across the chasms which now divide us' (Board of Education, 1921).

During the 1950s and 1960s the status of English as a school subject became more established, in particular at secondary level with the branching of English into two examinable aspects, language and literature, although debate continued over their content and purpose. Within primary education, while well established as a subject in its own right, the nature of primary English came into dispute. Essentially, the debate was between members or factions within the teaching profession and was not entered into by politicians, academics or others. Broadly different approaches emerged during this period concerning the questions of what primary English was and what purpose it served. On the one hand, the view of English having a culturally enriching, self-developing role had many adherents. For others, English was more of a means to an end, a more communications-orientated discipline. As one might expect, different pedagogic practices subsequently stemmed from such views: child-centred pedagogy, promoted by such influential bodies as the Plowden Committee (reporting in 1967), resonated with the ideas that the role of English was to provide a means of absorbing values, releasing self-expression and responding to literary experience. One example where this approach became especially prominent was the teaching of reading, where discovery methods enabled children's understanding of language features, forms and functions. Courses in language awareness and the celebration of multilingualism flourished. Others, however, saw all this as a threat to the view that culture was a 'given' (Dixon, 1975) and to the previously secure place of grammar teaching (Knight, 1996).

During the early 1970s, there was concern at policy-making levels that primary English needed to be reviewed and sharpened. Control over the debate moved away from members of the profession. Indeed, we may see what followed as a significant step by government to intervene in the hitherto education professionals' domain of setting the primary English curriculum. Attention began to focus upon the English language as a means of communication requiring the development of certain skills. In 1972 a Committee of Inquiry, chaired by Sir Alan Bullock, was established. It considered in relation to schools

> . . . all aspects of teaching the use of English, including reading, writing and
> speech; how present practice might be improved . . . and the role that
> initial and in-service training might play . . . and to what extent
> arrangements for monitoring the general level of attainment in these skills
> can be introduced or improved.
>
> (DES, 1975, p. xxxi)

The resulting Bullock Report, *A Language for Life* (DES, 1975), stressed the role of English as the medium through which teaching and learning is largely conducted. It promoted the notion of 'language across the curriculum', meaning that all subjects carried a responsibility towards developing pupils' language. The report had a sub-section on 'Language Study' (under 'Written Language') in which the development of pupils' understanding of how language functions is advised through teaching about language in context. *A Language for Life* did not support de-contextualised grammar teaching, that is, grammar teaching for its own sake, and eschewed a prescriptive approach to defining the grammar of English.

By *A Language for Life* taking the view that grammar was best seen as a description of real language, the controversy between prescriptive and descriptive grammatical schools of thought was temporarily laid to rest. Most importantly, however, from this report two linked themes emerged that would each provide grounds for dispute for many years: they are Knowledge About Language (KAL) and standard English.

Advocates of the importance of KAL as part of the English curriculum appeal to a deep-rooted sense of language as experience. In essence, they appeal for the teaching of the grammar of the English language *as it is used*. For them, the term grammar is a broad church, carrying no preconceptions as to one particular correct version. KAL allows for the exploration of how language changes under different conditions, how people speak differently from each other and from how they may write. It aims to develop language awareness (LA), in which pupils and teachers develop a sensitivity to KAL. Understanding and using grammatical terms are seen as useful in analysing and describing different forms and functions of language (Crystal, 1995).

Proponents of KAL take issue over stipulations that standard English 'should' be taught on the grounds of its being 'correct'. They would take the view that there is not one single variety of English, spoken and written, that should assume an exclusive position as *the* form of English language in the curriculum. Indeed, to reach a situation in which English in primary schools was based on standard English would be to risk reject-ing the validity of other varieties. Standard English itself has no local base, although it is seen by linguists as *a* variety of English, standing alongside, but not above, other dialects of English. Standard English is seen not as a matter of pronunciation; it may be spoken in a wide variety of accents. In England there exists a prestige accent, Received Pronunciation (RP) in which standard English is often spoken. Standard English is mainly distinguishable by its grammar and orthography (spelling and punctuation) and is recognised by adult members of the community as having prestige value.

During the 1980s, HMI published a series of discussion documents on curricular aims and content. *English from 5 to 16: Curriculum Matters* (DES, 1984) drew heavily upon the *A Language for Life* in its philosophy upon the centrality for learning of achieving competence in the use of English. It stated that

> All teachers, whatever their other responsibilities and whatever age groups they teach, have a contribution to make to this process . . . (of aiding their pupils to achieve competence in the many and varied uses of English).
>
> (DES, 1984, p. 1; brackets added)

English from 5 to 16 established four aims for the teaching of English, of which the fourth, admitted as likely to be the most controversial, was to teach pupils *about* language (that is, KAL). This was necessary as a means of increasing pupils' ability to use and respond to language. *English from 5 to 16* acknowledged the confusion that had existed for many years over whether grammar should be explicitly taught. Rejecting formal drills and exercises as the way to teach grammar, HMI stated its preference for teachers and pupils giving attention to language, examining its structure and how it works. The governing factor on the question of what and how much grammatical terminology pupils should be taught was '. . . how much they could assimilate with understanding and apply to purposes they see to be meaningful and interesting' (DES, 1984, p. 14).

In 1988 Professor Brian Cox was appointed to lead a working party to devise programmes of study and attainment targets for English within the National Curriculum. Cox had been a member of the Kingman Committee that had reported that year on what training teachers should have about English. Cox's working party's first report, which contained sections on standard English and grammar and linguistic terminology, was amended at the insistence of Kenneth Baker (the then Secretary of State for Education). Baker's insistence was upon the primacy of a Latinate style of English grammar to be unequivocally stated. This made it difficult for Cox and his working party to get across their Kingman-inspired view that while grammatical knowledge and understanding were important, they should be developed through descriptive, generative grammars, with appreciation of the diversity of grammars that exists for English. In the published version of the first report (DES, 1989), however, the concept of 'grammar' was given a more prominent role and expressed in firmer language than in the working party's first report. A section on standard English, however, was retained. This was later explained by Cox himself as possibly because of government confusion over the difference between Standard English and Received Pronunciation (Cox, 1991, p. 25).

The struggle between government and those charged with advising it over finding acceptable definitions of English and its purpose in the curriculum probably reached its height at the time of the Cox report (DES, 1989). Since then the decline of an independent voice that spoke for informed, apolitical views on the nature and role of English has been marked. An early casualty was the curtailment of the Language in the National Curriculum (LINC) Project (1989–1992). This was a government-funded initiative set up, as recommended in the Kingman Report, to provide training for serving teachers in Knowledge About Language. Its official materials, intended for publication, were banned in 1991. Government silence accompanied the prohibition. Since then, revisions to the national curriculum have contained sections on 'Standard English and Language Study' (DFE, 1995) and 'Standard English' and 'Language Variation' (DfEE/QCA, 1999) although their prescriptions have remained at the level of general blandishments.

English literature in the primary curriculum has also been exposed to some, but not so much, public controversy. Perhaps the debates over the place and nature of English literature in the secondary curriculum were sufficient. The close association in primary schools between quality reading material, whether literature or non-fiction, and successful English teaching was not seriously challenged. Yet for many years government agencies have made uninspired references to 'literature'. Banal requirements, such as the one that pupils should read '. . . poems or stories with familiar settings and those based on imaginary or traditional worlds . . .' (Key Stage 1, English AT1, see DFE, 1995, p. 6), are virtually unchanged in the curriculum for 2000 (see DfEE/ QCA, 1999, p. 46).

One potentially powerful legacy of those years is the model of the five roles for English that Cox presented (DES, 1989, paras 2.21–5). These were, in brief, that English in the curriculum:

- provides a means of 'personal growth';
- has a 'cross-curricular' role as a medium of instruction;
- meets an 'adult needs' role as a communication tool;
- carries a 'cultural heritage' function; and
- enables 'cultural analysis' through a critical understanding of the world.

WHAT ENGLISH SUBJECT KNOWLEDGE SHOULD PRIMARY TEACHERS POSSESS?

It would seem reasonable to suppose that the teachers who have to teach a primary curriculum for English do actually need to possess some relevant knowledge in order to teach it. What and how much is a problem. There does not appear to be a substantial body of evidence to answer this. Instead, there is more by way of worthy advice. From the previous section it is not surprising to find that the question of specifying what knowledge of English primary teachers should possess was highly politicised for most of the twentieth century, from the Newbolt Report onwards. The next landmark came in 1988, when the Kingman Committee was established by the then Secretary of State for Education, Kenneth Baker. The job of this committee was to recommend what training teachers should be given in order to understand how English works and to identify what, in general terms, pupils also need to know about how the language works (KAL again). The timing of this was critical: the Kingman Committee can be seen as pivotal, occurring between the appearance of the HMI papers including *English 5 to 16* and the formation of the working group, chaired by Brian Cox, to specify the English National Curriculum and Attainment Targets.

From the start the Kingman Committee sparked controversy. Its membership was widely seen as an insult to the teaching fraternity (Rosen, 1988, p. 2). Teachers were not represented and the views held by its members were assumed to be strongly pro-government (that is, in favour of Latin-based teaching of grammar, and supporting the view of the correctness of standard English, for example). When it reported, however, teachers and politicians were surprised. The Kingman Report (DES, 1988) contained a thoughtful, sensitive model of the English language that was novel to many, being descriptive rather than prescriptive, and influenced by a functional view of language. In answering its brief of specifying what training teachers should receive and what pupils needed to know it took full account of the preceding debates over KAL and LA (see above). It observed:

> We believe that within English as a subject, pupils need to have their attention drawn to what they are doing and why they are doing it because this is helpful to the development of their language ability. It is important, however, to state that helping pupils to notice what they are doing is a subtle process which requires the teacher to intervene constructively and at an appropriate time.
>
> (DES, 1988, p. 13)

Unsurprisingly, the report did not fully please government. This was widely seen at the time as mainly because it did not advocate a return to the traditional prescription and teaching of a Latinate grammar. At the time of its appearance, many major new developments such as the ERA and the introduction of the National Curriculum rather overshadowed Kingman's message, and its advice lay largely unheeded by government. The hand of governmental alterations to the Cox Report illustrates the weak impact of the Kingman Report.

There is some sign that during the 1990s there was a lessening of the overt tension between government and profession over specifying what knowledge of English primary teachers should possess. Questions over KAL and standard English were less often and less openly discussed. But beneath the apparent decline of those arguments a deeper struggle continued over who should identify the language knowledge that primary teachers should possess – professional educators (teachers, academics, researchers) or those ultimately employing teachers: the government. As the nineties drew to a close, definitive government directives appeared which signalled the end of those battles. The National Literacy Strategy Training Pack (DfEE, 1998b) is one example of such directives. These in-service training materials contain videos, teaching resource sheets and information for teachers. Widely used as preparation for the National Literacy Strategy, these materials, and more recent ones such as Additional Literacy Support (ALS) Materials (DfEE, 2000a), may have a major impact upon teachers' approach to language teaching. Embodying a government stance on what is 'best practice' and appearing firm and full of conviction, they offer primary teachers a 'security blanket', removing the necessity for them to explore and develop a well-formed philosophy of their own of the role and nature of English in the curriculum. They render unproblematic the role and nature of what knowledge of English teachers need to possess. This flies in the face of the concerns of previous decades.

WHERE ARE WE NOW?

There are other difficulties with these government-issued directives. The Framework for Teaching (both the original (DfEE, 1998b) and the second edition, DfEE 2000b) and the National Curriculum for Primary Initial Teacher Training, English (DfEE, 1998a) do not contain consistent messages about language information. DfEE Circular 4/98, *Teaching: High Status, High Standards* and the more recent TTA requirements for Initial Teacher Training (2002), rather blandly and blithely present the view that what is English subject knowledge is unproblematic. Yet the National Curriculum has moved towards seeing this differently. For example, as early as Key Stage 1 the English Programme of Study specifies that pupils should be '. . . introduced to some of the main features of spoken standard English and be taught to use them' (DfEE, 2000b, p. 45), as well as advising teachers, confusingly, that:

> The paragraphs on *standard English, language variation, language structure* and *language structure and variation* in speaking and listening, reading and writing provide a coherent basis for language study.
>
> (DfEE, 2000b, p. 45)

Perhaps this discord, between primary English being portrayed as an unproblematic subject that is amenable to positivist definition and direct transmission on the one hand and being acknowledged as variable, changing and flexible on the other, is not very important. Teachers may teach largely in accordance with their own beliefs about the subject matter they are attempting to convey. But is English too important to be abandoned in the centre of such a tug-of-war? While the debates have waxed and waned, and waxed and waned again, the actual content of primary English *as taught* has outgrown all definitions. Rather like a pre-adolescent child who has put on almost overnight a growing spurt that surprises even its parents, what is now commercially available to teachers as advice and materials for teaching language has grown enormously in recent years in range, quantity and quality. One thing this suggests is that we are about to lose the subject identity of 'English' in the primary school. Another is that teachers are steering a rudderless course through a sea of ideas and understandings about language and English. A professionally run review of where English is as a primary subject is urgently required. That way teachers will redefine their English subject knowledge and understanding for themselves.

REFERENCES

Board of Education (1921) *The Teaching of English in England* (Newbolt Report), London: HMSO

Cox, B. (1991) *Cox on Cox: An English Curriculum for the 1990s,* London: Hodder and Stoughton

Crystal, D. (1995) *The Cambridge Encyclopedia of The English Language,* Cambridge: CUP

DFE (1995) *English in the National Curriculum,* London: HMSO

DfEE (1998a) *Teaching: High Status, High Standards (Circular 4/98) Requirements for Courses of Initial Teacher Training,* London: DfEE

DfEE (1998b) *The National Literacy Training Pack,* London: DfEE

DfEE/QCA (1999) *The National Curriculum: Handbook for Primary Teachers in England,* London: HMSO/QCA

DfEE (2000a) *Additional Literacy Support Materials,* London: HMSO

DfEE (2000b) *The National Literacy Strategy Framework for Teaching,* 2nd edition, London: HMSO

DES (1975) *A Language for Life* (The Bullock Report), London: HMSO

DES (1984) *English from 5 to 16. Curriculum Matters 1: An HMI Series,* London: HMSO

DES (1988) *Report of the Committee of Inquiry into the Teaching of English Language* (The Kingman Report), London: HMSO

DES (1989) *English for Ages 5 to 6* (The Cox Report), London: HMSO

Dixon, J. (1975) *Growth through English – Set in the Perspective of the Seventies*, Oxford: NATE and OUP

Knight, R. (1996) *Valuing English*, London: David Fulton Publishers

Rosen, H. (1988) 'Struck by a Particular Gap' in A. West and M. Jones (eds) *Learning Me Your Language: Perspectives on the Teaching of English*, Cheltenham: Stanley Thornes

TTA (2002) *Qualifying to Teach: Professional Standards for Initial Teacher Training*, London: Teacher Training Agency.

3 **Reading**
EVE ENGLISH

INTRODUCTION

The question of how children are taught to read, especially in their first years in school, is one that is constantly being asked and debated. It is a question that is of interest not only to practitioners but also to the general public, to employers, to politicians and to the media. In 1990 the *Times Educational Supplement* published a story on reading failure in nine local education authorities that was picked up by the national media. Stories ran ('Children's Reading Ability Plummets', *Guardian*, 26 June 1990; 'Scandal of our young illiterates', *Daily Mail*, 30 June 1990) that criticised schools, local education authorities and teacher training institutions for their part in this failure. Decline in reading standards was blamed on the unstructured approaches to the teaching of reading linked to a 'real books' philosophy and practice. This chapter opens with a brief overview of some of the debates and approaches to 'beginning reading' that have existed in the past. It is important that you are aware of these developments because many have informed the approaches that we use today.

AN HISTORICAL PERSPECTIVE – BEGINNING TO READ

How far should we go back? Beard (1998) described how the 'alphabetic method' of teaching children to read was used for five hundred years, right up to the early twentieth century. Children learned to read by saying the names of the letters through which they learned to recognise and pronounce words. The emphasis was on the names and shapes of the letters. The assumption was that if children saw letters in words often enough they would learn to read because many consonants suggest their sounds. However, because the names of many letters are often very different from the sounds they represent in words and because individual letters can stand for several different sounds, it was very difficult for children to understand. These concerns were addressed to some extent by a phonics approach to the teaching of reading. Here the sound rather than the names of letters were used. This method emerged in the middle of the nineteenth century and by the early twentieth century many new books for teaching reading had adopted a phonic approach. One of the most successful phonic reading schemes was 'Beacon Readers' which was introduced from America in 1922. If teachers used a phonic method of teaching children to read explicit attention was given to the teaching of grapho-phonic knowledge, i.e. letter to sound correspondences and sound blending.

In the 1940s and 1950s there was a reaction to the phonics approach and a whole-word or 'look and say' method increased in use. This method was based on the idea that children see words as whole patterns. Children memorised the way a word looked and learned to associate the printed word with the meaning of the word. Flashcards would be used and children would often learn words in isolation before going anywhere near a book. This approach was also criticised, however, because it did not include a technique for attempting unfamiliar words and, because children were not able to learn a great number of whole words at a time, the reading material was often very restricted, repetitive and boring.

All the methods described up to now are skills-based approaches, sometimes known as 'bottom-up' approaches. In all of them children learn to recognise single linguistic units (sounds or words) first of all, before moving on to larger units such as sentences or whole texts. The teaching process emphasises the explicit teaching of word recognition and/or decoding skills. In these skills-based approaches children are not left to acquire the necessary skills through incidental learning but taught to read in a very structured way. Reading schemes based on skills-based approaches had a very controlled vocabulary, repetition of the vocabulary as a reinforcement of the learning process and simplified sentences. The child's reading was almost entirely dependent upon having a knowledge of sounds and letters and/or word recognition. Rarely in such schemes was the child given the support of sentence structure or meaning, although pictures sometimes gave clues. Learners were supposed to read the words correctly and risk taking was discouraged. Reading schemes containing pages of 'here' and 'look' or 'cats and mats' were the order of the day. Single words in tins went home and, sometimes, actual books were not even opened until all words were 'learned'.

It was perhaps not surprising that these approaches were considered to be so boring that there was a backlash. In the early 1980s there developed in Britain, America and Australia (Harrison, 1996) resistance to skills-based approaches to the teaching of reading. There was, particularly, criticism expressed at the formal teaching of phonics. This lack of confidence in a 'bottom-up' model led to the development of a 'whole-language' approach to language teaching, including reading. This approach to reading is often referred to as a 'top-down' model. According to whole-language practitioners, such as Goodman (1986) and Weaver (1990), children do not work up from the print to decode meaning but bring an expectation of meaning to the text that enables them to predict the word. The whole-language approach used 'real' books and environmental print rather than controlled and structured reading schemes. The main tenet of the whole-language approach was that children learn language more easily and effectively if they learn it within a context that is 'whole, real and relevant' (Goodman, 1986,

p. 26). Goodman presented a reading programme with the emphasis on a range of real materials. Children read familiar words such as T-shirt slogans, shop logos, cereal boxes. Environmental print was discovered in walks round the locality and role-play was seen as offering excellent opportunities for reading.

Waterland (1988) in England was very influenced by the work of Goodman and developed an approach to reading that she called the 'apprenticeship approach'. She saw the emergent reader as learning in the same way as an apprentice does, working actively with the tools of the trade alongside the craftsman, taking on more and more complex tasks as he or she became more efficient. Readers similarly were supported by adults until they became more confident and could take over more and more of the reading.

Not everyone, however, was so enthusiastic about the whole-language or apprenticeship approach to reading. A 1996 report by Her Majesty's Inspectorate commented on the significant omission in many schools of the systematic teaching of an effective programme of phonic knowledge and skills and said that 'because phonics is a set of culturally determined conventions it cannot be left to be "discovered"' (1996, p. 9).

The debate that ensued between those who supported a 'whole-language' approach to the teaching of reading and those who supported a structured and systematic approach to the teaching of phonics became very heated. Harrison described this debate as being '. . . often characterised by pugnacious rhetoric, evangelical allegiances and antipathies, and totemistic treatment of gurus' (Harrison, 1996, p. 9). Bayley (1996) described the debate as being dangerous in that '. . . polarised views were obscuring strengths and weaknesses in both approaches'.

Attempts were made to resolve the dispute. Stanovich and Stanovich (1995) felt that there were points of convergence and proposed a more integrated or interactionist model of teaching children to read. They claimed that the reading process combines elements of both 'top-down' and 'bottom-up' strategies and that a variety of sources of knowledge are used simultaneously during reading. Readers would draw upon appropriate cues, whether semantic, syntactic or orthographic, according to need. The efficient use of one type of knowledge (say Stanovich and Stanovich) can compensate for the inadequacies of another. If, for example, a reader has limited decoding ability then he/she will compensate for this by greater use of contextual cues. This interactionist approach was not seen as simply a compromise between 'top-down' and 'bottom-up' approaches but, as Cook and Young (1994, p. 17) said, a claim that reading is an activity that enables us to flex all our intellectual muscle in order to get meaning from text. Westwood et al. (1997, p. 228) believe that teachers who support an interactionist model of reading will take the best from both 'bottom-up' and 'top-down' models and carefully balance the two.

The National Curriculum and National Literacy Strategy (see below) require an interactionist approach to the teaching of reading but there is increasingly a greater emphasis on the teaching of phonics. An Ofsted report on the NLS (2002, p. 4) highlighted this emphasis. Alongside this, debate goes on about the relative advantages of teaching analytic phonics and synthetic phonics (Chew, 1997; Miskin, 1998; Bielby, 1999; Goswami, 1999).

> **Activity 1**   Try to remember how you learned to read.
>
> Did your teacher use flashcards and games to encourage whole-word recognition?
>
> Were you taught to use phonic strategies (perhaps just initial sounds – remember the 'b' table with the books, buttons and bows)?
>
> Were you, perhaps, part of the 'real books' or 'apprenticeship approaches' to reading where you were introduced to whole texts before breaking up words into their component parts?
>
> Did you work your way through one reading scheme or did you experience books from different schemes and even 'real books' from the very beginning?

RECENT DEVELOPMENTS

The Curriculum Guidance for the Foundation Stage

This guidance (QCA/DfEE, 2000) recommends a curriculum for children aged 3 to 5 years of age and identifies six areas of learning and early learning goals. One of these is 'Communication, Language and Literacy'. The guidance identifies 'stepping stones' that show the knowledge, skills, understanding and attitudes that children need to learn during the foundation stage in order to achieve the early learning goals. The section on 'Communication, Language and Literacy' comprises pages 44 to 67 and you need to make yourself familiar with this section. The reading advice comes on pages 60 to 63. On examining the stepping stones you will see that an interactionist approach to reading is being recommended. The 3 to 5-year-olds are to be taught letter/sound correspondence, the shapes of whole words but also those skills associated with the whole text, with being able to predict outcomes in stories, to understand that print can provide information and, most importantly, enjoyment. Teaching all these skills to children demands an interactionist approach to reading rather than a reliance on one method. As children work their way through the primary system the skills they have learned in the nursery and reception classes will be built upon and the National Curriculum (NC) and National Literacy Strategy (NLS) continue to promote the integration of 'bottom-up' and 'top-down' approaches.

The National Curriculum

This is a statutory document and the programmes of study for English at Key Stages 1 and 2 set out the curriculum for English in reading as well as in writing and speaking and listening. In terms of suggested approaches to the teaching of reading it may be interesting to know that with each revision of the National Curriculum there has been a greater emphasis on the teaching of phonics.

The National Curriculum English Orders were introduced into Key Stage 1 in September 1989. Up until this point teachers in schools devised their own curricula, with or without advice from local education authorities. To go from that to a statutory National Curriculum was a radical change. Attainment Target 2, which addressed reading, described how children should be able to recognise that print carries meaning, should be beginning to recognise individual words or letters in familiar contexts, show signs of being interested in reading and be able to talk in simple terms about the content of books. None of the statements at Level 1 pointed to any one method of teaching children to read. At Level 2 children were expected to be able to read signs, demonstrate a knowledge of the alphabet by using wordbooks, use picture and context cues, recognise some words on sight and use phonic cues. They were also expected to be able to describe what had happened in a text, predict possible outcomes, listen and respond to stories and read with fluency and accuracy. Level 2 was the level that the majority of children would be expected to attain at the end of Key Stage 1. There was nothing in the attainment targets that suggested that one particular method of teaching children to read was better than any other. As long as children had some awareness of phonics, had a sight vocabulary and responded to text then the methods of teaching those skills were left to the individual school. In particular, it is worth knowing that it was not necessary for pupils to have any phonic knowledge until the end of the key stage and, even then, only a limited knowledge was required.

The revised programmes of study and attainment targets for the National Curriculum (1995) brought changes for the teaching of reading as for all areas of the curriculum. The programme of study for reading at Key Stage 1, in the revised orders, described the range of texts that children should experience and also the key skills. Within that section on key skills, phonic knowledge was described in much more detail than it was in the original orders. Children were to be taught the relationship between phonemes and graphemes and be given the opportunity to identify a comprehensive range of letters and sounds including combinations of letter, blends and digraphs. Word recognition was also described as an important skill as was grammatical knowledge and contextual understanding. This Key Skills section was much more detailed and prescriptive than anything found in the original National Curriculum Orders. The most recent National Curriculum (DfEE and QCA, 1999) continued with the requirements that in reading at Key Stage 1 (DfEE and QCA, 1999, pp. 18–19) children should be taught reading strategies that involve phonemic awareness and phonic knowledge, word recognition and graphic knowledge, grammatical awareness and contextual understanding. It was also required that children need to be taught how to read for information and have experience and understanding of literature. This revised curriculum reflects the recommendations of the National Literacy Strategy (DfEE, 1998) that was introduced into schools in September 1998 following a pilot Literacy Project.

The National Literacy Strategy (NLS)

The NLS is not compulsory but it is expected that this programme will be adopted by schools unless a school can demonstrate, through its literacy action plan, schemes of work and performance in end of Key Stage tests, that existing arrangements are at least as effective. The NLS recommends that schools provide a dedicated, continuous hour of literacy teaching each day in all classes. The Framework for Teaching gives very clear directions on how the literacy hour is to be subdivided into whole-class shared reading and writing, guided and independent work and a plenary session. The teaching objectives are set out year by year and, from Year 1 onwards, term by term. They are divided into word-, sentence- and text-level work. The introduction to the framework describes a 'searchlight' approach to the teaching of reading where successful readers are seen as those who use as many strategies as possible including knowledge of phonics, grammar, word recognition and graphic knowledge and knowledge of context. This searchlight model sounds very like an interactionist approach but there is a very definite emphasis on the teaching of phonics (see, for example, the word-level objectives for Reception Year where an order is provided for the teaching of grapheme/ phoneme correspondences). There is also what can only be seen as a criticism of the 'real books' approach in the following sentence: 'Research evidence shows that pupils do not learn to distinguish between the different sounds of words simply by being exposed to books' (DfEE, 1998, p. 4).

SO HOW DO WE TEACH CHILDREN TO READ?

Hopefully, the introductory paragraphs to this chapter will have given you some understanding of the context within which you will be teaching children to read. When you go into schools you will realise that some teachers, while teaching according to the requirements of the NC and the recommendations of the NLS, may have very firm and individual views on how children learn to read most effectively. You, however, will be planning, teaching and assessing according to the Curriculum Guidance for the Foundation Stage, the National Curriculum for Key Stages 1 and 2, supported in many schools by the National Literacy Strategy. You will be using an interactionist approach in which children will be explicitly taught word-level, sentence-level and text-level strategies using a wide range of fiction and non-fiction texts.

The Foundation Stage for Reception-age children and Key Stage 1

The Foundation Stage covers the stage from 3-year-olds to the end of Reception Year. In the Reception Year the Foundation Stage objectives relate to the NLS objectives for the Reception Year. I am not going to address these objectives one by one but look at requirements more generally. Going through strategies for teaching reading it perhaps has not been made explicit enough that we teach children to read so that they can have access not only to information but also, perhaps more importantly, to one of the greatest pleasures in life – reading fiction. Certainly, the DfEE curriculum guidance, at all stages, although placing a lot of emphasis on reading strategies, does recognise that children's interest and enjoyment of reading should begin at a very early age and it is so important to remember this. Being able to read is not an end in itself, but a key to lifelong pleasure.

With this in mind I am going to start with **text-level work** – the books themselves. All the official curriculum guidance gives a range of texts that children are to experience. This range covers fiction: stories, plays and poems, traditional and modern, from familiar settings and different cultures. Similarly, non-fiction texts include print and ICT-based information texts from many different genres. The NLS has done much to broaden the range of texts that children experience in school and this begins at Foundation Stage and Key Stage 1.

Fiction

Hopefully, children come to school with an appreciation of books and will have enjoyed some precious moments with parents, curled up on a lap while a favourite story is read to them. We know, of course, that this is not always the case but whether, as teachers, we are introducing the world of stories to children or continuing the experience it must never be forgotten that stories are to be enjoyed. Opportunities have to be found during the day to read and tell stories either to the whole class or to smaller groups. In NLS terms this is often during 'shared text level' work and specific objectives have to be met, but when those objectives are examined closely many are associated with a response to the texts that encourages participation and enjoyment. In shared reading, stories can be read to a class of children that would be too demanding for them to read independently. The children are actively involved in the story telling. They imagine what might happen next or what they would do if they were in the story and are invited to share their thoughts with their classmates. These are the skills of prediction and projection that have traditionally been thought of as 'higher order' reading skills and, as such, part of the reading programme of much older children. The young readers also develop their 'primary skills' as they learn about print conventions, that there are units called words, that words, in English, go from left to right across the page and from top to bottom. They begin to understand terms such as 'beginning', 'end', 'page', etc. They also begin to recognise words and letters within the familiar texts. The children are being taught to understand print but within a context that is enjoyable and secure.

In shared reading the teacher has an opportunity to ask questions of children that are differentiated according to a particular child's knowledge and previous experience and are still related to the objectives planned for the session. However, as Fisher (1999) points out, shared reading cannot replace story time:

> Story time gives children the opportunity to get lost in a book in a way that they may not be able to do independently and which is inappropriate in a literacy hour where focused objectives and a brisk pace of teaching are important.
>
> (Fisher, 1999)

Chapter 4 considers in more detail the importance of stories in children's lives and, in meriting a whole chapter, indicates the importance we attach to the reading of fiction.

Non-fiction

Activity 2	Keep a diary for a week of all the reading you do.

How much of your reading has been fiction and how much non-fiction? While you, perhaps, are in a situation where you are reading more reference books than you will read at any other time in your lives you will also have had to read bits of information to enable you to function. Not only have you to be able to interpret information given to you but you need to be able to access useful information. While the value of reading fiction has long been recognised, non-fiction texts have, perhaps, not always been so explicitly part of the curriculum. All the recent curriculum guidance highlights the importance of teaching children to read non-fiction texts. The legal requirements of the National Curriculum in English at Key Stage 1 state that:

> Pupils should be taught to:
> A use the organisational features of non-fiction texts, including captions, illustrations, contents, index and chapters, to find information;
> B understand that texts about the same topic may contain different information or present similar information in different ways;
> C use reference materials for different purposes.
>
> (DfEE and QCA, 1999)

Wray and Lewis (1997) have been key players in the promotion of the importance of non-fiction texts. They point out the importance of reading information texts in the adult world, of recognising that the reading for information can be just as enjoyable as reading fiction and that there is evidence that boys prefer reading non-fiction to fiction. Wray and Lewis's EXIT (Extending Interactions with Texts) (1997) model is used as part of the NLS training material as a way of enabling pupils to interact meaningfully with information texts and communicate what they have learned. The model addresses the importance of using children's prior knowledge, establishing a purpose for reading before the reading begins and being taught effective strategies to locate information. This model can be as effective at Key Stage 1 as at Key Stage 2. The *Curriculum Guidance for the Foundation Stage* (QCA and DfEE, 2000) requires that children 'know that information can be retrieved from books and computers and (know) how information can be found in non-fiction texts to answer questions about where, who, why and how' (p. 62). Before pupils begin to look at information books on 'pets', for example, it is a good idea to find out what they already know about the topic. The next stage is to determine what they would like to know and then to teach them how to go about finding out the answers to their questions. They need to be taught about content pages, captions and how to use an index. Children also need at Key Stage 1 to begin the process of evaluating what they have read. At a simple level this would be an assessment of a book in terms of whether their original questions had been answered satisfactorily.

By considering text work first of all you should remember why you are teaching children to read. Alongside this, of course, you will be teaching reading strategies at what the NLS calls word and sentence level.

Word-level reading strategies include phonemic awareness and phonic knowledge, word recognition and graphic knowledge. You will remember from earlier paragraphs in this chapter that reading schemes based on the teaching of phonics were very limited in terms of interest and were one of the reasons why teachers embraced 'real books' so enthusiastically. The NLS has attempted to make phonics teaching more interesting by introducing, in *Progression in Phonics: Materials for Whole Class Teaching* (DfEE, 2000), games for the whole class that involve interactive, and, indeed, active, games. This booklet outlines the reasons why the NLS emphasises discrete phonics teaching while recommending that the skills learned should be applied to the reading of enjoyable texts:

> Although the structure of the phonic code can sometimes be revealed through poems and word-play texts, in most texts phonics patterning occurs too randomly to be discerned. Most quality stories, for example, in Big Books, will not repeat sound patterns with sufficient regularity to serve this purpose. Most focused phonics teaching should therefore be done through play, games and activities and then applied alongside other reading cues to meaningful reading of appropriately matched, good quality texts in other parts of the Literacy Hour, particularly in shared and guided sessions with the teacher.
>
> (DfEE, 2000, p. 7)

Before attempting to develop children's phonic skills it is essential to assess their phonological awareness and the NLS, particularly in *Progression in Phonics* (DfEE, 2000), gives you ideas for helping you decide whether a child can hear initial and final consonants, for example, and also for developing listening skills. Other schemes that have been designed to make phonics teaching more lively and multi-sensory are Jolly Phonics (Jolly Learning, Tailours House, High Road, Chigwell 1G7 6DL) and Letterland (Collins Educational).

It is important that you understand some of the terminology associated with the teaching of phonics:

Phonics is the understanding of the relationship between phonemes and graphemes.

Phonological awareness is the awareness of sounds within words. Children need to have this awareness before being taught phonics skills.

A **phoneme** is the smallest unit of sound, e.g. **a** *or* **sh**. There are approximately 44 phonemes in the English language.

A **grapheme** is the written representation of that sound. A grapheme may consist of one or more letters.

A **digraph** consists of two letters representing one phoneme (e.g. ba**th**, in which the **th** is a consonant digraph, and **rai**n, in which the **ai** is a vowel digraph).

A **split digraph** is something you may remember as a 'silent' or even 'magic' e. Two letters still represent one phoneme but they are separated by a consonant (e.g. ma**d**e, si**t**e, co**d**e).

A **trigraph** is three letters representing one phoneme (e.g. h**igh**, ma**tch**, e**dge**).

Synthetic phonics emphasises the sounding out and blending of sounds in words (synthesising), necessitating the explicit teaching of letters and phonemes (c-a-t).

Analytic phonics involves the analysing of whole words into sub-units, for example into onsets and rimes (r-at).

The **onset** is the initial consonant or consonant cluster of a word or syllable (e.g. the **r** in rat, the **ph** in phone, the **d** and **k** in **d**on**k**ey).

The **rime** is the part of the word or syllable that contains the vowel and final consonant or consonant cluster (e.g. the -**at** in rat, the -**one** in phone, the -**ash** in dash, the -**on** and -**ey** in donkey).

Activity 3 Underline the rimes in the following words:
cat stone late owl juice board sunshine petrol fight

The debate surrounding the relative effectiveness of analytic and synthetic phonics (mentioned above) was largely dismissed by the Director of the NLS:

> It is vital children are taught to identify and blend sounds for reading and to segment and spell sounds in words for writing . . . For the literacy strategy, the polarisation is largely irrelevant.
>
> (Stannard, 1999)

The emphasis on phonics teaching in this section reflects the emphasis placed on it by the NC and the NLS. However, as far as reading is concerned, word-level work also includes graphic knowledge and word recognition. Graphic knowledge is concerned with the recognition of words with common spelling patterns and the recognition of specific parts of words such as plurals, suffixes, prefixes etc. Children are taught to recognise these patterns through the analytic teaching of phonics, where, for example, onsets and rimes will be identified in rhyming words. Children will begin this work by learning rhymes and listening for common sounds.

Word recognition is the skill that many of you will remember from your own school days (e.g. the 'Look and Say' approach). You may have memories of flashcards and words in tins (separate from books). In current guidance this skill is taught to enable children to read on sight 'high-frequency' and 'medium-frequency' words that are not easy to decode using early phonic knowledge and are often difficult to predict from the context. However, they are words that are needed if an early reader is to make any sense of a text. Examples, of these words include **the, where, should**. The NLS Framework includes a list of recommended words that the children should be taught to read on sight. It is recommended that the words are not just taught in context while reading but reinforced through other activities. Games such as 'lotto' and 'snap' have long been used to encourage word recognition. Home-made books can repeat key words over and over again, as 'word detectives' children can hunt for the words in books and they can 'fish' for words using magnetic fishing rods. It must always be remembered, however, that although games can be enjoyable children should not spend too long reading words away from the context of a book. You may have memories of not being given a book until you could read all the relevant words out of context. This should certainly not happen today.

Sentence-level work consists of grammatical awareness. At Key Stage 1 pupils need to understand sentence order and begin to have an understanding of word classes. This is not as complicated as it sounds. If, for example, you read the following sentence, missing out a word: 'It was such a fine day when I — to school this morning that I felt like dancing', young children will be able to provide you with an appropriate word, a verb that might even be in the correct tense. Children develop an understanding of grammatical structure through hearing phrases and sentences repeated in stories and will bring this understanding to their reading.

Key Stage 2

Gone, hopefully, are the days when teachers of Key Stage 2 children saw their role as facilitating reading, having left the job of actually teaching reading skills to their colleagues in Key Stage 1. The NC programme of study for reading at Key Stage 2 requires the explicit teaching of reading strategies that will help pupils develop into competent and sophisticated readers. First of all, let us remind ourselves of why we want children to read and be encouraged by the NC requirement that

> During Key Stage 2 pupils read **enthusiastically** *(my emphasis)* a range of materials and use their knowledge of words, sentences and texts to understand and respond to meaning.
>
> (DfEE and QCA, 1999, p. 25)

We want children to read for pleasure and be able to access important information. How does the NC for English and the NLS help us to do that as teachers? Once again I want to consider text-level work first of all. The programme of study (Understanding Texts) requires that pupils should be explicitly taught to

> Use inference and deduction
> Look for meaning beyond the literal
> Make connections between different parts of a text
> Use their knowledge of other texts they have read.
>
> (DfEE and QCA, 1999, p. 25)

This has important implications for the way teachers question pupils about texts (both fiction and non-fiction) in order to ensure their understanding is beyond the literal.

The requirements are very reminiscent of comprehension taxonomies that categorised levels of understanding. Barratt (Clymer, 1972), for example, divided comprehension skills into five categories: literal comprehension, reorganisation, inferential comprehension, evaluation and appreciation. This taxonomy is very useful in terms of developing questions to elicit children's full understanding of a text. A summary of Barratt's categories and examples of questions will give you an understanding of how you need to plan carefully the questions you ask pupils.

- *Literal comprehension*, as you might expect, focuses on information that is explicitly stated in the text. Questions you might ask include, *What was the name of the boy in the story? When did a particular incident take place?* (The information must be clearly given.)
- *Reorganisation* requires the pupils to analyse or synthesise information. You might ask the pupils to summarise points made in the text, for example, *Summarise the events that led up to the fire?*
- *Inferential comprehension* involves, for example, predicting outcomes, inferring literal meanings from figurative language, inferring main ideas or, perhaps, morals that might not be explicitly stated in the text or inferring the motives of characters. Questions might be as simple as *What do you think might happen next? What is the moral of this story?*
- *Evaluation* includes the making of judgements based, for example, on the reader's own experience or the criteria set by the teacher. The evaluations could include considerations of whether the author has succeeded in supporting what he/she set out to do. Questions would include: *Could this really happen? Does the author prove his/her point?*
- *Appreciation* involves the pupils having an emotional response to the text, identifying with characters, reacting to the use of language or imagery. Questions could include examples such as: *How did you feel when Tom found out about his father? How did you feel when the author described the dungeon?*

Remember, however, that although the above comprehension skills have often been called 'higher order skills' we saw how, in the section on Key Stage 1, very young children can be asked questions that demand that they think beyond the literal.

Activity 4   Choose a passage from a book and devise questions that would elicit pupils'

- literal comprehension
- inferential comprehension
- appreciation

Reading for information

The EXIT model (Wray and Lewis, 1997) was mentioned briefly in the section on Key Stage 1 as a way of encouraging pupils to interact with non-fiction texts. This model is recommended by the NLS and has ten stages:

1   activating prior knowledge;
2   establishing purposes;
3   locating information;
4   adopting an appropriate strategy;
5   interacting with the text;
6   monitoring understanding;
7   making a record;
8   evaluating information;
9   assisting memory;
10   communicating information.

The NLS Literacy Training Pack (module 6) will take you through the model.

A range of non-fiction texts

The NC and NLS require that pupils should be introduced to a wide range of texts, non-fiction as well as fiction. Genre theory (Graham and Kelly, 1997) has shown that it is important that pupils are taught how to identify the language features and structures of different types of texts in order to be able to write in different genres. There is obviously an implication for reading in that pupils need to be introduced to a wide range of genres and have language features and structures explicitly described. The NC includes in its range of non-fiction and non-literary texts:

- diaries, autobiographies, biographies, letters;
- print and ICT-based reference and information materials;
- newspapers, magazines, articles, leaflets, brochures, advertisements.

(DfEE and QCA, 1999, p. 27)

The NLS (DfEE, 1998) provides a more detailed list of text types when it identifies the range that pupils should experience. These are identified at the top of each term's planning page (DfEE, 1998: Section 2). The reading objectives are directly linked to the writing objectives. For example, if we consider reading and writing objectives from Year 5, Term 1 (DfEE, 1998, pp. 44–5) we find that, in the non-fiction section (reading) one of the objectives is:

> To read and evaluate a range of instructional texts in terms of their
> - purposes;
> - organisation and layout;
> - clarity and usefulness.
>
> (DfEE, 1998, pp. 44–5)

The corresponding writing objective is:

> To write instructional texts, and test them out, e.g. instructions for loading computers, design briefs for technology, rules for games.
>
> (DfEE, 1998, pp. 44–5)

The range box at the top of that planning page identifies the need for pupils to read:

> Instructional texts: rules, recipes, directions, instructions etc. showing how things are done.
>
> (DfEE, 1998, pp. 44–5)

This is a good example of how the NLS links reading and writing throughout and also how it has encouraged teachers to widen the range of material that is presented to pupils.

Non-fiction, boys and Curiosity Kits

Curiosity Kits are book bags containing non-fiction books, related artefacts and activities. As you will see in Chapter 4 there has been evidence to show that book bags (Storysacks) have been very effective in encouraging reading but Curiosity Kits were created to address the needs of reluctant and struggling boy readers particularly in their attitude to reading at home and were based on non-fiction books rather than stories. They were also directed at Key Stage 2 children, unlike Story Sacks that tend to be used by younger children. The first Curiosity Kit project was set up and evaluated by Lewis et al. (2001) and set out to stimulate Year 4 boys' interest in reading. Another aim was to involve adult males at home by sending home a magazine on the same topic but aimed at adults. The research showed that the kits had an impact on the range of people sharing home reading and the number of books taken home. Certainly, the idea has been taken up by many schools and local groups, including those wishing to pursue environmental themes, for example (English and Machin, 2003).

Fiction

The other strand to text-level work is, of course, the teaching of literature (fiction). Chapter 4 deals with this in detail so I will only address a small number of issues here. Both the NC and the NLS recommend a wide range of fiction texts in the same way as they do for non-fiction.

The range includes, for Key Stage 2:

- a range of modern fiction by significant children's authors;
- long-established children's fiction;
- a range of good-quality modern poetry;
- classic poetry;
- texts drawn from a variety of cultures and traditions;
- myths, legends and traditional stories;
- playscripts.

The NLS, as with non-fiction, gives more detail so, for example, it is recommended that teachers give children experience of:

stories or short novels that raise issues, e.g. bullying, bereavement, injustice; stories by the same author; stories from other cultures.

(DfEE, 1998, p. 44)

It is laudable that it is now a requirement that children are introduced to a wide range of texts. It is important, however, that judgement is exercised when choosing specific books. There is a danger that books can be used simply because they fall within the required text type for that particular term. Marriott (1995) outlines five issues that we should take into account when considering children's books:

- Is the book physically attractive? Are the illustrations of good quality?
- Is the book well written? Is the language vivid and original yet accessible and easy to read?
- Does the book have a powerful story? Is it coherent, convincing and enjoyable?
- Are the book's social and moral assumptions, both explicit and implicit, positive and constructive?
- Is it a book that children will like?

(Marriott, 1995, pp. 45–6)

Marriott would be the first to dismiss, however, the notion of the 'the good book' and sees the teacher's role as guiding the children's reading rather than imposing too many restrictions (1995, pp. 59–60).

Activity 5	Choose two story books, one suitable for Key Stage 1 pupils and one for Key Stage 2 pupils, and apply Marriott's criteria.

It is important that Key Stage 2 teachers continue to develop their pupils' reading strategies and this includes **word- and sentence-level** strategies. You will know from your experience in school that primary school children now have a knowledge of language, particularly grammatical terminology, that you might find staggering. This, of course, reflects the lack of emphasis that was placed on grammatical knowledge when you were at primary school. Before you panic, however, do not forget that, while you may lack an explicit knowledge of rules about language, you will probably have an excellent implicit knowledge. Chapter 8 of this book will give you the grammatical knowledge you need to enable you to discuss with pupils the way authors have made use of language in their texts.

The emphasis at Key Stage 2 in the word-level work requirements is on spelling strategies and vocabulary extension that bring reading and writing skills together. During shared and guided reading sessions pupils need to have words drawn to their attention in order that these words can be spelled correctly and used effectively in the children's own writing. For example, analogies should be made between words with common endings to aid spelling and vocabulary can be enhanced through a discussion of an author's use of a particular word or expression. It is, perhaps, a very obvious thing to say, but writing cannot come from nowhere. As well as having first-hand experiences to write about children need to read, and have read to them, a variety of books that they then have the opportunity to discuss in order to be able to write interesting texts themselves.

So I end this chapter with the books themselves and this is as it should be. You will, hopefully, have an understanding of the debates and tensions that have always dogged the teaching of reading but you will also be experiencing the excitement of providing children with the key to the world of books.

| **Answers to Activity 3** | cat; stone; late; owl; juice; board; sun; petrol; fight |

REFERENCES/SUGGESTIONS FOR FURTHER READING

Bayley, R. (1996) 'The Tyranny of Black and White', *Language and Learning*, 8, 2, pp. 32–3

Beard, R. (1998) *National Literacy Strategy, Review of Research and other Related Evidence*, Sudbury: DfEE

Bielby, N. (1999) *Balanced Phonics and the Teaching of Reading*. United Kingdom Reading Association Conference Paper

Chew, J. (1997) 'Traditional Phonics: What It Is and What It Is Not', *Journal of Research in Reading*, 20, pp. 171–83, Oxford: Blackwell for the United Kingdom Reading Society

Clymer, T. (1972) 'What is "Reading"? Some Current Concepts' in A. Melnick and J. Merritt (eds) *Reading Today and Tomorrow*, London: University of London Press

Cook, D. and Young, D. (1994) *The Teaching of Reading*, Derby: University of Derby

DfEE (1998) *The National Literacy Strategy Framework for Teaching*, London: DfEE

DfEE and QCA (1999) *English: The National Curriculum for England*, London: DfEE and QCA

DfEE (2000) *Progression in Phonics: Materials for Whole Class Teaching*, London: DfEE

English, E. and Machin, J. (2003) Environmental sacks in *Curiosity Kits* edited by M. Lewis and R. Fisher, Reading: National Centre for Language and Literacy

Fisher, R. (1999) 'Literacy Inside and Outside the Hour' in R. Fisher with A. Arnold (eds) *Understanding the Literacy Hour*, Royston, Herts: United Kingdom Reading Association

Fisher, R. with Arnold, H. (eds) (1999) *Understanding the Literacy Hour*, Royston: United Kingdom Reading Association

Goodman, K. (1986) *What's Whole in Whole Language?*, Ontario: Scholastic

Goswami, U. (1999) *Balanced Phonics*, a paper for Ofsted meeting, 29 March, 1999

Graham, J. and Kelly, A. (1997) *Reading under Control*, London: David Fulton

Harrison, C. (1996) *The Teaching of Reading*, Shepreth, Herts: United Kingdom Reading Association

Her Majesty's Inspectorate (1996) *The Teaching of Reading in Inner London Primary Schools*, London: DFE.

James, F. (1996) *Phonological Awareness, Classroom Strategies*, Royston: United Kingdom Reading Association

Lewis, M., Fisher, R., Grainger, T., Harrison, C. and Hulme, P. (2001) 'Curiosity Kits: The Impact of Non-Fiction Book Bags on Boys' Reading at Home', *Topic – Practical Applications of Research in Education*, Spring, 25, Slough: NFER

Marriott, S. (1995) *Read On*, London: Paul Chapman

Miskin, R. (1998) *Best Practice Phonics*, London: Heinemann

Ofsted (2002) *The National Literacy Strategy: The First Four Years 1998–2000*, London: Office for Standards in Education

QCA and DfEE (2000) *Curriculum Guidance for the Foundation Stage*, London: QCA

Stannard, J. (1999) 'Letter' from Director, National Literacy Strategy, *Times Educational Supplement*, 5 March

Stanovich, K. and Stanovich, P. (1995) 'How Research Might Inform the Debate about Early Reading Acquisition', *Journal of Research in Reading*, 18, 2, Oxford: Blackwell for the United Kingdom Reading Society

Waterland, E. (1988) *Read With Me: An Apprenticeship Approach to Reading*, 2nd edn, Stroud: Thimble Press

Weaver, C. (1990) *Understanding Whole Practice*, Portsmouth, USA: Heinemann

Westwood, P., Knight, B.A. and Redden, E. (1997) 'Assessing Teachers' Beliefs about Literacy Acquisition', *Journal of Research in Reading*, 20, 3, pp. 224–35, Oxford: Blackwell for the United Kingdom Reading Society

Wray, D. and Lewis, M. (1997) *Extending Literacy – Children Reading and Writing Non-fiction*, London: Routledge

4 Fiction

GEORGE ENGLISH

This chapter is going to consider the role of fiction in children's lives. Some of this has been addressed in Chapter 3 but I want to go beyond the National Curriculum and explore the importance of stories and readers' response to stories.

The world of fiction is a world of stories. Stories are very important to us all – think of the audience of millions that television soaps attract. This enjoyment starts at a very early age as young children have stories told to them or read to them in a very secure and pleasurable environment, sitting on an adult's lap or tucked up in bed. Leeson (1985) described the importance of stories to children:

> Every children's story is, in the broadest sense of the word, a story about growing up. Stories told by adults to children cannot help but teach, because of the difference in age and experience. The story is the gateway through which the young pass in discovering the difference between facts and the truth, between observation and understanding, which is the essence of all experience and thus all growing up.
>
> (Leeson, 1985, p. 16)

Activity 1	Take a trip down memory lane and make a list of the stories (either told to you or read) that you enjoyed as a child.

What an important role the teacher has in ensuring that young children continue (or begin, in some cases) to hear stories and, as they learn to read for themselves, to be introduced to books that will turn them into readers for the rest of their lives. As children stumble with their early reading skills somehow the contest is entered between the child thirsty for stories and the printed text which may not give up its messages easily. This is where careful choice of books is important and by this I mean a careful choice of picture books. Picture books and illustrated books are not the same things. In picture books the text and the pictures are equally important in moving the story along. Some picture books may have no text at all but still tell an excellent story. Jan Ormerod's *Sunshine* and *Moonlight* are good examples of this. Illustrated books include pictures but these are not vital to the story. However, good illustrations can reinforce what is being said in the text and often enhance it. We tend to think of picture books as being produced for young children while older, more able readers have books with only a few illustrations, the reasoning being, presumably, that once children can read well they don't need the support of pictures. There are, however, picture books that have very sophisticated ideas. Look, for example, at Mitsumasa Anno's complex picture books (*Anno's USA*, for example, with its wealth of detail) or Anthony Browne's *Changes* where both the ideas and the pictures are very complex.

Good pictures and illustrations glow and have their own magic. The writer and illustrator Brian Wildsmith was once visiting a school when a boy suddenly leapt up and shouted, 'Here, are you the feller what wrote them books?' Wildsmith answered that he was, wondering what the boy would say next. The boy went on, 'I loves them. I likes to lick 'em.' If you see a Wildsmith illustration with its vivid illustrations you can understand what the boy meant. What a compliment that his pictures didn't just fit the story, they had a life of their own and what a pleasure for the boy, the feeling that the illustrations were so tangible that his engagement with the book was physical. Wildsmith is just one of the many brilliant illustrators British children's books are blessed with. Nicola Bayley has quite a different style, detailed and reflective, showing a passionate eye for detail, seen to great effect in *The Patchwork Cat*. Quentin Blake meanwhile is the master of the furious line, with illustrations so full of energy they almost fizz of the page. He has illustrated other writers' work, but he is equally at home with his own texts, *Mr Magnolia* being a particularly dazzling example of his gifts. These are just a few of the classic children's illustrators and new illustrators come along regularly to add to their store.

Pictures are crucial at this stage and a good early reading book should be well stocked with them. Also important are stories with repetition so that children can predict language patterns and events. A wonderful book, *The Three Little Wolves and the Big Bad Pig* by Eugene Trivizas and Helen Oxenbury is an excellent example of this. With an environmental twist on the traditional tale of the three little pigs, this book has the same repeated 'huffing and puffing' as the original with an additional 'But the pig wasn't called big and bad for nothing' repeated after every failed attempt to blow up the cuddly wolves' homes. Rhythm and rhyme also play an important role in books for young children, just as they are important in oral story telling for children and adults. Nicola Bayley and William Mayne's *Patchwork Cat*, already mentioned for its glorious pictures, is a firm favourite with children who love Mayne's rhymes.

> She says good morning and good yawning to the people living in the house.
> (Bayley, and Mayne, 1981, p. 2)

Good story and picture books are essential to the teacher's task of motivating children to read so that they become young people and adults who both 'can' and 'do' read. Stories can also help children structure their thoughts and increase their vocabulary and their understanding of increasingly complex grammatical sentences. However, fiction has other functions, even if it means simply escaping everyday problems and realities. It also helps the child to make sense of a complex and contradictory world.

At some point in their young lives children have to negotiate their way from the world of the spoken story to the complex world of print and the even more complex world of progressing as readers in understanding how language functions in more complex ways. The struggle between the child and the printed word is a complex one which is not part of this chapter but it continues to influence their enjoyment of the text, their confidence as readers and their eventual continuance in the world of print.

Fortunately a wide range of texts is available that cater for the developing reader in a diverse and diverting way. Bob Wilson's *Stanley Bagshaw* lives 'up north where it's boring and slow'. But his life is far from boring as the reader discovers in a series of sophisticated picture books. Similarly, in Russell Hoban's *How Tom Beat Captain Najork and his Hired Sportsmen*, Quentin Blake's fabulous illustrations support a text full of deft wit which shows the indomitable Tom winning out against the terrifying Captain Najork in a series of crazy athletic games. Jill Murphy's *Worst Witch*, meanwhile, shows Mildred Hubble as a modern and very determined witch triumphing against the repressive regime of Miss Cackle's academy for witches. It is important to understand that once children master the picture book stage then their reading lives become like a game of hop-scotch – they don't just throw their marker forward and proceed in a straight line reading more and more complex texts. Sometimes they leap forward but they also leap backward and enjoy catching up on an old and venerated picture book that has been with them for a long time. Equally important, they jump sideways and read books that are sometimes neither taxing nor imaginative nor very literary. For a teacher of 7 to 11-year-olds this can be disconcerting and hard to resource within the classroom. This is where a well-stocked school library, available to children as regularly as possible, even if it is just in the corner of a hall, is so important.

> The best we can do by way of a creative environment is to fill the shelves with the best books and persuade children to read them.
>
> (Inglis, 1981, p. 6)

The key word here has to be persuade, because often children will not come to books on their own, even if they are on the shelf in front of them. Crucial to their safe development as readers is that they are supported. This can mean listening to a story read by a teacher or parent or an older brother or sister or a friend. Certainly it is very important as we begin to look at longer texts, for example *The Pie Makers* by Helen Cresswell or *Charlie and the Chocolate Factory* by Roald Dahl, that the first encounter of the text is in a supportive situation. Hearing a book read and discussing it as part of a large group is an important part of the process of developing the child's faculties as critical readers, able to formulate an opinion on a text and engage in a reflective analysis when questioned. As teachers you will need to practise your 'reading aloud' skills, supporting your reading with the necessary dramatic intonations that will help children understand more complex and sophisticated texts than they would be able to if they relied on their own reading of stories. This is a good place to mention the usefulness of puppets to support your stories. I am constantly surprised by the way children respond to puppets. Sometimes a demanding group of children will sit up and take notice of a puppet after all other attempts at getting through to them have failed: a useful strategy to remember for behaviour management! Story Sacks are also widely used in schools to support story telling and can be very effective.

STORY SACKS

Story Sacks, the brainchild of Neil Griffiths (1998), have taken off in such a way since their inception that it is the rare school that does not use them. They are being used by schools and libraries to lend to individual children, by teachers to support their teaching in school and also as part of family literacy projects. The words 'Story Sack' very much describe what it is – a sack containing a story – but it is much more than this. Griffiths makes great claims for these sacks and the enthusiasm with which they've been adopted by schools would perhaps support the claims. A typical cloth sack, simply or elaborately decorated, contains a storybook, a non-fiction book picking up on the theme of the storybook, an audio-tape of the story, puppets, games, activities and other artefacts connected with the story. On the video produced to introduce the Story Sacks, Griffiths (1998) describes how they are a fresh approach to enjoying books, how they bring stories to life and how they instil in children a love of books that might well turn them into lifelong readers. The video shows parents describing how, when children bring the sacks home, the play and activities can last for days and the children become really motivated to read. Similarly, when a whole class of children has access to the sacks in the classroom, Griffiths (1998) claims that the children's motivation to read increases, interest in a book is sustained for longer periods of time, the children learn to listen more attentively and the active interaction and participation in a story increases the children's confidence and self-esteem. As well as benefiting the children, the making of the sacks brings parents and community members together in a very purposeful way.

READING ALOUD

The importance of reading aloud to children has been mentioned. Remember how crucial this is to introducing children to stories that will be at their interest level but perhaps at a higher reading level. Do not make the mistake of thinking that reading a story is just a way of filling in a few minutes at the end of a day. The following is an abridged version of Trelease's (1982) 'Do's and Don'ts of Read Aloud', and should help you prepare for this very rewarding task.

- Read as often as you and the class have time for.
- Remember the art of listening is an acquired one. It must be taught.
- Avoid long descriptive passages until the child's imagination and attention span are capable of handling them.

- Allow your listeners a few minutes to settle down and adjust their feet and minds to the story. An authoritarian 'Now stop that and settle down! Sit up straight. Pay attention' is not conducive to a receptive audience.
- If you are reading a picture book, make sure the children can see the pictures easily.
- Remember that reading aloud comes naturally to very few people. To do it successfully and with ease you must practise.
- Use plenty of expression when reading. If possible, change your tone of voice to fit the dialogue.
- Adjust your pace to fit the story. During an exciting part, slow down, draw your words out, bring your listeners to the edge of their chairs.
- The most common mistake in reading aloud is reading too fast.
- Preview the book by reading it to yourself ahead of time.
- Don't read stories that you don't enjoy yourself.

(Trelease, 1982, pp. 73–5)

Activity 2 Choose a story that you think would 'read aloud' well. Read it a number of times and then find an appreciative audience to read the story to, bearing in mind the advice given above.

CHOOSING BOOKS

The only way to choose books for your pupils is to make sure you make frequent visits to bookshops and your local authority's Schools Library Service. It would also be useful to become a member of the National Centre for Language and Literacy (www.ncll.org.uk) or the Federation of Children's Book Groups (www.fcbg.org.uk). New books are reviewed in such journals as *Books for Keeps* (6 Brightfield Road, Lee, London, SE12 8QF) and *Carousel* (7 Carrs Lane, Birmingham, BA 7TG). While working as co-editor for *Books for your Children* I was in the wonderful position of having almost every published children's book pushed through my letter-box. Fortunately, my family shared my love of children's books and it was, for all of us, like Christmas every day. It only became an issue when floors and ceilings began to collapse under the strain. Some of the books I reviewed for the magazine became firm favourites and I would like to share some of those reviews with you. These reviews have been reproduced with kind permission of Ragdoll Productions UK (Ltd).

Books for younger children

Ladybird, Ladybird by Ruth Brown (Anderson)

Ruth Brown has a justified reputation as an illustrator of almost photographic skill. *Our Puppy's Holiday* was excellent and *Ladybird, Ladybird* continues a winning streak with variations on the traditional rhyme:

> Ladybird, ladybird, fly away home,
> your house is on fire and your children are gone.

Happily, this book takes a more reassuring line but not before the ladybird has had a whole series of adventures. There's also a James Herriot story, *Blossom Comes Home*, illustrated by Ruth Brown that is well worth grabbing (Michael Joseph).

The Moonlit Journey by Peter O'Donnell (ABC)

There are a number of books that deal with night-time fears. Often there's a drab sameness about them, no matter what good intentions their author might have had in writing them. Occasionally as with the Berenstain's *Bears in the Night*, Sendak's *In the Night Kitchen* or Martin Waddell's *The Park in the Dark* the fear of the dark that so many children experience is explored with great intensity and often humour. This picture book follows in that great tradition. Thomas, the hero, safe at home in bed, is nevertheless terrified that wolves are coming for him as the storm beats against his house. Then a fox appears to guide him through the wild winter night into the dark world where he sees for himself that there really is nothing to be afraid of except his own imagination. But just when the reader feels safe O'Donnell has a master stroke to play. And play it he does in a masterly fashion. A striking and very original picture book.

Wild Wild Sunflower Child Anna by Nancy White Carlstrom, illustrated by Jerry Pinkney (Macmillan)

Anna runs through the summer countryside ruffling sunflowers, blowing dandelion clocks and falling dizzy with delight into the vivid greenery. This delightful book makes you want to pick it up straight away, glowing as it does with Jerry Pinkney's dazzling sunshine illustrations. And that sunshine is reflected in Nancy Carlstrom's poetic text, which flows and falls, as Anna dances and skips, eats berries and splashes in frog pools. My one reservation about this lovely book is that there might be a slight discrepancy in the age of the child portrayed and the age of the potential reader. Not a first picture book, but lovely for the sixes to sevens.

Can It Be True? by Susan Hill, illustrated by Angels Barrett (Hamish Hamilton)

A Christmas story with a difference, told in beautiful free verse by a writer who knows not only how to make language flow, but is keenly aware of the sounds it makes. Set against a traditional countryside background it tells how the owl, the fox, the huntsmen and the great whales, far out at sea, hear the news of Christ's birth. Angela Barrett's glowing illustrations, set against blustery winter landscapes and billowing oceans and surrounded by illuminated borders, give it an exceptional quality which makes it special among Christmas books.

Hold Tight Bear by Ron Maris (Julia MacRae Books)

Following on from his very successful *Are You There Bear?* Ron Maris has taken the same set of toy characters and used them to illustrate an imaginary adventure. As usual Maris's drawing is excellent and the teddy bear and assorted toy dolls are portrayed affectionately but also with a great deal of humour. Bears getting into scrapes seem to be very popular with more than one author using the theme.

Eat Up Gemma by Sarah Hayes, illustrated by Jan Ormerod (Walker)

These happy snapshots from the life of a middle-class black family, especially their baby Gemma, make a smashing pre-school book. Every parent knows what it's like trying to encourage toddlers to eat the right sorts of food and every young rebel will surely identify with a heroine who knows what she wants and is determined to get it. A simple, clear text is beautifully brought to life by Jan Ormerod's crisp illustrations.

Somebody and the Three Blairs by Marilyn Tolhurst, illustrated by Simone Abel (ABC)

What if a bear took on Goldilock's role and came to a house owned by three people? That's the concept behind this marvellously entertaining picture book, which is just complicated enough to prompt questions from a 6-year-old reader. This being a modern story, what the bear does is quite different from the original story: he finds the shower too hot and the lavatory too small, but the wash basin is just right for drinking from. The illustrations are richly comic and the words are just right.

Let's Go Home, Little Bear by Martin Waddell and Barbara Firth (Walker)

This is a wonderful picture book with Martin Waddell working his own particular style of magic. The story is simply constructed around two bears walking home through the woods, with the younger one hearing all kinds of worrying sounds that he takes to be mysterious followers. Big bear is sensitive to his fears and eventually carries him back to their warm and safe home. Martin Waddell is a master of the picture book form, knowing when an idea needs repeating, knowing when to push the narrative along and how to resolve the tensions of the story in a satisfying climax. The illustrations are warm and strong and convey, effortlessly, the difference between the cold snowy wastes of the forest and the warm safety at home.

Books for older children

The Talking Car by Nicholas Fisk (Macmillan)

Writing for the seven to nines isn't all that easy but here Nicholas Fisk does it with great ease. It's a simple story about a boy whose father gets a talking car, one of those with the micro-processor voices. But the boy can really communicate with the car and it pours out all its feelings to him. Then his father sells it and the boy is devastated. A lively, fast-moving, warm and comic book which it is hard to imagine any child not liking.

The Tunnel by Anthony Browne (Julia Macrae)

Only a few, very talented, children's author/illustrators have managed to take a familiar and much-loved folk tale and attempted to recreate it in their own individual way. This is Anthony Browne's 'Little Red Riding Hood' brought up-to-date. There is no grandmother to visit and no wolf to threaten but there is a nightmare forest to be traversed and a daring rescue to be affected. The strength of the book is in the narration, both in pictures and in words. But it is the relationship between the bold brother, who becomes the frightened victim, and the timid sister, who saves him from death, which gives it emotional resonance.

Miss Fanshawe and the Great Dragon Adventure by Sue Scullard (Picturemac)

Sue Scullard's work is a bit like Nicola Bayley's in its fineness and attention to detail, but her imagination is all her own. Miss Fanshawe, a suffragette explorer, sets off into the mountains in search of a stolen dragon's egg. High in the mountains she finds a volcano into which she descends. And the reader descends with her through a series of cut-out holes in the centre of the page into a fantastic world of butterflies and dark leopards, where glowing lava is replaced by a lost city. Dazzling to look at if occasionally a bit scary.

The Blemyah Stories by William Mayne, illustrated by Juan Wijngaard (Walker paperback)

This is a 'great' book in every sense of the word. On the feast of Tiffany the Blemyahs come to the priory-kirk and at Midwinter they leave. Misshapen as they are, with gigantic heads where their bodies should be, they nevertheless carve beautiful misericords on the choir stalls. But first out of their carving comes Ruffin the demonic imp who rampages through the book determined to be evil but who in the end is overcome by his own goodness. Mayne, as usual, is a master craftsman, writing with elegance and style, yet suffusing the text with a wild humour. All this is neatly underlined by Juan Wijngaard's illustrations which can be menacing or atmospheric in the colour plates and comically inventive in the cartoon sketches which border each page. A haunting book, which will repay more than one visit.

The Lives of Christopher Chant by Dianna Wynne-Jones (Methuen)

The figure of Chrestomanci is always popping up in Dianna Wynne-Jones's novels and this time the story is based on his early years. As usual with a novel from this author there is richness of invention which is astonishing and the story roars along at breakneck speed as Chrestomanci stumbles from adventure to adventure, eventually learning the meaning and responsibility of power. I loved every minute of it and was sorry when it had finished. For readers who adore wild fantasy novels, with a surprise at every turn, this is an absolute must.

The Adventures of a Railway Cat by Phyllis Arkle (Puffin)

Alfie is the kind of cat who's always getting into adventures, which makes him popular with some of the characters using the railway but unpopular with Hack, the station porter. Children know only too well what it is to be disliked by an adult and Alfie is an easy character for them to identify with in these thoroughly modern but gently narrated stories.

Ultramarine by Jenny Nimmo (Methuen)

Riddles in the sand, ancient sea myths and the terrors and joys of family life are all elements in this wonderful story about two children who are left in the care of their aunt while their mother goes on her honeymoon. During this brief season their lives are radically changed; old uncertainties disappear to be replaced by other, newer ones and the children are involved in a heartbreaking rescue of oil damaged sea-birds. All the while, in the background, is the sea itself, the smell and sound of it and the many dramatic moods it can summon up. This is a rich and magical book with a strong emotional resonance.

Wild Robert by Diana Wynne-Jones (Methuen)

At first sight this little book bears the hallmark of a cliché-ridden ghost story. A young girl whose parents are caretakers of a big house makes friends with a ghost and they have adventures. What makes it special is Diana Wynne-Jones's inventive handling of the story and the throwaway humour. The ghost is far from friendly and turns out to be a nuisance that the girl is glad to get rid of. Knockabout fun for rainy summer afternoons.

Funny Stories by Michael Rosen (Kingfisher)

Anthologies are usually the death of readers. They sit like accusing dinosaurs on the shelves of public and school libraries, mouldering, unwanted and unread. Michael Rosen's collection isn't a bit like that, as you would expect from a writer who can be hilarious and disconcerting within the same page. For a start, the stories aren't only funny 'ha-ha' they're also 'funny peculiar', strange and often quite frightening. Jan Mark rubs shoulders with Joyce Grenfell, James Thurber complements Italo Calvino and Tunisian folk tales take their place alongside those from Pakistan. But the oddest of all for me in this very rich collection is *The Hole* by Eric Partridge. In the space of three pages it manages to be one of the most disquieting accounts of the penalty for keeping up with the Joneses.

Hairline Cracks by John Robert Taylor (Armada)

This elegant little thriller shows how much television has shaped and changed our expectations of certain types of story. From the moment he walks through the door to find his mum missing we identify with the hero's growing panic as he tries to find out the reason for her disappearance. As the story grows we learn just enough to keep us guessing, until it builds to a special climax. Some interesting asides about public corruption and the nuclear industry give it that extra edge.

RESPONDING TO FICTION

Martin (1999) is critical of the National Literacy Strategy in that 'responding to fiction' does not appear as one of the key areas at text level. The learning objectives make reference to the importance of response but there is no real examination of what that process entails.

Traditional approaches to the study of literature have focused on trying to understand what the author has intended. Increasingly, we now encourage readers to interact with the text and bring their own experience and understanding to their reading. This is known as 'responding to text'. Marriott (1995) sums up the importance of reader response:

> To enable children to reflect on what they read, to evaluate it, and to
> share it, is to make it possible for them to interact with texts more
> effectively and thus to construct meaning more skilfully, and to learn a
> little more about themselves and others and the world they live in.
>
> (Marriott, 1995, p. 88)

Responding is an active process and it is important that teachers encourage children to reflect on their reading. Discussion needs to be encouraged that will help children to picture characters and what is happening in a story, to predict what might happen next and project themselves into the situations described.

Prediction begins by looking at the book cover and the title and trying to decide what the story might be about. This would also be the time to remember books written by the same author or books written on the same topic. As the book is read to the children, stop and ask them about the characters and what they, the children, would do in similar situations. Discuss how the author has made a particular character appear friendly or frightening. The following activities will encourage children's response to texts. They can be used, with different levels of support, for children of all ages.

- Make puppets and use them to retell the story.
- Write letters in role, as a character explaining or justifying actions to other characters or readers.
- Report the major events in the story in the form of a newspaper report.
- Write a day/week of one character's life in diary form.

- Make a 'radio play' of a story, using a tape recorder and sound effects.
- Create a story sack (see above) for the story.
- Predict what will happen after a certain point in the story, perhaps writing the next scene.
- Look at the vocabulary, kinds of sentences etc. to see how they are used to build up suspense, tension or humour.
- Write book reviews. Young children could use symbols to indicate whether or not they liked the book. Older children could organise a 'Book Programme': a live or taped programme with chairperson and reviewers offering their views of the book.
- Write letters to another class, perhaps in another school, explaining why they would recommend the book.
- Use drama activities such as 'hot seating' or 'freeze-frame'. The 'hot-seating' technique involves the teacher or a child taking on the role of a character from the story. Questions are asked of the character (in role) by the rest of the class. A 'freeze-frame' involves a group choosing a particular moment from the story and freezing that moment by holding it in position, rather like a photograph.

(See end of chapter for further reading that will give you other suggestions for encouraging children's response to text.)

> **Activity 3** Visit bookshops and libraries and start to build up a repertoire of stories that you would enjoy reading to children. Make brief notes on the books, basing your 'reviews' on those compiled above. Have a good time!

This is an appropriate place to finish this chapter. I hope that the reading of children's fiction will enhance your lives as well as those of the children you teach.

REFERENCES/SUGGESTIONS FOR FURTHER READING

Anno, M. (1983) *Anno's USA*, London: Bodley Head

Atterton J. (2001) 'Waking Quests' in F.M. Collins and J. Graham (eds) *Historical Fiction for Children – Capturing the Past*, London: David Fulton

Bayley, N. and Mayne, W. (1981) *The Patchwork Cat*, London: Cape

Browne, A. (1990) *Changes*, London: Julia MacRae Books (Walker)

Cresswell, H. (1976) *The Pie-makers*, Harmondsworth: Puffin

Dahl, R. (1967) *Charlie and the Chocolate Factory*, London: Allen and Unwin

Dahl, R. (1995) *Charlie and the Chocolate Factory*, illustrated by Quentin Blake, London: Puffin

Gamble, N. and Yates, S. *Exploring Children's Literature* (2002), London: Paul Chapman

Griffiths, N. (1998) *Story Sacks* (Video), Bury: Story Sacks Ltd

Inglis, F. (1981) *The Promise of Happiness*, Cambridge: Cambridge University Press

Leeson, R. (1985) *Reading and Righting*, London: Collins

Marriott, S. (1995) *Read On*, London: Paul Chapman

Martin, T. (1999) 'Becoming Readers' in Goodwin, P. (ed.) *The Literate Classroom*, London: David Fulton

Murphy, J. (1978) *The Worst Witch*, Harmondsworth: Puffin

Ormerod, J. (1981) *Sunshine*, Harmondsworth, Middlesex: Kestrel Books

Ormerod, J. (1982) *Moonlight*, Harmondsworth, Middlesex: Kestrel Books

Read and Respond Series (Scholastic), for example:

    English, E. (2001) *The Leopard's Drum*, Leamington Spa: Scholastic (Key Stage 1)

    Scott, A. (1997) *The Secret Garden*, Leamington Spa: Scholastic (Key Stage 2)

Trelease, J. (1982) *The Read Aloud Handbook*, Harmondsworth: Penguin

5 Writing

SUE BEVERTON

The ability to write is an essential element of modern life. Writing is not only an art, to which perhaps only a small proportion of the population is drawn as a means of making a living, it is also an activity often expected of us in a literate society almost as casually as reading. The assumption that everyone possesses the skill to communicate in writing has increased enormously, rather than receded, as technology has made its rapid advances through the twentieth and now the twenty-first century. Think of how often we write text messages. Think of the power we feel in doing that, in being able literally to drop a line to someone whenever we wish. The creative potential that writing can unleash is as powerful as ever.

Of course there are far more contexts than text messaging in which the skills of writing are essential. In this chapter we shall visit some of them, and hopefully you will begin to acquire a clear basis from which to construct your approach to teaching writing as you move through your preparation as a teacher and into the first stage of your early teaching career.

The chapter is planned as follows: we will first trace briefly some key points in the history of the teaching of writing. Naturally, as we come to recent times we will consider how the current requirements concerning writing placed upon teachers have evolved. We will then go on to look at current curricular documentation and teaching frameworks, starting with Reception Year, and moving on into Key Stages 1 and 2. Then, we will look in more depth at theories and practices through which writing may best be taught throughout the primary age range. As we go along, there will be points at which activities are suggested for you to complete. These amplify the themes of the chapter: they are not arduous and are intended to assist you in your understanding.

AN HISTORICAL PERSPECTIVE ON BEGINNING TO WRITE AND TEACHING WRITING

For much of the twentieth century, how to teach children to write was an under-researched issue. Little was known about how children learnt to write, so teachers were largely following their own experience as children. I was born in 1950. I can remember learning to write, both at home and at school, by practising letter shapes, first following dotted lines then on blank paper, until I was good enough to be allowed to copy whole words. Then I graduated onto copying sentences. Finally, I was 'let loose' on putting together my own choice of words – the beginning at last of my being the creator of what I was writing! This pattern of learning to write had largely been unchanged since the beginning of the twentieth century, and harked back to times well before in the preceding century at least. However, from the early 1960s onwards far more interest in how children learn to write and how best to teach them to write has developed.

During the 1960s, considerable change in educational values and attitudes took place. There were many drivers for this change, some considered more extreme than others. An important landmark event was publication of the Plowden Report (Central Advisory Council for Education, 1967), which stressed the need for children to be more at the centre of their education, with teachers working from their existing levels of knowledge and skills and raising their performance by leading them up to higher levels. This child-centred approach coincided with growing interest in educational spheres in developing children's abilities to write creatively. More emphasis began to be placed on capturing children's interest and enthusiasm, harnessing these with their natural creativity and thereby providing ways for them to expand their writing abilities.

During the 1970s and early 1980s interest in raising children's writing abilities continued, with now a more research-based underpinning to theories being presented to teachers. One significant author was Donald Graves (1983). His work, in North America, was among the first to point out to teachers the benefits of allowing children to draft and redraft their written work. He outlined what is known as a *process* approach to written composition, in which children learn and apply a strategy for evolving their writing through a series of stages. With the teacher aiding and leading them, working in small groups, then working individually when their ideas are more clear, children plan out their work in a deliberate process. Instead of being asked to write 'cold' on a topic (which all too often leads to children sitting and staring at a blank piece of paper), Graves's approach is to start with a brainstorming of ideas that may be relevant, to edit these and organise them into a set of subheadings, to write a first draft, to check it against another person (often but not necessarily the teacher) and to then rewrite it up into 'best'. More than one draft may be written, depending upon circumstances.

Of course, my description here is a rough approximation of Graves's ideas. However, they have proved seminal and still carry great weight. As we shall see later, many aspects of his thinking have been incorporated into current thinking on good practice in the teaching of writing.

One reason why Graves's ideas had, and still have, appeal is that children's experience of writing from scratch to the finished product was broken down into manageable steps. As we shall see later, this has been developed more recently into the notion of supporting children's growing abilities to write by providing them with forms of *scaffolding*, which are removed once they become sufficiently capable. Also, Graves stressed the importance of children preparing their writing with a clear audience in mind, and with a specific purpose. These ideas, too, have remained valuable in today's widely accepted views on good practice in writing. Again, as we shall see shortly, *purpose* and *audience* figure strongly in recommended approaches to teaching writing.

During the late 1980s and into the 1990s, broad interest in the teaching of writing and how children develop as writers flourished. There was a government-funded National Writing Project (directed by Pam Czerniewska, which ran from 1990 to 1993). The NWP opened up valuable insights into how sensitive and expressive children's writing can be and simultaneously showed us that many teachers applied clear, insightful approaches to their teaching of writing. As an outcome from the NWP, a number of useful publications were produced that supported teachers who were interested in trying to elevate and expand their pupils' writing performances.

Further refinements were also taking place in terms of research. Bereiter and Scardamalia (1985) researched over a long period of time, but among their earliest work was a chapter on difficulties children encounter when composing text, which appeared in 1985. Working in the USA, they pointed out the significant differences between the act of writing and the act of speaking, participating in a conversation. Again, as we shall see later, many of their ideas have become well established in good practice. Essentially, their work started from the basic point that writing involves the act of composing and is an act of construction. Hitherto, attention had not been fully paid to the *compositional* aspects of writing. Rather, the *transcriptional* aspects (again, we shall deal more with these two later) of writing predominated in the classroom.

Activity 1	This is in two parts.

1   I mentioned earlier my own first memories of learning to write. Recall how you learnt to write, or at least an instance very early on in your learning to write. (*Here are some memory prompts: is there anything you can remember about your own first learning experiences as a writer? Are they clear or fuzzy memories? Are they of an experience at school or at home, or both? What did you have to do? Can you recall how you felt? Was the experience at all laden with emotion?*)

Given what you have remembered, can you identify with any of the points in time that I have outlined so far about views on teaching of reading?

2   Think of how you generally approach the idea of writing. How would you describe yourself as a writer? (e.g. *Naturally given to setting things down on paper? Or someone who agonises for hours before committing themselves in writing? How much do your answers to those two depend on the situation? Do you compose easily at the word processing screen? Have you picked up keyboard skills sufficiently for your word processing writing purposes?*)

Can you see any link between your earliest experiences and your later development into adulthood as a writer? If not, what are the differences between then and now?

LOOKING AT THE DOCUMENTATION – RECEPTION YEAR

When you read Chapter 3 on Reading, you were introduced to the Curriculum Guidance for the Foundation Stage (CGFS) (DfEE/QCA, 2000). The first year of compulsory school, Reception Year, follows this guidance. This makes for a particularly pressing role for Reception teachers, who have to respond to the CGFS at the same time as preparing their pupils for entry into Key Stage 1 where the National Curriculum (NC) (DfEE/QCA, 1999) is followed. Writing comes under the same area of learning and early learning goals as reading: the area of communication, language and literacy (see DfEE/QCA, 1999, pp. 44–67). The representation of meaning via writing has a clear role in this area. The CGFS advocates a 'print rich environment', meaning that classrooms and play areas, corridors etc. should take maximum opportunities to display information, messages, ideas etc. in writing. It also stresses the need for children to become used to expressing their ideas on paper in ways that are alternatives to writing. Signing, codes, pictures, texts in Braille, labels, lists, texts in languages other than English, are examples of the variety of forms in which writing can communicate.

Activity 2	The Teacher Training Agency (TTA) standards for the award of Qualified Teacher Status (QTS) (2.1a) require you to be familiar with the CGFS areas of learning and early learning goals.

Read through pages of the 'Communication, Language and Literacy' learning area of the CGFS.* As you do so, look for opportunities in which writing (meaning 'writing' both as an activity for the children and as pieces of writing) can be incorporated in some way into the language development basis of the curriculum. Begin to build up a file of different ways in which written texts of a variety of types can be introduced into Reception Year work.

You should begin to see how widely 'writing' can be interpreted and applied in early years classrooms and where play is the basis for learning to be developed.

*In the web-based copy of the CGFS these are pp. 44–7. (See www.qca.org.uk/)

As the earlier chapter on reading explained, the CGFS uses a system of Stepping Stones as a means of structuring progression. These give teachers clear indications of what is helpful to provide for their pupils. As that chapter also explained, the ways in which children are taught and make their first advances in learning are very important bases, quite literally 'Foundations', for their later learning. So whatever age group in the primary phase you begin your teaching career in, I strongly recommend you read carefully the CGFS requirements. They will help you make sense of the teaching and learning experiences your own class has received.

The CGFS takes a play-based approach to developing children's learning. You may think that writing is a skill area that can wait, given a play-based orientation to learning in the Reception Year. This is far from the case. Children reaching Reception

Year will have encountered many structured occasions in which they have attempted writing – if only writing their own name in a variety of play contexts. So while the NC proper does not commence until Year 1, the National Literacy Strategy (NLS) (DfES, 2001) provides throughout guidance for the Reception Year (DfES, 2001, e.g. p. 7 and pp. 18–19).

In the NLS, objectives for Reception Year (YR) are subdivided into the usual NLS language levels: word, sentence and text, and there are writing objectives at each level.

Activity 3   The TTA standards for QTS (2.1a) require you to have a knowledge and understanding of the NLS framework, methods and expectations for Reception-age children.

Consult pages 17 and 18 of the NLS. Identify those objectives which you think relate to writing. Now think of a topic to act as the context for binding the following part of this activity (a topic might be a particular story or information book, or poem, for example). Taking each language level (word, sentence and text), select two objectives you have identified and note down how you might tackle them in the classroom, given the topic you have identified, i.e. how might you, if you had a Reception Year class, get the children to meet those objectives using a play-based approach?

Begin to build up a dossier of word-, sentence- and text-level teaching ideas. This will develop and expand as you progress through your training and will be helpful in your first post.

Finally, read pp. 106–9 of the NLS Framework. There you will find guidance about teaching 'Children of Reception Age'. It may be helpful to refer back to this should you be teaching YR at some future point.

LOOKING AT THE DOCUMENTATION – KEY STAGE 1

In the Key Stage 1 classroom (Years 1 and 2), the National Curriculum applies to the teaching of writing. You will already have read in earlier chapters of this book or picked up from elsewhere some knowledge of how the NC is broadly structured. Since the NC was first established, English has been a core subject (i.e. occupying a central place and role), and so is subject to regular testing via standard assessment tasks (SATs). The first and second versions of the NC (DES, 1989 and DfEE/QCA, 1999) had three Programmes of Study (PoS): reading, writing and speaking, and listening. The current version (DfEE/QCA, 1999) has retained these three PoSs and resequenced them by presenting speaking and listening first, followed by reading and writing. Of course all three PoSs are important and are taught alongside each other. In fact, they strongly interrelate and children best develop them when they are taught interdependently.

Within the KS1 Writing PoS, the content is divided along the same two divisions as in other PoSs: 'Knowledge, Skills and Understanding' and 'Breadth of Study'. Under 'Knowledge, Skills and Understanding' are seven further subdivisions, some containing yet further subdivisions. So we have:

- composition;
- planning and drafting;
- punctuation;
- spelling (further subdivided into 'Spelling strategies' and 'Checking spelling');
- handwriting and presentation;
- standard English;
- language structure.

| Activity 4 | The TTA standards for QTS (2.1b) require you to know and understand each of the NC core subjects. |

Turn to En3 for Key Stage 1 (DfEE/QCA, 1999, pp. 48–9 in the *Handbook for Primary Teachers in England* version). Note in particular the left-hand column of print on the first page. These are important because they help establish the parameters of the contexts and contents in which you will operate. For KS1, En3 this includes a statement on 'Building on the Early Learning Goals'.

Read this short section, then read through the rest of En3 for KS1.

Note down for each of the seven subdivisions under Knowledge, Skills and Understanding, one way in which building on ELGs may be tackled through a classroom activity suitable for Year 1 or 2. Draw upon your own observations of teachers at work and your reading from earlier in this chapter and other recommended texts.

'Breadth of Study' is the second main category for the En3 at Key Stage 1. (In fact, this two-way division, into 'Knowledge, Skills and Understanding' and 'Breadth of Study' is used across all subjects' PoSs.) The useful thing about this section is that it tells you how to apply the content in the previous category, KSU. The significant issue for us here is that the Breadth of Study, although brief, points out to you the potential for a very rich interpretation of the preceding KSU.

| Activity 5 | Read the 'Breadth of Study' statement for En3 at Key Stage 1. |

Notice the strong messages it contains regarding the range of purposes for writing, the importance of writing itself, the different audiences for children's writing and the many forms that writing can include.

You will have read in the 'Reading' chapter, and have probably already heard from your experience so far, about the 'literacy hour' – the classroom approach recommended in Section 1 of the NLS Framework to teaching literacy. Rather than repeat the earlier points, I will just say here that it is important to become very familiar with the structure of and intent behind the literacy hour. Although a number of schools do not necessarily follow it to the letter, and take a different approach for good reason, your training standards do require you to know it well.

The NLS Framework for Teaching contains considerable detail about teaching literacy at Key Stage 1. You will find that in Section 2, The Termly Objectives, the same aspects of language – word, sentence, text – are used as for the Reception Year, although the subheadings within each aspect are sometimes different. The subheadings used for Y1 are followed throughout the Framework for each year group. You will see that under 'Word-level Work' there is a subheading for 'Handwriting'. While this is an important aspect of writing, do not assume it is the only writing-related aspect that concerns writing under 'Word-level Work'. You will find that a great deal of other word-level work is concerned with writing, although not always directly stated as such. The same applies to 'Sentence-level Work'. At 'Text-level Work', there is more of a distinction between reading and writing, with 'Writing Composition' as a subheading both under 'Fiction and Poetry' and 'Non-fiction'.

Activity 6   Choose either Year 1 or Year 2. Turn to the relevant termly objectives in Section 2. Notice first the 'range statement' box at the top of the page. This should relate to the relevant 'Breadth of Study' section from the NC.

Now read closely the word-, sentence- and text-level objectives, paying particular attention to the aspects that relate to writing.

Turn to the Summary of the Range of Work for Each Term (Section 3, p. 66 for KS1). Read it through and as you do so begin to develop a sense of how the NLS operates in setting objectives and ensuring coverage of the NC.

Sections 3 and 4 of the NLS Framework contain valuable reference and planning materials across the primary phase. Rather than overload you at this point with new material, I will take you further into these when talking about Key Stage 2 and the NLS Framework for Teaching.

LOOKING AT THE DOCUMENTATION – KEY STAGE 2

The NC structure of the En3 at Key Stage 2 is the same as that for Key Stage 1. You will find the most striking difference is the more sophisticated level of work required of the children, which is only to be expected. As you read through En3 for Key Stage 2, you will find it very helpful in setting out the scope of what you have to teach.

Activity 7   Turn to the NC En3 (DfEE/QCA, 1999, pp. 56–8 in the *Handbook for Primary Teachers in England* version). Read these pages through carefully, noting how each subdivision develops on from its KS1 precursor.

Some aspects may seem to require you to possess further knowledge than you have as yet. Make a note of these for future action. For example, some aspects may require you to brush up on your grammatical knowledge and you may find John Williamson's chapter on Grammar (Chapter 7) helpful.

You may wish to make annotations on the text itself, or make separate notes if you are maintaining a learning file on your English work.

Now we will consider how the NLS deals with Key Stage 2. You will find the approach taken in Section 2, the Termly Objectives, familiar as it extends and refines key skills introduced in Key Stage 1. We have already begun to broach Sections 3 and 4 in earlier activities, but in order to expand a little more your familiarity with them I suggest one final activity for this chapter.

| Activity 8 | Turn to the Technical Vocabulary List in Section 3 (starting on p. 69). Note the considerable amount of knowledge already covered in YR and Key Stage 1. Look in more depth at the terms used with reference for Key Stage 2. These terms are a checklist for teachers. |

Identify those terms, at word, sentence and text level for each year group, which have a very clear application to the task of writing. For example, at text level in Y3 you would need to ensure your teaching paid due attention to establishing purposes of writing. You may find you need to check out the meanings of some terms, in which case refer to the Glossary (p. 73) which follows on from the technical vocabulary list.

HOW TO TEACH WRITING – PROCESS

There are two important aspects to how we teach children to write today. One is the development and increasingly widespread practice of a process approach to writing, mentioned briefly in the introduction to this chapter, and the other is an appreciation of the role of genres in broadening the range of types of writing which children produce. The importance of process as an approach to teaching writing is well explained by Hodson and Jones (2001). It is an approach which places children at the centre of the writing process. It requires the teacher to understand that as children come to see themselves as authors, they will grow in confidence and their enjoyment of the writing experience will increase. This means the teacher's role is to enable children to make decisions and choices and guide them through a sequence of stages as their particular pieces of writing evolve. This replaces the more traditional approach where the teachers would expect perfect, 'finished' pieces of writing at short notice.

A central feature of the process approach to teaching writing is that the child goes through stages in the construction of a piece of text, and that each stage fulfils an important role towards reaching the final product. Typically, those stages will start with the setting of a task, which gives some impetus to the start of the process. Often, of course, this will come from you, the teacher, but remember the importance I have already mentioned about the value of having a clear audience and purpose for the children's writing. The more these can be authentic, such as writing invitations or thank you letters to visitors, rather than contrived, such as your telling the class to imagine that they have to write such letters, the more you are going to create a strong sense of purpose.

There is no absolute rule about what the stages are that the writing process has to go through. Indeed, as children become more accomplished writers, they may not need all the stages they have been using in the past. Figure 5.1 shows a possible set of such stages.

Figure 5.1 Example of possible stages in process approach to writing

- Choosing an idea – getting a title
- Considering various possible items of content – things associated with title
- Making decisions about what to include and what to reject – putting the selected content into some form of sequence – structuring the content
- Writing a first draft – making sense in prose
- Receiving a response (from another) – checking for meaning, order of ideas
- Redrafting
- Possible final redraft, checking handwriting and spelling, making presentable
- Reviewing/thinking about the process

As you progress in your teaching career, you encourage the children in your class to become adept responders to others' first (or even second) drafts. Responding is a role to be taken seriously – you may wish to set up children in pairs, with each member of the pair being a response partner for the other. Responding should involve saying whether the ideas are clear, whether the meaning of the text comes across and whether there are any parts that might need changing.

Also, notice how transcriptional features (mainly handwriting and spelling) do not get dealt with until towards the end of the process. This is because the emphasis from the start is upon encouraging children to think, to decide, to compose their own piece of writing. Once these have been achieved, then the matters of handwriting and spelling can be attended to. To do so earlier would be a distraction from the task of constructing meaningful, valid text. Children should be encouraged to check their spellings and meanings by consulting dictionaries and to look for alternative words by using thesauruses.

Children need to be taught how to reflect on a piece of their writing. This should be done before a new piece of writing is begun, so that any lessons learnt can be picked up and applied if appropriate to the next. The sorts of lessons in question might be that they have rushed a particular stage, or that they need to think more carefully about different options for how they are going to present their writing. Reflecting might involve a talk with the teacher or classroom assistant, or it might be noting down some points in their own writing log or diary.

HOW TO TEACH WRITING – GENRES

Children need to be taught that different types of text are suitable for different purposes. This is the second of the two important aspects about teaching writing that I mentioned a few paragraphs ago. 'Genre' means, understandably, text-type. Of course there have always been different types of text, such as narrative fiction, instructional text and so on. They differ from each other in many ways: the register of language used (e.g. a vocabulary range related to a specific topic, formal, informal expressions, addressing the reader in the second person, using third person), the layout (e.g. paragraphs, numbered points), the nature of the content (e.g. factual, fictional) and the purpose (e.g. to deliver a report on a particular matter, to persuade the reader to adopt a particular viewpoint). What has only relatively recently been realised is the need to draw children's attention specifically to these text types and their particular features. The NLS Framework is very helpful in suggesting when different genres of text need to be taught. There are many books available which identify and explain in depth the features of different genres (e.g. Hodson and Jones, 2001).

A useful technique in teaching children to write in different genres is to use writing frames. You can, if you wish, create these for your own class. They need only be very simple. Writing frames simply help the children to organise their ideas into an appropriate order and assist them by giving them ways into the type of language appropriate for the genre they are tackling. Figure 5.2 shows a possible writing frame for a recount of an event. It is the sort of genre that would be relevant for the task of writing about a class visit to a place of interest, or about a visitor to school who came to talk to them.

Children need to learn the different styles of writing and different vocabulary and phrases that different genres employ, so you may wish to support children by giving them examples of the different words they may find useful. For example, in a recount genre, such as in Figure 5.2, they may need to call upon words which show how different events relate to each other over time. This means you can include a box of useful words, such as 'after, later, before, at first' with young children, or 'beforehand, subsequently, therefore', etc. with older children.

You can create frames yourself, for your own use in your classroom, or you can purchase sets of them from reputable publishers – many examples exist. You will probably find that schools where you are on placement will have writing frames as part of their writing resources. As children become more familiar with the needs of different genres, they may require less support from writing frames. However, even without any support from you by way of a frame, you can see how children can employ their own as part of the planning stages in a process approach to writing.

TEACHING WRITING IN THE FOUNDATION STAGE AND IN KEY STAGES 1 AND 2

As you may have realised from reading the early part of this chapter, we now recognise that most if not all children arrive in school with some awareness at least of writing. Children see adults who write, and they see books, newspapers, even television screens of text, being read. It is important for teachers to capture this very early awareness and develop it into a clearer understanding of the role of writing in communicating our thoughts, ideas and knowledge to others. Children don't always understand straightaway the concept that print or written text conveys meaning. From

Figure 5.2   Possible writing frame for a recount of an event

Recount of a visit made by the class

Possible title: _____

1   When was the visit?

2   Who went?

3   Where did we go?

4   What happened?

5   Was there anything special or unusual about the visit?

6   What I think about the visit?

their earliest arrival in Reception children should be encouraged to make marks on paper and to do so as part of some kind of meaning-making activity. For example, making shopping lists may seem a task too difficult for such children, but if those lists are pictures with accompanying marks, scribbles, that is beginning to get the idea across.

If children have attended Nursery, they may well already have reached the stage of being able to write their name. They may have progressed as far as knowing the alphabet and being able to write each letter. Some will arrive knowing all this and how to write their name. Others will arrive not having held a pencil before. This shows you what a challenging and exciting task the Reception teacher has. You will need to be alert, through careful monitoring, to the progress that children can so quickly make, especially at this age.

As children move through Reception, they will make a series of advances with their writing. You need to be ready to guide them and anticipate their learning needs. If you imagine the earliest stage as that of making marks on a page, then you can encourage them into a comfortable and efficient grip on their pencil and show them how to write their name.

Often you will find that a next stage is children writing their own scribble. Encourage this to develop in lines, working from the top to the bottom of the page, and from left to right.

As you teach letter recognition as part of their learning to read, naturally you will show them how to write the letters they are learning, and give them plenty of opportunities for practice – labelling groups of items which all start with a given letter, for example, or drawing then labelling their own ideas of such items.

You can encourage them to bring into their scribbles the letters they are learning with you. You will notice that as their concept of words develops, so they need to be shown that words are written with spaces between them. Speech is usually a stream of noise, but words have to be separately written. Children need to be provided with lots of opportunities to practise their writing. Many early years' classrooms have a writing area where the children are encouraged to write freely. This area should be as attractive as possible, constantly changing and containing writing tools and stationery that the children will not be able to resist. Play or role-play situations also demand that purposeful marks are made. Think of the 'cafes' or 'hospitals' that are set up in classrooms. 'Waiters' write menus, 'doctors' write prescriptions; these are situations that require children to write. Even when children's writing consists of mainly scribble with a few letters gradually being introduced, it is not difficult to see that they are already writing in different genres. For example, they soon understand that the 'shopping list' is written in a different way to the continuous text of a story.

In shared writing sessions you will be encouraging them to see how writing is used for many purposes. One important role for you as the teacher is to act as their scribe on occasion, giving them the sense of putting into a permanent form their own ideas, for a story perhaps, or record of an event that they experienced.

Even at this early stage, in guided and independent writing you can provide them with ways of reflecting about their writing, talking over what they have written and what they want to write.

During Key Stage 1 children learn a great deal about the interrelationship between writing and reading. An early skill to establish with them is that of recognising and writing each letter of the alphabet unaided. Once this has been grasped, you will find that the interplay between reading and writing proceeds more smoothly. The termly objectives in the NLS Framework for phonological awareness and spelling, for example, can be taught through reading and writing sets of phonemes, making the work far more fun and interesting.

You will find that by the end of Y2, the amount of writing that children are capable of producing has increased considerably. If you follow the guidance of the NLS Framework as well as applying the principles of a process approach and genre theory, you will be establishing a good basis for their later writing development in Key Stage 2. As was pointed out in Chapter 3, the NLS ensures that at text level reading and writing objectives are clearly linked. For example, in the Year 2, Term 2 objectives you find a reading, text-level objective: 'to identify and describe characters, expressing own views and using words and phrases from texts'. This is related to the writing objective: 'to write character profiles, e.g. simple descriptions, posters, passports, using key words and phrases that describe or are spoken by characters in the text'. The texts that are to act as vehicles for teaching the objectives are identified in the range described at the top of each planning page. This is the case for non-fiction as well as fiction and poetry. Only by reading and discussing texts can children begin to write. Remember also that children are motivated by the requirement to write for real purposes and audiences whenever possible.

In Key Stage 2 the principles of process and genre in writing really show their worth, provided the basis has been laid, with strong gains in writing progress capable of being made each year. You will find the sophistication of children's writing will evolve if you develop more and more refined writing frames to support their writing. Of course, do not overdo this, and ensure you cater for all abilities by differentiating the frames you use with different ability groups. For example, some children will find the notion of a discussion text, with points of argument and counter-argument with supporting examples of evidence, easy to digest. Others will not. Do not forget, however, that ability to write is not a necessary indicator of a child's ability to think. You may find that pairing pupils into writing partners is a successful way of extending the writing skills of one child while at the same time promoting the thinking skills of another.

Many of the principles involved in the teaching of writing at Key Stage 2 are the same as those discussed for Key Stage 1. Reading and writing should still be linked. Pupils should have the opportunity to read and discuss a wide range of fiction, poetry and non-fiction if they are to write successfully. They should be provided with real purposes and audiences for their writing whenever possible. The teaching of transcriptional skills and compositional skills should be balanced.

REFERENCES/SUGGESTIONS FOR FURTHER READING

Berieter, C. and Scardamalia, M. (1985) 'Children's Difficulties in Learning to Compose' in G. Wells and J. Nicholls, *Language and Learning: An Interactional Perspective*, Lewes: Falmer Press

Central Advisory Council for England (1967) *Children and their Primary Schools: A Report of the Central Advisory Council for Education (England) Vol. 1. The Report* (The Plowden Report), London: HMSO

Czerniewska, P. (1992) *Learning about Writing*, Oxford: Blackwell

DES (1989) *The National Curriculum*, London: HMSO

DES (1995) *The National Curriculum*, London: HMSO

DfEE (2000) *The National Literacy Strategy. Grammar for Writing*, London: HMSO

DfEE (2001) *The National Literacy Strategy. Developing Early Writing*, London: HMSO

DfEE/QCA (1999) *The National Curriculum: Handbook for Primary Teachers*, London: HMSO

DfEE/QCA (2000) *Curriculum Guidance for the Foundation Stage*, London: HMSO

DfES (2001) *The National Literacy Strategy. Framework for Teaching*, London: DfES

Evans, J. (ed.) (2001) *The Writing Classroom*, London: David Fulton Publishers

Fisher, R. and Williams, M. (eds) (2000) *Unlocking Literacy. A Guide for Teachers*, London: David Fulton

Graham, J. and Kelly, A. (1998) *Writing under Control: Teaching Writing in the Primary School*, London: David Fulton

Graves, D. (1983) *Writing: Teachers and Children at Work*, London: Heinemann

Hall, N. and Robinson, A. (eds) (1996) *Learning about Punctuation*, Clevedon: Multilingual Matters

HMI (2001) *The Teaching of Writing in Primary Schools: Could Do Better*. A Discussion Paper, London: HMI

Hodson, P. and Jones, D. (2001) *Teaching Children to Write. The Process Approach to Writing for Literacy*, London: David Fulton

Medwell, J., Moore, G., Wray, D. and Griffiths, V. (2002) *Meeting the Standards for QTS. Primary English Knowledge and Understanding*, 2nd edn, Exeter: Learning Matters

Sedgwick, F. (2001) *Teaching Literacy. A Creative Approach*, London and New York, NY: Continuum

6 Speaking and Listening

SUE BEVERTON

ROLE OF ORAL SKILLS

Oral skills – which encompass both speaking and listening – are important. Fluent speech in everyday life is central to our lives. We need to know and use many rules and conventions of spoken language. Participating in conversation requires both listening and speaking. Think how often we forget what someone, a friend or relative, has told us, because our thoughts were elsewhere or how often we have had to repeat something to someone, often just because they weren't fully attending. Skills of conversation need practice. Many children arrive in school without much experience of quality conversation so they also need to be shown how to ask and answer questions, how to take part in a conversation without interrupting, how to follow what someone is saying, as well as how to keep within the normal conventions of sociable behaviour and use appropriate speech at appropriate times.

Apart from the obvious value of enabling communication with those around us, our speech carries strong cultural significance. Although we may not always realise it, our background, gender, character and ethnicity are all implicated in our speech. Fluency of speech and facility in listening and comprehending what people say create powerful impressions about us in other people's minds. Think how helpful it is, when meeting a potential employer, to be able to speak and listen with ease. Of course, you would need to have something sensible to say in such a situation, and that is of overriding importance. And I am not suggesting that as teachers we should be in the business of creating stressful situations in which children practise speaking and listening! Far from it.

Conversation is natural. It is a spontaneous, informal and cooperative form of verbal communication. It involves sharing ideas, knowledge, feelings, experiences and perceptions. Our conversations are deeply situated in our everyday lives. We can start and close conversations, halt them abruptly, pick them up and recommence them with almost unconscious ease, usually. As we do so, we are constructing meaning jointly with our interlocutors. This is a clue as to why conversation is an essential component of children's learning. Participating in cooperative talk has a major role in children's cognitive development. It aids the development of their thinking and reasoning skills. Furthermore, as well as being a source of pleasure, gossip and play, conversing has a central role in the process of our becoming a member of society. Learning how to communicate effectively is a means of entering a culture (Bruner, 1996).

FEATURES OF ORAL LANGUAGE

It is worth taking a little time to consider the range of features that encompass oral language. First, we need to realise oral language includes aural and visual aspects, not spoken aspects alone. Aurally, not only do we listen to the words people use, but we notice their intonation patterns, the pitch of their voice, the stress or emphasis they give to certain words or groups of words. We notice where they pause, often in mid-flow. We notice whether they are hesitant or worried, eager or sad. We notice whether they use such expressions as 'you know', 'kind of' or 'like' as fill-ins. We notice their accent (the way they pronounce words) and their dialect (the words and expressions they actually use). Visually, when we are physically with our interlocutors, we tend to notice facial expressions and their body language. These can reveal much about their state of mind and attitude towards what is being said.

These features, and the degree to which people use them or respond to them, may be very individual. When children arrive at school, they have begun learning and detecting them. Children still need to learn a great deal more to be sensitive to them.

There are also some basic rules of oral language that growing children need to acquire. Turn-taking is one such rule. Conversing is a two-way process involving turns, usually alternately taken by the participants, that relate to each other. However, links may not always be signalled until after one speaker has begun his or her turn, or even finished it. This is an example of where thought and language can be very closely mapped upon each other. Sometimes, our thoughts are ahead of the words we are using. Sometimes we are trying to express a thought but can't find the right words. In conversation, gaps between turns may be long, or short, or may not even exist, when one person overlaps his or her turn with another. This can especially happen in telephone conversations, when we do not have the support of visual clues to help us follow what someone is saying. Conventions exist for who takes the next turn. Children especially may need to be taught about not interrupting, and waiting for the speaker to finish.

Conventions also exist for how conversations are opened and closed – you would not open or close a conversation with a close friend in the same way that you would with a pupil. These are all culturally significant aspects of oral language. Lastly, an overriding point to bear in mind is that in conversations the meanings of utterances are usually highly context-dependent. This is why it is so easy for a person to be misunderstood or to cause an upset when they report out of context something said by someone else. It is also why, by the way, in judicial proceedings, care has to be taken with reported conversations as opposed to recorded interviews.

| Activity 1 | Think of the last telephone conversation you held with a close member of your family. What were its main features in terms of how it was conducted? Note down how you felt during it in terms of what you had to do to sustain your end of the conversation, how you may have had to work at ensuring you got your message across. Was it a comfortable and straightforward conversation, or rather different from that?

Now think of a face-to-face conversation you have held recently, but with someone you know far less well. How did that go in terms of its conduct? Again, did you have to work at sustaining it, at getting your point across? What did you have to do? |
|---|---|

These two situations may have shown you something of the range of skills you have developed in order to converse in everyday life. We will now look at some developmental aspects of those skills.

DEVELOPMENT OF CHILDREN'S ORAL SKILLS

One view, common in the 1970s and into the 1980s, was that children arrive in school without many of the speaking and listening skills that they need. This is called a deficit model: it implies that the role of the teacher and school is to supply what's missing, to implant and then nurture what's lacking. However, over the last two decades researchers have established that very young children can possess many oral skills long before they arrive in Reception, but that they have them in embryonic form, not fully fledged. This is based on evidence that babies and toddlers do engage in turn-taking and can check on their listener's attention. Think of how we, as adults, react when we are shown a young baby. We instinctively smile, coo and make encouraging noises. We try to gain eye contact. We are delighted when we succeed and get a reaction. We endorse that reaction by making even more attempts to engage their attention. So babies learn from a very young age that they will be rewarded when they take a turn, even if a turn is only a smile, in a conversation. Think also of how young children, before they are able to conduct fluent speech, can initiate a conversation, or instigate an urgent communication by crying when they want something.

We may wonder what happens to the promising early development of such oral skills if young children, arriving in Reception, are unable to put together more than just a handful of words. This has often been said to me by Reception teachers – where has all that communicative potential gone? One plausible viewpoint is that in fact it is submerged, under a mound of worrying, perhaps terrifying, concerns that children accrue as they grow more and more aware of their surroundings and of adults being 'rulers of their worlds'. When you think about it, young children may not have lost these skills altogether. In fact, they may have been developing them and approximating them to adults' ways of doing things. Like adults, they can use paralinguistic features (that is, literally, things that we do as we speak) like gesturing, pointing, using facial expressions. They can make eye contact. When conversations seem on the point of breaking down, they can make repairs and restore contact. They can correct themselves if they make mistakes – maybe not all mistakes, but the fact that they can self-correct at all shows they monitor their own speech. Given the embryonic presence of all these skills, teachers' roles are to work on extending, enriching and developing them into more effective and sophisticated forms.

SOME EXAMPLES OF MAJOR RESEARCH AND THEIR FINDINGS

The Bristol Study (Wells, 1986) is a seminal piece of work on the pre-school development of oracy and its implications, or lack of implications, for children's future academic success. The study took 128 children and followed them closely from the age of 1 until their entry into school. Thirty-two of these children were then monitored until they were 10 years old. Findings showed that conversations between children and members of their family are embedded in shared activities of mutual interest. They revealed that talk at home during the pre-school phase is largely purposeful and goal-directed. Children are in the business of using talk to make sense of their world and their own place in it. The amount and quality of talk varied considerably in Wells's sample. Wells was looking to see if the language of the home and language at school differed greatly, and whether there was a connection between lack of oral competence and later problems with progress at school.

As teachers we often face tricky problems in our dealings with people. One that can occur and is especially delicate is that of children's (and their families') dialects. The NLS Glossary explains clearly the difference between accent and dialect, so I will just briefly explain that while accent is only concerned with pronunciation, dialect concerns features of grammar and vocabulary (such as 'owt/nowt' for anything/nothing). Accent and dialect may often be regionally determined, but not always. Standard English is a variety of English which is used, as the NLS explains, in public communication, especially writing. I am using it now to write this chapter. Standard English may be spoken with any accent. One of Wells's conclusions was that non-standard dialect did not significantly impact upon school progress, nor did it seem to matter whether children spoke in standard English. While this research was conducted before the strong SATs-orientated culture that has developed, this is nevertheless an important conclusion because it means that children's home language is valuable and to be valued. As we shall see later, the National Curriculum requires us to teach primary children to understand and use standard English. This requirement does not mean, however, that we demote or relegate non-standard forms of spoken language. It is a matter of appropriate language being learnt and used for different purposes and circumstances.

Another of Wells's (1986) conclusions was that the evidence from the Bristol study did not support the usually held view that pre-school children's oral language is strongly related to social class.

> . . . up to the age of 5, there were no clear differences between the
> middle and lower-class groups of children in their rate of development,
> in the range of meanings expressed, or in the range of functions for which
> language was used.
>
> (Wells, 1986, p. 142)

Wells made the strong point that it is important not to reject the rich oral language that children from all groups bring to school. Where difficulties were highlighted relating to social class these were associated with literacy (reading and writing) rather than oracy and so another important point made was that 'talking to learn is just as important as reading and writing to learn' (Wells, 1986, p. 146). This is a message for all teachers.

In 1987, hard on the heels of both Wells's study and, in fact, the National Writing Project, the National Oracy Project was established. The School Curriculum Development Committee set up the NOP and it was administered by the National Curriculum Council (NCC). The NOP ran for six years and took the form of an action research project in which teachers participated. The idea was that the role of speech in the learning process for 5 to 16-year-olds needed to be explored, expanded and generally improved. While the NOP has perhaps not had quite as wide public recognition as the NWP received, it was nevertheless very important in providing ideas for the content of the Speaking and Listening strand of the English programme of study. In particular, because of its action research nature, the NOP reached a large number of teachers and its positive influence has been felt across the whole profession.

Another valuable outcome of the NOP was the realisation by many teachers that collaborative talk was an aid to learning. This had long been suspected by many researchers. Vygotsky had seen the social interaction in talk as enabling children to learn more with assistance than they would doing simpler tasks on their own. Bruner, in a similar vein, saw the use of teacher–pupil talk as a scaffold, which could slowly be withdrawn, while the difficulty of the task remained constant. Barnes stressed the importance of exploratory talk as a means of pupils gaining a stake in their own learning. Taking these points forward, the NOP presented a clear and coherent picture of the central role of talk in the classroom, with pupils sharing and developing ideas, discussing possibilities and reshaping them as a consequence. Reflection on their learning is an avenue into developing their ability to think critically.

SPEAKING AND LISTENING AND THE NATIONAL CURRICULUM

The revised National Curriculum (DfEE/QCA, 1999) positioned speaking and listening at the forefront of the English PoS by emphasising a significant role for oracy as the prime medium for learning. As with other strands of NC PoSs, Speaking and Listening is structured into two broad elements: Knowledge, Skills and Understanding and Breadth of Study.

The KSU element has a number of subdivisions. These are:

- speaking;
- listening;
- group discussion and interaction;
- drama;
- standard English;
- language variation.

Each of these has further information and some have useful notes.

Activity 2   Turn to the Speaking and Listening (En 1) strand for Key Stage 1. Read carefully the content of the KSU element. As you familiarise yourself with these points, begin to think about how each one may be incorporated into everyday classroom activities.

From your existing experience of observing teachers at work you may begin to see how teachers integrate these requirements into their practice. As with so much of the English NC, your continuing task is to develop your own repertoire of teaching styles to ensure you cover the range of requirements. This Activity provides you with the start of this process in Speaking and Listening.

Try not to feel daunted by the depth of knowledge, skills and understanding that the Key Stage 1 teacher should be developing in their pupils' speaking and listening skills. Remember, children bring a great deal of oral knowledge with them. Indeed, there may be times when your pupils are more talkative than you would wish. However, as you may have seen from the earlier sections of this chapter, a talkative classroom, under good teacher control, is usually a good learning context!

Activity 3   Read through the 'Breadth of Study' content of the En 1 for Key Stage 1. As you do so, note down illustrations of teaching opportunities that might accompany each activity. For example, under point 8b, 'Reading Aloud and Reciting', you may wish to note down some short poems that especially appeal to younger pupils because of their catchy rhythm or amusing sounds.

As with some other activities in this book, you may wish to consult a teaching resource library for this activity. Or you may have other access to the kinds of materials that might be suitable. The idea is that you need to build up your own ideas list of what might be used.

Turning now to Key Stage 2, you will see that the Speaking and Listening content across both elements of KSU and Breadth of Study continues with the same approach as that laid down in Key Stage 1. This helps to encourage the growth and expansion of children's oral skills in a steady manner.

The English NC advises us, before the content of each key stage's English PoS, that 'Teaching should ensure that work in speaking and listening, reading and writing is integrated.' The importance of integrating these four skill areas into classroom activities cannot be overstated. Long gone are the days when teachers made sure that classes of children always practised their reading and writing as separate entities. Now that speaking and listening are at last being rightly valued, we must not lose sight of the importance of maintaining an integrated approach when teaching language skills. You will find that your pupils will be helped, not confused, when you invite them to talk about their reading and written work, the parts they like and the parts they find tricky. They will enjoy talking about what being a reader feels like, about what mastering a particular reading book means to them and so on.

Drama is an aspect of Speaking and Listening that is becoming more appreciated and recognised for its contribution to learning. Its potential for cross-curricular work is also being realised more and more. Two simple techniques from within the 'Drama' teaching tradition that are especially useful when your class is doing a project in any topic are 'freeze frame' and 'hotseat' work. A freeze frame is a picture or tableau that the children create in the classroom, or similar display area, to illustrate a moment in time from the project they have been studying. The children each take on the role of a character in the display. This works best if the children have discussed in a group or as a class the picture, or frame, they wish to compose (you could divide the class into a number of groups, each producing their own freeze frame). You need to guide them through the whole process, from choosing their frame, planning it, getting props and setting it up through to deciding who is take which part and how they are positioned. Of course, much of the purpose is to get the children to take responsibility, to collaborate, discuss, make decisions, so do not become too heavily directive! It is their freeze frame, not yours!

After the freeze frame is presented, characters may take it in turn to sit on the 'hotseat'. You'll probably be familiar with this idea from other contexts. And of course hotseating may be used on its own, without a freeze frame beforehand, or in conjunction with some other activity. There are two essential points about a hotseating session: first, pupils in the hotseat become the characters they represent; they assume that identity. So they answer questions from the rest of the class or group in role. Successful hotseating is when pupils drop any worries about being themselves. The second essential point is that hotseating can only work if the pupils know something about the character they have assumed. This is where the cross-curricular use of hotseating is especially potent. Information learnt about a character from history, say, becomes far more relevant and important when you are hotseated about it!

Activity 4   Read through the KSU element of the En 1 for Key Stage 2. Taking the Drama strand (Section 4), choose one of the four points, a, b, c or d and plan out in rough how you might use one or more of the dramatic techniques it mentions in teaching a class about either an historical period or the characters in a class novel of your choice.

The idea behind this activity is to give you an opportunity to think about applying dramatic techniques outside the context of an actual drama performance. Once you start to do this, you will find that you begin to see such opportunities in quite a number of teaching contexts.

Activity 5 Select a particular year group. Consult the Breadth of Study statements from the National Curriculum for Writing (En 2) and look at the final entry, which is about forms of writing. How many ideas can you come up with for writing in role that draw upon the suggestions in that range?

Here are some to get you started:

Formal letters written in role (to newspapers, etc.); diagrams or maps from scenes in books; public notices; coded messages . . .

Another way of incorporating drama into your wider teaching is to use the idea of writing in role. Teachers use this very frequently, perhaps without fully realising that they are borrowing a technique from drama. Often teachers invite pupils to write a diary entry as if they were a character from history, or from a novel. This is an example of writing in role.

Finally, I would just like to suggest that if you are following or adapting the literacy hour and NLS approach to teaching Reading and Writing, you nevertheless ensure you pay full regard to developing your pupils' Speaking and Listening skills. The NLS has been written specifically to address literacy standards, by which are meant, to be blunt, reading and writing. As we have seen already, good English teaching requires the integration of reading, writing, speaking and listening in the classroom. In fact many of the classroom practices advocated in the NLS training materials do exactly that, and combine oral skill development with literacy work, to the benefit of all aspects of language.

However, it is just possible that as the NLS offers a range of planning for reading and writing, and these seem to be popular, then you may find yourself with fewer planned opportunities for integrating oral skills. So I'll finish by inviting you to do one more activity, in which all four modes of language are integrated. Don't worry if you find this a demanding activity, or if you wish to leave it until later in your training. It is a planning exercise which requires thought, care and imagination to bring together the different language modes.

Activity 6 The purpose of this activity is to bring together into one classroom exercise opportunities for speaking, listening, reading and writing.

Select a year group and consult the relevant key stage's Breadth of Study statements for Drama in En 1, and for Literature in En 2. Think of a suitable piece of literature that you know well enough to plan some work from. With that in mind, what oral activity can you devise that could fit into a scheme of work based on that piece of literature? Finally, try to devise a writing task that could lead on from the oral work.

Once you have completed this, you will have succeeded in combining all four language modes of the English National Curriculum. Well done!

REFERENCES/SUGGESTIONS FOR FURTHER READING

Bruner, J.S. (1996) *The Culture of Education*, Cambridge, MA: Harvard University Press

DfEE/QCA (1999) *The National Curriculum: Handbook for Primary Teachers*, London: HMSO

Goodwin, P. (ed.) (2001) *The Articulate Classroom*, London: David Fulton

Grugeon, E., Hubbard, L., Smith, C. and Dawes, L. (2001) *Teaching Speaking and Listening in the Primary School*, 2nd edn, London: David Fulton

Howe, A. (1997) *Making Talk Work*, Sheffield: NATE

Wells, G. (1986) The Meaning Makers – *Children Learning Language and Using Language to Learn*, Portsmouth, NH: Hodder and Stoughton

7 Grammar

JOHN WILLIAMSON

INTRODUCTION

Quotation 1	Why care for grammar as long as we are good?
	Artemus Ward

Do not think we are arguing against goodness but as student English teachers you need to care for grammar because of the requirements of the National Curriculum for English.

Not all of this chapter is required reading for the Primary elements of the National Curriculum (some of the details have been included so that those who wish may develop a fuller understanding of English grammar); sections which are not essential from a National Curriculum point of view are clearly marked. However, the National Curriculum for Key Stage 1 requires that:

In composing their own texts, pupils should be taught to consider:

a   how word choice and order are crucial to meaning;
b   the nature and use of nouns, verbs and pronouns;
c   how ideas may be linked in sentences and how sequences of sentences fit together.

(DfEE and QCA, 1999, p. 21)

The programme for Key Stage 2 goes much further and requires that

pupils be taught to identify and comment on features of English at word, sentence and text level, using appropriate terminology.

(DfEE and QCA, 1999, p. 26)

As part of the writing programme,

Pupils should be taught:

a   word classes and the grammatical functions of words . . .
b   the features of different types of sentence, including statements, questions and commands . . .
c   the grammar of complex sentences, including clauses, phrases and connectives;
d   the purpose and organisational features of paragraphs, and how ideas can be linked.

(DfEE and QCA, 1999, p. 29)

Your grammatical knowledge will also play a part in your understanding of some of the issues surrounding the place of standard English in the National Curriculum and we feel that working through the whole of this chapter will better enable you to grasp the necessary elements, so we advise you to try not to skip the additional information.

| Quotation 2 | I will not go down to posterity talking bad grammar. |
| | Benjamin Disraeli |

The term grammar has a variety of meanings; Disraeli in Quotation 2 is using the term *prescriptively* – that is to say he sees grammar as telling people how they should use their language. Such grammar is prescriptive in the sense that it *prescribes* how we ought to speak. For the rest of this chapter we will be using the term 'grammar' *descriptively* – that is, to describe to us the patterns of organisation found in English. These patterns can conveniently be split into two categories – organisation up to the level of the sentence and organisation above the level of the sentence.

GRAMMAR TO SENTENCE LEVEL

There are five levels of grammar up to and including the sentence, as follows:

sentence;
clause;
phrase;
word;
morpheme.

The relationship between these elements is essentially hierarchical. (The exceptions implied in the *essentially* of the last sentence will be outlined later.) Each element consists of one or more of the elements below it until we come to the morpheme which is the lowest constituent of grammatical structure. For reasons of clarity of exposition, we are not going to deal with the elements of grammatical structure in the order given above.

THE MORPHEME

Crystal (1994, p. 90) offers us a version of one of the clearest definitions of this unit: 'The smallest meaningful elements into which words can be analysed are known as *morphemes*.' Let's look at what this means through some examples.

If we consider the word 'happy', we can see that it cannot be segmented into any smaller *meaningful* units: it does not consist of 'ha + ppy' or 'happ + y' – there is no meaning in 'ha', 'ppy', 'happ' or 'y'. 'Happy' is therefore a word which consists of only one morpheme – 'happy'. If we now think about 'unhappy' we can see two meaningful units: one is our old friend 'happy' but the other is a new meaningful unit, 'un', which carries the meaning 'not'. 'Unhappy' is therefore a two morpheme word, consisting of 'un + happy', each element of which conveys meaning. There is a difference between 'un' and 'happy' in that 'happy' is a *free morpheme*, that is to say one which can stand by itself as a word and 'un' is a *bound morpheme*, one which will normally only occur as part of a word.

Morphology, which is 'the study of the structure of words' (Greenbaum, 1996, p. 626), appears in the National Curriculum for English (DfEE and QCA, 1999, p. 28) as early as Key Stage 2. You will need to be able to help pupils learn about *prefixes* and *suffixes*. A prefix is a morpheme which appears at the start of a word, a suffix one which appears at the end of words. Thus, in 'unhappiness' we have a prefix 'un' and a suffix 'ness' (don't worry about slight changes of spelling like 'happy/happi' which sometimes occur when morphemes are combined to make up words). In English, prefixes usually change the sense of words in terms of their overall meaning – so, as we have seen, 'unhappy' means 'not happy', 'rediscover' means 'discover again' and 'mis' has a meaning 'wrongly' in such words as 'misinterpret'. The meaning of suffixes, however, is typically a grammatical meaning. So, our earlier example of 'ness' has the 'meaning' of changing an adjective 'happy' into a noun 'happiness'. One of the commonest uses of suffixes is as an inflection in nouns, to indicate number and possession, and verbs, to indicate such features as person and tense. So, one of the characteristics of many nouns is that they have a set of forms like:

	Singular	*Plural*
Non-possessive	bo**y**	boy**s**
Possessive	boy**'s**	boys**'**

Here plurality and possession are indicated by the suffixes **s**, **'s** and **s'**.

In the case of verbs, suffixes show differences in person in the present tense: 'I/you/we/they **climb** versus he/she/it **climbs**' where the third person singular forms are marked by the morpheme 's'.

Similarly, many verbs use suffixes to show whether they are in the past or present tense:

> 1   I **climb** versus **climbed**;

and to indicate the past or present participle form:

> 2   I have **climbed**; I was **climbing**.

Verbs like those in 1 above, which directly show tense, that is whether the verb refers to present or past time, are called *finite verbs*. The participles in 2 above, along with the infinitive form ('to climb' in this example), are called *non-finite verbs*.

As always seems to be the case in grammar, there are exceptions to these regular patterns. Some verbs don't simply add a morpheme to show past tense or the past participle, so we have forms like: 'I **saw** him yesterday' and 'I have **seen** him'. These are perhaps most easily thought of simply as special cases of the past tense and past participle morpheme.

Activity 1	Analyse the following words into morphemes; remember that all the parts of any word you segment have to be meaningful units.

talk   word
boyish   happening
elephant   disinter
quick   misinformed
quickly   dogs

Answers to all grammar activities appear at the end of this chapter.

THE CLAUSE

We are going to go back to our hierarchy of elements now and work outward from the *clause*. The essence of the clause is that it 'typically consists minimally of a subject and a verb' (Greenbaum, 1996, p. 618). We will come to the complications implied by 'typically' later. Research by Williamson and Hardman (1995) suggested that well over 90 per cent of student teachers could identify a verb. If you suspect you are one of the remainder, please do Activity 2. If you still have problems, read the section on verbs later in this paper.

| Activity 2 | Identify the verbs in the following sentences: |

I like chocolate.
I remember it very well.
I gave him some good advice.
I was very busy when he came to see me.
The doctor examined me but she found nothing wrong.

So, now we've cleared that up, the *verb* element in a clause consists of either a single verb like those we have just been identifying or a group of verbs acting as a verb phrase (see below for details of the verb phrase – we'll just use single verbs for the moment).

The other element in clause structure which we have said is central is the *subject*. The subject of a clause comes before the verb in statements, and in the present tense the subject determines the form taken by the verb. So, for example, we have 'I **sing**' but 'She **sings**'. The subject can either be a noun or pronoun acting on its own or it can consist of a noun phrase (see below) in which a number of words act together as a single unit as in '**The woman** was a solicitor' or '**My friend** is unhappy'. (Subject in bold type.) One distinction which is often made is that between the *subject* and the *predicate* where the subject is the topic under discussion and the predicate is what is being said about it, including the verb and the other clause elements discussed in the following sections.

| Activity 3 | Identify the subject in the following clauses: |

The bride was married on Thursday.
The children dressed up for the party.
The blackbird returned to its nest.
A baby cried for food.
Jerry Springer is a chat show host.
Five sealions were basking on the rocks.
My television is broken.
She wore a blue suit.
The dragonflies landed on the marsh.
Nepal is very hilly.

OBJECTS AND COMPLEMENTS

This is a more complex aspect of clause structure but the good news is that you don't absolutely need to know about this to deal with the National Curriculum. This section and the next are included to give you a complete picture of clause structure.

Some verbs require an additional element to complete their sense – look at the following sentences:

1   Everyone likes chocolate.
2   She became a student.

In both of these sentences there is an element coming after the subject and verb. They look very similar but there are some important differences between sentences 1 and 2. 'Chocolate' in 1 is an *object*, 'a student' in 2 is a *complement*. There are two main differences between these elements. An object can usually be made the subject of a *passive* clause. So, we have an *active* clause ('Everyone likes chocolate') which can be transformed into its passive equivalent 'Chocolate is liked by everyone'. In the passive, the active object becomes the subject and part of the verb 'be' is introduced to the verb phrase.

We cannot do this with sentence 2 – *'A student was become by her'. (An asterisk introduces an ungrammatical utterance.) 'A student' in sentence 2 is not an object but a complement. Complements, however, have a feature which is not shared by objects: in sentence 2, the subject 'she' and the complement 'a student' refer to the same person. This *co-referentiality* is characteristic of complements. A complement which is co-referential with a subject is called a *subject complement*. Another feature of complements is that they, unlike objects, can consist of adjectives: 'She became unhappy'.

Activity 4	Which of the following contain objects and which contain subject complements?

> The boy ate the sweets.
> The girl kicked the ball.
> The girl seemed nice.
> My father was a sailor.
> Pavarotti sang the aria.
> The forecast predicted rain.
> The bridegroom cancelled the wedding.
> The bride was left.
> Northumbria has many coastal castles.
> *The Lord of the Rings* was a very popular film.

Unfortunately, the complexity of objects and complements doesn't quite end there. Consider sentences 3 and 4:

3   My father gave me the book.
4   The university made him a professor.

Again, these look very similar but again there are hidden differences. Sentence 3 contains two objects – an *indirect object* ('me') and a *direct object* ('the book'). Both 'me' and 'the book' in sentence 3 can be made the subject in a passive:

5   I was given the book by my father.
6   The book was given to me by my father.

So both are objects. Broadly speaking, if you only have one object, it's a direct object; if you have two objects the first one is an indirect object.

Now let's look at sentence 4 above. We can say:

7   He was made a professor by the university.

So 'him' in sentence 4 is an object, but we can't say:

8   *A professor was made to/for/by him by the university.

So what do we have in sentence 4? The clue lies in co-referentiality. If we look at 'him' and 'a professor' in sentence 4 we find again that both refer to the same person; since 'me' is the object, we refer to 'a professor' as an *object complement*. (In other instances, the object and object complement may refer to the same object, creature, quality and so on − it's not always a person.) Like subject complements, object complements may consist of an adjective − in 'I like my coffee white', the object 'my coffee' and the complement 'white' are co-referential.

So far, we have the following possible patterns in clauses:

Subject	*Verb*		
Henrietta	dreams.		

Subject	*Verb*	*Direct object*	
Ranjit	eats	chocolate.	

Subject	*Verb*	*Subject complement*	
John	is	a student	

Subject	*Verb*	*Indirect object*	*Direct object*
Susan	sent	Henry	a message

Subject	*Verb*	*Direct object*	*Object complement*
The group	elected	him	chairman

Activity 5   Analyse the following sentences into subject, verb, direct object, indirect object, subject complement and object complement. Just use the criteria we have been discussing and it shouldn't be *too* daunting.

I wonder.
That girl gave Jane a present.
James adores Mabel.
Nobody eats spaghetti cold.
The police searched the room.
Truth is beauty.
The dog is an Alsatian.
John lent me his pen.
The teacher called him an idiot.
That was difficult.

ADVERBIALS

Another section which is not absolutely essential reading.

The final element of clause structure is the *adverbial*, which is in some ways harder to tie down in a definition than subjects, verbs, objects and complements. Greenbaum (1996, p. 615) notes only that 'An adverbial is an optional element in sentence or clause structure. There may be more than one adverbial in a sentence or clause.' Burton-Roberts (1986, p. 97) cites another feature: 'A very prominent characteristic of adverbials is that they can appear in all sorts of positions in the sentence.' So, adverbials are (usually) mobile and optional. Consider the following:

9   I read novels.
10   I read novels in the evening.
11   In the evening I read novels.

'In the evening' is a 'typical' adverbial in that, as we can see from sentence 9, it is totally optional in the sense that we have a complete grammatical clause without it. As Burton-Roberts says (1986, p. 92) '[Adverbials] give additional, though not essential, information.' Further, sentences 10 and 11 show that 'in the evening' is movable – it can appear at the start or end of the sentence. Neither of these criteria can be absolutely relied on, however, as we can see from the following examples:

12   I was in the park.
13   *In the park I was.

Not all contexts will permit the moving of adverbials, as sentence 13 shows. Furthermore, in the case of 12 it's not easy to see how we can regard 'in the park' as non-essential information – it's not just giving additional information to the proposition 'I was'. In some ways, the easiest way to identify an adverb is by checking that it is not the subject, verb, object or complement of the clause in which it appears.

Another guideline is the kind of information given. Adverbials will often tell you things like when, where, how or why something happened:

14   I saw him on Tuesday.
15   I saw him in the dining room.
16   He writes carefully.
17   He was selected because of his good looks.

Sentences 14–17 are examples of adverbials of time, place, manner and reason. Other concepts expressed in adverbials include: condition (often introduced by 'if' – 'Your teeth will be healthy **if you brush them**'); concession (often introduced by 'though' or 'although' – 'He gave me a Mars bar **although I asked for a Twix**') and purpose – 'He stayed up late **in order to watch the game on TV**').

The next activity will help you clarify your understanding of adverbials through considering some examples.

Activity 6   Identify the adverbials in the following:

I watch football on Saturdays.
She studied in Lancaster.
She dances effortlessly.
Last week they went to Manchester.
I like him because he's funny.
Penguins eat fish every day.
If you're lucky you may win the lottery.
I watched him as he worked.
There was mistletoe over the door.
John had known Sally since 1987.

THE SENTENCE

The sentence is the unit above the clause in our hierarchy and consists of one or more clauses. The sentence is one of many important linguistic elements which are notoriously difficult to define – some have suggested there are 100 available definitions (LINC, undated); Crystal (1994, p. 94) raises this to 'over 200'. But as teachers of English we need something to work with since the National Curriculum (DfEE and QCA, 1999, p. 29) requires that pupils be taught about 'the features of different types of sentence'. There are traditional definitions of the sentence, but there are serious problems with them. One approach is to relate the sentence to punctuation, but this is inevitably circular: a sentence ends where you would put a full stop in writing; but if you ask 'where do you put full stops' the only sensible answer is 'at the end of sentences'. We know where full stops go because we have a concept of the sentence which is independent of punctuation. Another traditional definition runs along the lines that a sentence contains a complete idea. Again, it is easy to show that this does not work; consider:

18   Mary came home. John made tea.

In so far as the concept of 'ideas' can be made to work, we can see 18 as containing two ideas and, indeed, 18 consists of two sentences. But what about:

19   Mary came home and John made tea.

We have the same two 'ideas' but now we have only one sentence. We can take this even further:

20   Mary came home because John made tea.

Arguably here we have three ideas – the original two plus one, expressed in 'because', that there was a causal relationship between these two events.

This sort of difficulty arises because the sentence is a *grammatical* unit, not one which is centred on ideas. We can express as many ideas as we like in one sentence providing we meet the appropriate grammatical criteria. The essence of the *sentence* is that it consists of a single clause or more than one, provided that they are linked together. We shall see shortly that there are two forms such linkage takes – co-ordination and subordination. Greenbaum (1996, p. 618) summarises neatly: 'A set of clauses interrelated by co-ordination or subordination (or minimally one clause that is independent of any such links) constitutes a sentence.' This provides us with an explanation that we can easily use to help pupils in their understanding of what a sentence is: if you have a new subject and verb, you have a new sentence *unless you join them together*. Clearly, this presupposes they have already been taught what a subject and verb are – which should not be beyond the bounds of possibility considering that pupils at Key Stage 2 should be taught about 'subject–verb agreement' (DfEE and QCA, 1999, p. 29).

We have, then, an idea of a sentence as consisting of either a single clause (in which case we have a *simple sentence*) or a series of linked clauses. Let us consider first the simpler of the two ways of linking clauses: *co-ordination* 'links items of equivalent grammatical status' (Greenbaum, 1996, p. 86) and 'typically each [clause] could be an independent sentence' (Greenbaum, 1996, p. 45). So, with co-ordination we simply tag clauses on to one another joined usually by 'and' (much the most common, especially in children's writing), 'or' or 'but'. Sentences in which clauses are joined together exclusively through co-ordination are known as *compound sentences*. What is deemed to be excessive use of co-ordination is often seen in children's writing – 'I got up and I got dressed and I had breakfast and I went to school and I . . .'.

The second way in which clauses are joined together is more complex (although children at Key Stage 2 (DfEE and QCA, 1999, p. 29) should be introduced to it). *Subordination* occurs when one clause is made part of another clause. There are many forms which this can take and we have space here to consider only some of the possible patterns. Think about the following sentence:

21   I eat fish on Fridays.

We should by now be able to say that this is a clause and that we can analyse it thus:

Subject	*Verb*	*Object*	*Adverbial*
I	eat	fish	on Fridays

'On Fridays' is clearly an adverbial: it could be omitted and still leave an acceptable sentence ('I eat fish'); it could be moved ('On Fridays I eat fish'); it tells us *when* the fish is eaten so is an adverbial of time. Now look at:

22   I eat fish when I feel hungry.

'When I feel hungry' meets all the criteria of an adverbial which we have just cited in respect of 'on Fridays': it is deletable, movable and tells us *when*. 'When I feel hungry' *is* an adverbial, just like 'on Fridays'. But there is a major difference: 'when I feel hungry' has its own subject, verb and subject complement. So it is a clause. It is a clause functioning as part of the structure of another clause and it is to precisely such a relationship that we apply the term *subordination* which 'is a non-symmetrical relation, holding between two clauses in such a way that one is a constituent or part of the other' (Quirk and Greenbaum, 1973, p. 309). Sentences in which clauses are only joined through subordination are known as *complex sentences*. (Where both co-ordination and subordination are present, we have *compound-complex sentences*.)

| Activity 7 | All of the following sentences contain two clauses; one consists of the whole sentence, the other is a subordinate clause. Identify the latter. |

Jane goes to the theatre when she can.
As soon as the bell goes the pupils leave.
Surinder likes maths because she is clever.
If Newcastle win they will go to the top of the league.
I don't like him although he is nice.
This saw cuts wood like a knife cuts butter.
I saw him where the two roads meet.
If you take the rabbit to the vet he will cut its nails.
You will die unless you drink.
The woman had no grey hair after she visited the hairdresser.

This is perhaps the point at which to mention the exceptions to a generalisation made earlier. We have been assuming that clauses always have subjects but there are some situations in which this is not the case. One occurs in imperative sentences, in explicit commands of the type 'Shut the door' or 'Be quiet'. Omission of the subject is the defining grammatical characteristic of imperatives. Another common case of subject omission arises when two clauses in the same sentence have the same subject: we can say either 'I came home and I had tea' or 'I came home and had tea'. When the second subject repeats the first we can choose what is called 'identical subject deletion' and omit the second instance of the repeated phrase.

PHRASES

Phrases, you will remember, come between the clause and the word in the hierarchy of grammatical elements mentioned above. Fowler (1974, p. 103) offers the following definition: a *phrase* 'is a sequence of words which as a group fulfils a single structural function'. Remembering that a 'sequence' can consist of a single word, this gives a clear idea of the phrase. Think about the structural functions we identified in the clause (subject, verb, object, complement and adverbial). Each of these will frequently (though not always) consist of a phrase of one or more words.

23	*Subject*	*Verb*	*Object*	*Adverbial*
	Jane	met	Margaret	weekly.

Each of the one word phrases in sentence 23 could be expanded as, for example in sentence 24:

24	*Subject*	*Verb*	*Object*	*Adverbial*
	The woman	may meet	her friend	on Tuesday.

Let's look now at the types of phrase we use in English and the ways in which they can be expanded.

THE NOUN PHRASE

The key element in the noun phrase is a noun or pronoun which acts as the *head*, by which we mean the central element around which the rest of the phrase (if any) is centred. If there is only one word in the noun phrase, as in 'Jane' or 'Margaret' from sentence 23 or 'I' from sentence 21, it will be the head, which is the only obligatory element in the noun phrase.

In addition to the head, we may also have one or more *premodifiers* which come before the head in the noun phrase. There are very many types of premodifier and we will illustrate only four of the more common ones here. Very often, the noun phrase starts with a determiner; the commonest determiners are the articles, 'a/an' and 'the', but we also find words like 'all', 'both', 'this', 'some' and numbers such as 'two' introducing noun phrases. The next category which we shall consider is adjectives – used either on their own ('pretty woman') or preceded by a determiner ('the pretty woman'). Also commonly used are personal pronouns, in their possessive form – 'my', 'your', 'his', 'her', 'its', 'our', 'their'. Finally, for our purposes, nouns are frequently premodified by other nouns, either in their simple form or as possessives: 'paper boy' or 'Henry's son'. (For the difference between 'pretty' and 'paper' see the section below on adjectives.)

The other structural possibility in the noun phrase is that we may have *postmodifiers*, which come after the head. There are two common types of postmodifier, the first of which is a prepositional phrase. Most frequently, *prepositional phrases* consist of a preposition followed by a noun phrase. This leaves open the question of what a preposition is and that is much more easily exemplified than defined. Words like 'in', 'on', 'under', 'over', 'above', 'below', 'near', 'up', 'down', 'beside' and so on can function as prepositions. So we find noun phrases like the following:

Premodifier	*Head*	*Postmodifier*
The clever	girl	in my class
The big	house	beside mine
The dark	cupboard	under the stairs
The	king	over the water
The	man	in the iron mask
The butter	knife	across the table
Our	friend	from Mongolia

Note that our hierarchy of grammatical elements has once again been violated: we have here phrases (prepositional phrases) acting as part of other phrases (noun phrases) instead of functioning directly as part of clause structure. The same kind of thing happens with the last type of postmodification which we are going to consider here.

Think again about the first of the last group of phrases:

Premodifier	Head	Postmodifier
The clever	girl	in my class

Now, suppose we changed that to 'the girl who is in my class'. The segment 'who is in my class' is clearly functioning in the same way as 'in my class' did in the first sentence in terms of having as its purpose an extension of our understanding of which girl is being discussed; it is therefore a postmodifier in the noun phrase 'The girl who is in my class'. But there is a major difference between 'in my class' and 'who is in my class'. The latter has its own verb, 'is', and has 'who' acting as subject. So 'who is in my class' is a clause. Like the adverbial clauses we looked at earlier, 'who is in my class' is a subordinate clause because it forms part of the structure of another clause. This particular kind of clause, acting as the postmodifier in a noun phrase, is known technically as a *relative clause*.

Let's look at some more examples of relative clauses:

Premodifier	Head	Postmodifier
The	man	who shot Liberty Valance
The	car	which is in the drive
The	girl	I met
The	information	that I got from the web

All of the postmodifiers above are clauses because they all have their own subject verb structure but are postmodifiers because they add information about the head.

Activity 8	Identify the premodifiers, heads and postmodifiers in the following phrases:

> The ball
> The big ball
> The red ball
> The big red ball
> The big red beach ball
> The ball in the cupboard
> The red ball in the cupboard
> The ball I gave to Jane
> The ball in the cupboard which I never use

THE VERB PHRASE

You will be pleased to know that structurally this is much simpler than the noun phrase. The *verb phrase* consists of a main verb which may be preceded by one or more auxiliary verbs. So, at its simplest, the verb phrase may consist simply of a single verb, as in almost all the examples we have cited up this point – 'Jane **sings**'. It may be preceded by part of the verb 'be', in which case the main verb will take the present participle form: 'Jane **is singing**'; 'Jane **was singing**'.

Either the main verb alone or 'be' plus a main verb may be preceded by part of the verb 'have', in which case the following verb will take the past participle form: 'Jane **has sung**'; 'Jane **had sung**', 'Jane **has been singing**'; 'Jane **had been singing**'.

Finally, all or any part of the above can be preceded by a *modal verb*. The modal verbs are 'can, could, may, might, shall, should, will, would, must'. These verbs have certain unique features not shared by other verbs including the lack of an infinitive form with 'to' – so we have 'to sing', 'to walk', 'to cry', 'to have', 'to be' but not 'to would' or 'to must' and so on.

The overall structure of the verb phrase looks like this, then, with brackets indicating the elements which may not always be present, although where they are present they appear in the order below: (modal) (have) (be) main verb.

ADJECTIVE AND ADVERB PHRASES

Adjective and adverb phrases are similar enough to be dealt with together. They consist, respectively, of an adjective or adverb with the possibility of premodification and postmodification.

Both adjectives and adverbs are typically premodified by adverbs, which usually indicate to what degree the head adjective or adverb applies to the situation:

Premodifier	*Adjective or adverb*	
very/quite/rather/extremely/pretty/fairly	quick	quickly

Postmodification of adjective and adverb phrases is broadly similar to that of noun phrases, with prepositional phrases and clauses being among the elements acting as postmodifiers: 'I was **fond of him**'; 'I am **confident that he will do well**' where the adjectives 'fond' and 'confident' are postmodified respectively by a prepositional phrase and a clause. In the case of adverbs, we can look to examples such as '**Fortunately for us**, it is near the end of term' and 'You sing **better than I do**'.

We have now covered the five types of phrase found in English clauses and sentences – noun phrase, verb phrase, adjective phrase, adverb phrase and prepositional phrase – and noted that although generally these form parts of the structure of clauses we do find phrases used as part of other phrases and that we can find clauses being used as part of phrases. Try the following activity to see how much of this you have grasped.

Activity 9	Analyse the following sentences into phrases:

The table is very heavy.
My friend from Liverpool has been to China.
The train went to Birmingham very quickly.
The drink which I ordered was terrible.
The white parrot has yellow head feathers.
The pond was full of weeds.
Two men were fishing by the riverside.
Some people are rowing the boat.
A duck has landed on the village pond.
Your poodle may have had an ear infection.

WORDS

The word has always been a problematic unit to define although one which literate speakers have found relatively simple to handle; Seiler (1964) commented that the word is an easy concept for the layman but a difficult one for the linguist. You can probably assume that you know what a word is (although we all have difficulties with some examples, especially where hyphenation is involved – do you prepare 'well-planned lessons' or 'well planned lessons', for example). One attempt at offering a definition is to say that 'a word is any segment of a sentence . . . at which pausing is possible' (Hockett, 1958, p. 166) – but, as with pausing as a means of determining sentences, this begs the question of how we know where pausing is possible. Indivisibility has also been used as a criterion – we can add extra items between words but not within them – so, 'my friend' can become 'my best friend' but not 'my fribestend'. Also, this definition applies equally well to the morpheme – as you can see from 'friend' above. One of the best attempts to define the word was that of Bloomfield (1933); he characterised words as minimal free forms – 'the smallest units of speech that can meaningfully stand on their own'. However, many words, such as 'the', are extremely unlikely to stand on their own as sentences. None of these definitions, then, is perfect but all give some insight into the general characteristics of words.

The main interest of the National Curriculum at word level is in the parts of speech and it is to these that we will now turn.

NOUNS

Both nouns and verbs have traditional definitions which are all that many people remember of language work from their own days in primary school. These usually run along the lines that a noun refers to a person, place or thing and that a verb is a doing word or a word which refers to an action. In some ways these are quite useful notions in that they cover many nouns and verbs; you should, however, be aware that these definitions are problematic in many cases. Think about:

25   He can jump 24 feet.
26   His best jump was 24 feet.

Now, ask yourself whether 'jump' is a noun or a verb in these sentences. Your answer (hopefully) was that 'jump' was a verb in 25 and a noun in 26. But does the latter refer to a person, place or thing? Surely 'jump' has the same reference in both sentences; the noun 'jump' refers to an action in sentence 26, just as the verb 'jump' does in 25. This phenomenon occurs with many common noun/verb pairings such as 'talk', 'walk', 'thought', 'smile' and so on. If we really want to know what a noun or a verb is, we need to look to grammatical criteria, rather than looking at the meanings conveyed. Unfortunately, as you might expect by now, there is no *simple* alternative to the traditional definitions.

We have already mentioned some of the *formal* criteria for identifying nouns and verbs in the section above on the morpheme. (Formal criteria relate to the characteristic patterns or forms adopted by the class of words in question.) So, a word which changes form to mark number and possession will be a noun:

	Singular	*Plural*
Non-possessive	table	table**s**
Possessive	table**'s**	tables**'**

Unfortunately, not all nouns follow this pattern – 'furniture', for example, has no plural forms and neither do many nouns which refer to abstract qualities – 'honesty', 'truthfulness', 'fidelity' and so on.

Perhaps more useful for understanding nouns are *functional* criteria (which define a word class by the way it functions). Even here we need to be careful – Greenbaum (1996, p. 627) defines a noun as 'a word that (alone or with modifiers) is capable of functioning as subject . . . or direct object'. But this would include pronouns, which have very different formal properties from those of nouns. Perhaps we are better to think of a series of frames (we need a series rather than a single frame because not all nouns will occur in all contexts) like: 'The_____ was on the table.' Any word which can fill the space is a noun. Think of as many examples as you can: 'book, apple, paper, stripper, napkin' or even 'hippopotamus' (it may be being operated on by a vet) can all appear here and are all nouns. Abstract nouns may not work with that frame but we could use 'I admired his_____' where the blank could be filled not only by a wide range of concrete nouns but also abstract ones such as 'honesty', 'truthfulness' and 'fidelity' which did not meet our formal criteria above. The tests outlined in this paragraph may have already suggested to you one very easy way of helping pupils to develop their concept of the noun – through the use of cloze procedures in which, instead of deleting words at random, you can delete only nouns (or any other part of speech); the pupils will generate words which fit into the blanks and all the teacher has to do is make sure to attach the label 'noun' to the pupils' offerings.

Formal and functional criteria do not give an easy answer to the question 'what is a noun' because the category 'noun' is a complex and varied one. As I have just suggested, pupils need to build up their understanding through experience of the different features which nouns possess. If you, as a teacher, feel the need for a definition then perhaps there is not too much harm in using the traditional ones as long as you realise that children may sometimes be confused rather than helped by them and supplement them with activities like cloze procedure.

VERBS

Formal criteria are perhaps more useful with regard to the verb than to the noun. A word which can change its form by adding 's' to mark third person singular ('I **seem**' versus 'he/she/it **seems**'), which has a form with 'ing' (**speak/speaking**'), a form to show past tense (**speak/spoke**) and a past participle form which is usually used when the preceding verb is 'have' ('**speak/spoken**') is a verb.

As with nouns, we can use functional criteria, and cloze procedure, as in 'I _____ the book', where the blank could be filled by 'read', 'borrowed', 'bought', 'stole', 'destroyed', 'lost', 'hated' and so on. Again, as with nouns, not all verbs will be usable in all contexts but a frame of this *pattern* should cover all verbs which take an object or complement. Other verbs will work with an adverbial in place of 'the book': 'I _____ quickly' would suggest verbs like 'thought', 'spoke', 'ate', 'ran', 'went', 'vomited' and so on.

ADJECTIVES

Most adjectives can be used either as the premodifier in a noun phrase or as the complement in a clause; so we can say 'the clever girl' and 'the girl is clever'. This marks the distinction between adjectives and nouns as premodifiers mentioned above in the section on noun phrases: we can say 'the garage mechanic' but not 'the mechanic is garage'.

Many adjectives undergo a formal change to mark the comparative and superlative forms: 'bright', 'brighter', 'brightest' and others (those containing more than one syllable) mark the same distinctions using 'more' and 'most': 'more beautiful' and 'most beautiful'. Note however that this does not apply to all adjectives: 'single' and 'dead' for example do not allow comparative and superlative forms.

ADVERBS

A great many adverbs 'are formed from adjectives by the addition of *-ly*' (Burton-Roberts, 1986, p. 61), such as 'wisely', 'neatly', 'foolishly' and so on, although not all adverbs follow this pattern – 'often', 'fast', 'late', 'soon' and 'hard' (as in 'work hard'), for example.

Like adjectives, many adverbs can be made comparative or superlative, usually taking the expanded forms '**more** rapidly, **most** rapidly'.

In functional terms, adverbs generally act as adverbials in clause structure: 'He will finish the work **quickly**' (see under 'Adverbials' above) or as premodifiers for adjectives: 'She was **extremely** nice' (see above, under Adjective phrase).

OTHER PARTS OF SPEECH

To meet the demands of the National Curriculum from Key Stage 2 onwards, you also need to have some understanding of pronouns, prepositions (these are covered above, in the section on the noun phrase) and conjunctions.

PRONOUNS

Pronouns are a class of words which can be substituted for nouns in various contexts. Perhaps the most important group consists of *personal pronouns* which directly replace noun phrases. So for 'the girl' in 'the girl kicked the ball' we can have 'she kicked the ball' as long as the preceding context has given us some idea of to whom 'she' refers. Personal pronouns are characterised by person and number:

	Singular		Plural	
	As subject	As object	As subject	As object
First person	I	me	we	them
Second person	you	you	you	you
Third person	he/she/it	him/her/it	they	them

Each of these also has *possessive* forms: as determiners we have 'my', 'your', 'his', 'her', 'its', 'our'; as subjects or objects we have 'mine', 'yours', 'his', 'hers', 'ours' as in 'Mine's a pint' or 'I don't think much of yours'.

Other types of pronoun include: *demonstrative pronouns* ('this', 'that', 'these', 'those'); *indefinite pronouns* ('anyone', 'someone'); *relative pronouns*, which introduce relative clauses ('who', 'which', 'that'); *reflexive pronouns* ('myself', 'yourself' and so on).

CONJUNCTIONS

Conjunctions serve to join grammatical units together. There are two types: co-ordinating conjunctions and subordinating conjunctions. *Co-ordinating conjunctions* join two units of equal status, which may be clauses, phrases or individual words. The commonest co-ordinating conjunctions are 'and', 'but', and 'or': 'I like coffee **but** I hate tea'; 'toil, envy, want, the patron **or** the gaol'; 'Jack **and** Jill went up the hill'. *Subordinating conjunctions* link subordinate clauses to their main clause; examples include: 'before', 'until', 'when', 'while', 'where' (showing time relationships); 'where' (place); 'if', 'unless' (condition); 'if', 'although' (concession); 'because', 'since' (reason); 'to', 'in order to' (purpose); 'so', 'so that' (result). (Examples taken from LINC, undated, p. 335.)

| Activity 10 | Identify the parts of speech in the following sentences: |

The magnolia was in flower.
Foreign investment is at a low level.
The elderly man bred pigeons as a hobby.
The church was destroyed by fire.
The city baths are used by children and adults.
They want tickets for the cup final.
The electricity man read the meter.
Her diamond and sapphire ring shone brilliantly.
The weather will become cooler and wetter.
It was very foggy at the coast.

BEYOND THE SENTENCE

We should by now have a fairly good idea of the structural patterns up to the level of the sentence. But we do not write or speak in a random collection of sentences – there are relationships between sentences in both writing and speech. Think about the following sentences, taken from a children's book on jungles (Catchpole, 1983, p. 7):

| Activity 11 | Put the following sentences into the correct order: |

1 To stop this, some passion flowers have poison on their leaves.
2 The eggs hatch into caterpillars who then eat the leaves.
3 In the jungle, animals and plants depend upon each other a great deal.
4 The poison protects them from the birds, who learn that certain coloured butterflies taste nasty.
5 Their caterpillars are immune to the poison, which is stored and passes over to the adult butterflies.
6 Although flowers attract insects to pollinate plants, there is a risk that butterflies will lay eggs on the leaves.
7 But certain butterflies only lay their eggs on passion flower leaves.

Hopefully, you put the sentences into more or less the original order. But how did you *know* how to order them? Sentence 1 is a fairly typical *topic sentence* in that it serves to orientate the reader to the topic that is going to be considered in the sentence. The rest of the sentences contain various linguistic clues as to their order. Sentence 2 contains the noun phrase 'eggs'; characteristically if we encounter a plural noun with no determiner or a singular noun premodified by 'a', we are seeing the first mention of whatever the noun refers to. Sentence 3 must therefore follow 2 because here we have 'the eggs' with 'the' implying that the eggs have been mentioned earlier. In sentence 4, 'this' must refer back to something which has been raised in an earlier sentence – here, quite clearly, it refers to the attempts of passion flowers to stop their leaves from being eaten. 'But' in sentence 5 implies a relationship of contrast between what precedes it and what follows it. (Sentences 4 and 5 could have been written as a single sentence – probably the writer was trying to avoid facing his young readers with overlong sentences.) The relationship between sentences 4 and 5 is also highlighted by lexical repetition (*lexical* is a linguistic term derived from *lexis*, which means vocabulary); both sentences contain the words 'passion flower' and 'leaves'. Sentences 5 and 6 are linked through the relationship between 'certain butterflies' and 'their caterpillars'. Sentence 7 is related to Sentence 6 through the use of the pronoun 'them', which relates back to 'the adult butterflies' of sentence 6 (we know that 'them' refers to butterflies because of the use of 'certain coloured butterflies' later in 7).

It is not intended to suggest that there is only *one* appropriate ordering of these sentences – you may like to see if you can justify your own ordering through examination of features like those mentioned in the preceding paragraph. The central point is that the sentences that make up this paragraph are linked together through the use of a range of cohesive devices. *Cohesion* 'refers to lexical and grammatical devices for linking parts of a written text or spoken discourse' (Greenbaum, 1996, p. 619). Learning to make texts function as cohesive wholes is a skill which pupils need to acquire, especially since written language tends to make more use of some cohesive devices than spoken language. Cohesion across sentences is a focus of the National Curriculum requirements both at Key Stage 2 and Key Stages 3 and 4.

COHESIVE DEVICES

There are many ways of making texts cohesive entities and we have space here only to introduce you to some of the major ones. You will be able to spot others for yourself once you have seen the kind of feature we are looking at.

Lexical repetition is a widely used device; we saw this in the 'Jungles' paragraph where there was repetition of 'plants', 'eggs', 'leaves', 'caterpillars', 'passion flower(s)' and 'butterflies'. We often seek to discourage children from excessive repetition in their writing, but a certain amount will pull the text together.

The use of *lexically related* words also functions as a cohesive device; these may be words with similar meanings – 'kill', 'murder' or words with opposite meanings – 'live', 'dead', or words with more subtle relationships – 'butterfly', 'caterpillar'.

Of great importance is the use of *cataphoric* and *anaphoric* reference. 'References to what comes earlier in the text are anaphoric, whereas references to what comes afterwards are cataphoric' (Greenbaum, 1996, p. 375). We have seen several examples of anaphoric reference in 'Jungles': 'To stop **this**', where 'this' refers back to 'caterpillars who eat the leaves'; '**Their** caterpillars' where 'their' refers to 'certain butterflies' in the preceding sentence; 'The poison protects **them** from birds' where 'them' refers to 'the adult butterflies'. Cataphoric expressions are probably less important in cohesion, but would include instances like: 'Have you heard **this**? Scotland won the championship.'

The use of *pronouns* is very widespread – these may be possessive as in 'Their caterpillars' or may act as substitute for whole noun phrases: 'The boy was angry. **He** had not been picked.' Words like 'this', 'these', 'that' and 'those' can serve a similar function: 'To stop **this**' from 'Jungles', for example.

The verb 'do' behaves with relation to verbs in very much the same way as pronouns do to nouns. 'I like to lie in the bath and drink Chablis. Whenever I **do** this, I feel very relaxed.'

More explicit forms of cohesion involve the use of a wide range of *connectives*, which can express a variety of relationships between sentences. Place connectives relate sentences on a spatial basis: 'The police station is situated in the main road. **Nearby**, there is a pub. **Just along the road** is an off-licence.' Time connectives indicate a temporal relationship: 'Every morning I get up and shave. **Then** I get dressed. **After that** I have breakfast. **Meanwhile**, my wife is sleeping.' The co-ordinating conjunctions 'and' and 'but' are often used to indicate relationships between sentences as well as functioning within sentences: 'To stop this, some passion flowers have poison in their leaves. **But** certain butterflies only lay their eggs on passion flower leaves.' Many connectives suggest a logical link between sentences. This may simply take the form of listing, as 'first', 'second', 'third', 'in addition', 'furthermore', 'finally', 'in conclusion' and so on. Other relationships include: contrast ('on the other hand'); result ('consequently'); concession ('nevertheless', 'however', 'in spite of that').

COHERENCE

We have exemplified some of the ways in which texts are made cohesive. Well organised texts go beyond this, however, in that they are also coherent. LINC (undated, p. 334) neatly outline the difference between these two concepts:

> For a text to be fully satisfactory to a listener or reader it needs not only appropriate grammatical links between sentences (*cohesion*) but also the concepts, propositions or events to be related to each other and to be consistent with the overall subject of the text. This semantic and propositional organisation is called *coherence*.

Greenbaum (1996, p. 386) summarises some of the main conceptual relationships that can hold between sentences in a paragraph or larger text:

generalization	refutation
particularization	chronological narration
exemplification	description
supporting with factual evidence	definition
supporting with argumentation	offering solution
restatement	evaluation
elaboration	contrast
qualification	comparison
concession	summarization

It is not being suggested that you teach all these types of paragraph to your pupils, but the list provides a useful guide to you in developing your own understanding of some of the ways in which sentences in a paragraph can relate to each other and form a satisfying whole.

TEACHING GRAMMAR

We cannot provide here a complete guide to the teaching of grammar – that will come from experience of working with pupils in a range of contexts and from working with experienced teachers and tutors who will help you develop your skills. However, two important principles can be stated here.

First of all we would stress the importance of teaching grammar in context. When the teaching of grammar last ceased to be a central component of English (in the 1960s and 1970s) it was largely because it had become a sterile set of exercises, removed from any real world context of language use. From the Cox Report on, there has been substantial agreement that good practice links the teaching of grammar to the everyday contexts of the English classroom. So, for example, work on adjectives might focus on the study of texts which use adjectives in interesting ways, or work on subordinate clauses could be linked to development in the pupils' own writing. There is ample scope in the English curriculum for wandering along the byways of grammar without making the work dry or disconnected from the reality of pupils' experience with language and literature. Stubbs (1990) shows to good effect how an examination of grammar can illuminate the presuppositions in a text through a close examination of a *Daily Mail* article published at the time of Nelson Mandela's release from jail in South Africa. Stubbs's article is long and densely argued, but the following should give an idea of the kind of insights gained:

> . . . in the *Daily Mail* article, when Blacks are reported as doing things, committing violence or issuing threats, they are in subject position, and at the beginning of the clause, e.g.:
>
> – Mobs of Mandela's followers ran wild and looted shops . . .
> – Mandela supporters knifed a man repeatedly . . .
> – The youths hurled bottles and rubbish at the police
>
> (Stubbs, 1990, p. 6)

Examples like these are contrasted with the presentation of violence by whites, for example:

> There are only four examples in the text where the police are in grammatical subject position. Three put the police in the subordinate clause, thus presenting their violence as a reaction to preceding actions and not as initiated by them:
>
> – in Capetown, where police fired on the crowds
> – outside Durban, when police fired at a celebration
> – at the police, who immediately responded with more shotgun blasts

In the fourth instance, the police are explicitly presented as responding:

– police immediately resorted to birdshot, teargas and baton-charges.

(Stubbs, 1990, p. 7)

Stubbs (1990, p. 7) goes on to address the significance of this analysis:

> The general point is as follows. The article does not anywhere say explicitly that 'the Blacks are the cause of the violence', but the grammar expresses this message. Position 1 in the clause in English expresses what the clause is about, its theme. This article is about Blacks causing violence, although this is never said in so many words. The meaning is deniable. Alternative, rather obvious interpretations, are not proposed: for example that the violence is caused by the Whites and by the system that they have set up.

Stubbs's analysis has been considered in some detail here because it serves as a model of the ways in which a consideration of grammar can interrelate with our reading of a text to show factors not immediately apparent on a cursory or superficial reading. You can probably immediately see ways in which such an analysis would help you to explore the language of advertisements, for example, or poetry.

The second principle is rooted in the fact that children come to school with considerable *implicit* knowledge about language. The role of the grammar teacher is to make that implicit knowledge *explicit*. So, for example, children know all there is to know about how nouns function in clauses in the sense that they use them appropriately every day of their lives. They may use non-standard forms but they will use them in accordance with the grammatical rules with which they handle language. This is true even of people who have never heard the words 'noun' or 'clause'. What we are trying to do is to make them consciously aware of what they know implicitly and the more we build on that implicit knowledge, the easier it will be for children to learn grammar and the more successful they will be.

Let's look at some examples of what this might mean in practice. Consider the following cloze procedure text (the numbers in the gaps are simply to make the following discussion easier):

The . . . 1 . . . goes to school early every . . . 2 . . . His first . . . 3 . . . is English, which he enjoys. He reads interesting . . . 4 . . . and sometimes discusses them with his . . . 5 . . . His English . . . 6 . . . is friendly and helpful and helps the boy with his . . . 7 . . .

Now, think about some of the words that could go in these spaces: 1 – boy, lad, child, pupil; 2 – morning, day, Monday; 3 – lesson, period; 4 – books, stories, things; 5 – friends, fellow-pupils; 6 – teacher; 7 – work, writing.

What all these have in common is that they are all nouns. Pupils can fill in blanks like these with nouns because of that implicit knowledge we have been discussing which tells them the kind of words that can be used. To help develop the concept 'noun' explicitly all we need do is to remind the children that the words they have been using are, in fact, nouns.

Take another, more difficult example – the subordinate clause. These are quite difficult to pick out of texts which have already been written but are relatively easy for children to produce themselves, given appropriate stimuli such as asking children to complete the following sentences.

1   I like English because . . .
2   School is good when . . .
3   You will do well at school if . . .

These could be completed with subordinate clauses like:

1   . . . it is interesting/I like my teacher/we read good books.
2   . . . we have English/the teachers help us/it's dinner time.
3   . . . you work hard/you are clever/you are a swot.

The point again is that pupils are simply doing what they do all day long – making up sentences; all you have to do is to reinforce the point that what they have produced are subordinate clauses.

You may be saying at this point, why weren't the activities in this chapter based on the principle you have just outlined? The answer is that to work in this way you need to be able to give feedback; closed questions were used here so you could be given the answers – this is a drawback of textbooks that doesn't apply in classroom teaching.

WHY TEACH GRAMMAR?

Quotation 3	What's a' your jargon o' your schools, Your Latin names for horns and stools; If honest Nature made you fools, What sairs your grammars?
	Robert Burns

Burns is asking here the age old question 'So what?' There are many reasons for teaching grammar, some of which should be clear from what you have read in this chapter.

Quotation 4	The proper study of mankind is man.
	Alexander Pope

The first argument relates not merely to grammar but to the development of knowledge about language in all its forms. The human species has been characterised as 'The

Articulate Mammal' (Aitchison, 1976, quoting Ogden Nash) because the possession of language is one of the most fundamental characteristics of humanity. Human language is richer, more complex and more widely enabling than the communication system of any other species, so far as has been established hitherto. There can be no study more beneficial to our understanding of ourselves and the meanings we construct for ourselves as individuals and members of society than the study of language, which must include a study of our use of grammar.

More prosaically, the possession of a shared *metalanguage* (a language for talking about language) enables teachers and pupils to discuss language in ways which are very useful for a variety of purposes: it enables teachers to discuss pupils' work in ways that allow them to explain the features that are being used and ways in which the pupils can develop; it allows for the kind of discussion of a wide range of texts illustrated in the example from Stubbs discussed above; it will help students to understand about differences between standard English and other dialects and give them a deeper understanding of features which they will need to acquire in order to use standard English in their speech and writing, as required by the National Curriculum; it can afford them linguistic self-respect through an understanding that their own, non-standard, dialects are fully formed grammatical systems; it is a useful tool for the learning of foreign languages.

For teachers, a knowledge of grammar is extremely useful in developing their understanding of what their pupils can and cannot accomplish in their language use. A knowledge of grammar can help teachers make judgements which go beyond the superficialities of spelling and punctuation that often provide the only yardsticks against which pupils' linguistic capabilities are measured.

Finally, of course, you need to know about grammar because it is an important part of the National Curriculum and the Literacy Strategy.

ANSWERS TO THE ACTIVITIES

Activity 1		
	talk	word
	boy + ish	happen + ing
	elephant	dis + inter
	quick	mis + inform + ed
	quick + ly	dog + s

Activity 2	
	Identify the verbs in the following sentences:
	I **like** chocolate.
	I **remember** it very well.
	I **gave** him some good advice.
	I **was** very busy when be **came** to see me.
	The doctor **examined** me but she **found** nothing wrong.

Activity 3   Identify the subject in the following clauses:

The bride was married on Thursday.
The children dressed up for the party.
The blackbird returned to its nest.
A baby cried for food.
Jerry Springer is a chat show host.
Five sealions were basking on the rocks.
My television is broken.
She wore a blue suit.
The dragonflies landed on the marsh.
Nepal is very hilly.

Activity 4   Which of the following contain objects and which contain subject complements?

The boy ate **the sweets** (object).
The girl kicked **the ball** (object).
The girl seemed **nice** (subject complement).
My father was **a sailor** (subject complement).
Pavarotti sang **the aria** (object).
The forecast predicted **rain** (object).
The bridegroom cancelled **the wedding** (object).
The bride was **left** (subject complement).
Northumbria has **many coastal castles** (object).
The Lord of the Rings was **a very popular film** (subject complement).

Activity 5   Analyse the following sentences into subject, verb, indirect object, direct object, subject complement and object complement:

Subject	Verb		
I	wonder.		

Subject	Verb	Indirect object	Direct object
That girl	gave	Jane	a present.

Subject	Verb	Direct object	
James	adores	Mabel.	

Subject	Verb	Direct object	Object complement
Nobody	eats	spaghetti	cold.

Subject	Verb	Direct object	
The police	searched	the room.	

Subject	Verb	Subject complement	
Truth	is	beauty.	

Subject	Verb	Subject complement	
The dog	is	an Alsatian.	

Subject	Verb	Indirect object	Direct object
John	lent	me	his pen.

Subject	Verb	Direct object	Object complement
The teacher	called	him	an idiot.

Subject	Verb	Subject complement	
That	was	difficult.	

Activity 6   Identify the adverbials in the following:

I watch football **on Saturdays**.
She studied **in Lancaster**.
She dances **effortlessly**.
Last week they went **to Manchester**.
I like him **because he's funny**.
Penguins eat fish **every day**.
If you're lucky you may win the lottery.
I watched him **as he worked**.
There was mistletoe **over the door**.
John had known Sally **since 1987**.

Activity 7	All of the following sentences contain two clauses; one consists of the whole sentence, the other is a subordinate clause. Identify the latter.

Jane goes to the theatre **when she can**.
As soon as the bell goes the pupils leave.
Surinder likes maths **because she is clever**.
If Newcastle win they will go to the top of the league.
I don't like him **although he is nice**.
This saw cuts wood **like a knife cuts butter**.
I saw him **where the two roads meet**.
If you take the rabbit to the vet he will cut its nails.
You will die **unless you drink**.
The woman had no grey hair **after she visited the hairdresser**.

Activity 8	Identify the premodifiers, heads and postmodifiers in the following phrases

Premodifier	Head
The	ball

Premodifier	Premodifier	Head
The	big	ball

Premodifier	Premodifier	Head
The	red	ball

Premodifier	Premodifier	Premodifier	Head
The	big	red	ball

Premodifier	Premodifier	Premodifier	Premodifier	Head
The	big	red	beach	ball

Premodifier	Head	Postmodifier
The	ball	in the cupboard

Premodifier	Premodifier	Head	Postmodifier
The	red	ball	in the cupboard

Premodifier	Head	Postmodifier
The	ball	I gave to Jane

Premodifier	Head	Postmodifier	Postmodifier
The	ball	in the cupboard	which I never use

| Activity 9 | Analyse the following sentences into phrases. |

(Key: NP = noun phrase; VP = verb phrase; PP = prepositional phrase; Adj. P = adjective phrase; Adv. P = adverbial phrase. Phrases that are in bold act as part of other phrases.)

NP   *VP*   *Adj. P*
The table   is   very heavy.

NP   *PP*   *VP*   *PP*   *NP*
My friend   **from Liverpool**   has been   to   **China**.
(Liverpool is also an NP)

NP   *VP*   *Adv. P*   *Adv. P*
The train   went   **to Birmingham**   very quickly.
(Birmingham is also an NP)

NP   *NP*   *VP*   *VP*   *Adj. P*
The drink which   **I**   **ordered**   was   terrible.

NP   *VP*   *NP*
The white parrot   has   yellow head feathers.

NP   *VP*   *Adj. P*   *PP*
The pond   was   full   **of weeds**.
(Weeds is also an NP)

NP   *VP*   *PP*   *NP*
Two men   were fishing   by   **the riverside**.

NP   *VP*   *NP*
Some people   are rowing   the boat.

NP   *VP*   *PP*   *NP*
A duck   has landed   on   **the village pond**.

NP   *VP*   *NP*
Your poodle   may have had   an ear infection.

Activity 10   Identify the parts of speech in the following sentences:

(Key: det. = determiner; prep. = preposition; con. = conjunction; pro. = pronoun.)

det.	*noun*	*verb*	*prep.*	*noun*
The	magnolia	was	in	flower.

adjective	*noun*	*verb*	*prep.*	*det.*	*adjective*	*noun*
Foreign	investment	is	at	a	low	level.

det.	*adjective*	*noun*	*verb*	*noun*	*prep.*	*det.*	*noun*
The	elderly	man	bred	pigeons	as	a	hobby.

det.	*noun*	*verb*	*verb*	*prep.*	*noun*
The	church	was	destroyed	by	fire.

det.	*noun*	*noun*	*verb*	*verb*	*prep.*	*noun*	*con.*	*noun*
The	city	baths	are	used	by	children	and	adults.

pro.	*verb*	*noun*	*prep.*	*det.*	*noun*	*noun*
They	want	tickets	for	the	cup	final.

det.	*noun*	*noun*	*verb*	*det.*	*noun*
The	electricity	man	read	the	meter.

pro.	*noun*	*con.*	*noun*	*noun*	*verb*	*adverb*
Her	diamond	and	sapphire	ring	shone	brilliantly.

det.	*noun*	*verb*	*verb*	*adjective*	*con.*	*adjective*
The	weather	will	become	cooler	and	wetter.

pro.	*verb*	*adverb*	*adjective*	*prep.*	*det.*	*noun*
It	was	very	foggy	at	the	coast.

Activity 11   The original order was:

1 In the jungle, animals and plants depend upon each other a great deal.
2 Although flowers attract insects to pollinate plants, there is a risk that butterflies will lay eggs on the leaves.
3 The eggs hatch into caterpillars who then eat the leaves.
4 To stop this, some passion flowers have poison on their leaves.
5 But certain butterflies only lay their eggs on passion flower leaves.
6 Their caterpillars are immune to the poison, which is stored and passes over to the adult butterflies.
7 The poison protects them from the birds, who learn that certain coloured butterflies taste nasty.

RESOURCES

There are a number of works to which you can turn if you wish to develop further your own knowledge of the material covered in this chapter. Several of the works to which reference has been made in this chapter are helpful, although you should be aware that grammarians often vary from each other in respect of their use of terminology. Probably the most accessible book, and one which is not too expensive to buy, is:

Crystal, D. (1988) *Rediscover Grammar*, London: Longman

In addition, you may find it useful to consult the following text specifically addressed to the National Curriculum which, despite its title, goes beyond the knowledge needed at primary level and contains valuable self-auditing activities which will enable you to check your knowledge:

Wray, D. and Medwell, J. (1997) *English for Primary Teachers: An Audit and Self-Study Guide* London: Letts Educational

There are now some good materials available for use in the classroom. At primary level the best is probably:

Bain, R. and Bridgewood, M. (1998) *The Primary Grammar Book*, Sheffield: NATE

As with any published material, none of the works mentioned here should be used uncritically but together they provide a wealth of varied, stimulating ideas which can be adapted for your own purposes.

On a smaller scale, you will find useful ideas in both of the following:

Hudson, R. (1992) *Teaching Grammar*, Oxford: Blackwell
Hunt, G. (1994) *Inspirations for Grammar*, London: Scholastic Publications

REFERENCES/SUGGESTIONS FOR FURTHER READING

Aitchison, J. (1976) *The Articulate Mammal*, London: Hutchinson
Bloomfield, L. (1933) *Language*, New York, NY: Holt
Burton-Roberts, N. (1986) *Analysing Sentences: An Introduction to English Syntax*, London: Longman
Catchpole, C. (1983) *The Living World: Jungles*, London: Walker Books
Crystal, D. (1994) *The Cambridge Encyclopaedia of Language*, Cambridge: CUP
DfEE/QCA (1999) *English: The National Curriculum for England*, London: DfEE and QCA
Fowler, R. (1974) *Understanding Language*, London: Routledge and Kegan Paul
Greenbaum, S. (1996) *The Oxford English Grammar*, Oxford: OUP
Hockett, C.F. (1958) *A Course in Modern Linguistics*, New York, NY: Macmillan
LINC (Language in the National Curriculum) (undated) *Materials for Professional Development*, no publisher

Quirk, R. and Greenbaum, S. (1973) *A University Grammar of English*, London: Longman

Seiler, H. (1964) 'On Defining the Word' in H. G. Lunt (ed.) *Proceedings of the Ninth International Congress of Linguists*, The Hague: Mouton

Stubbs, M. (1990) *Knowledge about Language: Grammar, Ignorance and Society*, London: Institute of Education, University of London

Williamson, J. and Hardman, F. (1995) 'Time for Refilling the Bath? A Study of Primary Student-Teachers' Grammatical Knowledge', *Language and Education* 9, 2, pp. 117–134

8 Standard English and Language Study

JOHN WILLIAMSON

INTRODUCTION

Many students come into teacher training with little or no formal training in language study. This partly reflects the relatively low priority which was placed on this area during their own school years; priorities have changed, especially since the advent of the present pupils' National Curriculum, and Standard English and Language Study is now an element in each profile component (Speaking and Listening, Reading, Writing) at each key stage. Even among English graduates knowledge about language is often limited because their prime interest lies in the study of literature and they do not choose Language or Linguistics options. This chapter provides an introduction to an aspect of knowledge about language whose importance is highlighted by its being afforded a separate heading in each profile component in the National Curriculum at both Key Stage 1 and Key Stage 2.

STANDARD ENGLISH

Standard English and other dialects

> **Quotation 1** And the Gileadites took the passages of Jordan before the Ephraimites: and it was so that when those Ephraimites which were escaped said 'let me go over' that the men of Gilead said to him, 'Art thou an Ephraimite?' If he said 'Nay' then they said unto him, 'Say now "Shibboleth"'; and he said 'Sibboleth' for he could not frame to pronounce it right. Then they took him and slew him at the passages of Jordan; and there fell at that time of the Ephraimites forty and two thousand.
>
> Judges XII: 5–6

As the above quotation suggests, forms of language have been important for a very long time and they continue to arouse strong feelings today. In countries such as Canada and Belgium, there are major divisions between groups of people who are separated from each other through the use of different languages. One of the main languages of former Yugoslavia is generally known as Serbo-Croatian but even before the troubles of recent years it was important to Croats and their sense of identity to maintain that there was no such language; they argued that there was Serbian and there was Croatian but no Serbo-Croatian (Wardhaugh, 1992).

Historically, England has known no such divisions (although the same cannot be said of Ireland, Scotland or Wales). In the years since the Second World War, England has become a multilingual country but only English has official status and English is essentially the language of education so we will not be dealing in this section with the rich variety of languages from around the world which many of us encounter in our everyday lives.

This does not mean, however, that there is no variation in the English used in this country. In fact, English varies in many ways but our focus in this section is on differences in dialect and accent. The distinction between these terms is important and these two aspects of linguistic variation are treated quite differently from each other in the National Curriculum. The term dialect 'refers to a variety of the language that is identified geographically or socially by certain vocabulary or grammatical features' (Carter, 1995, p. 37). 'Accent' refers only to varieties of pronunciation. It should be noted that by definition every speaker of English speaks with an accent and in a dialect (or, quite commonly, with more than one). Your accent is simply your way of pronouncing English and your dialect is the collection of vocabulary and grammatical features which you use. Accents and dialects are not the prerogative of foreigners, or people from rural or inner-city areas.

We mentioned geographical and social factors in the definitions; in fact the relationship between these factors is quite complex. In essence, the higher up the social scale you go, the less regional distinctiveness there tends to be. So, for example, working-class speakers from Newcastle have an accent which is easily distinguished from the accent of similar people from Sunderland and Ashington, neither of which is more than 15 miles away. On the other hand, middle-class speakers – doctors, lawyers, most teachers and so on – might be identified as having a northern rather than a southern accent but probably couldn't be precisely located. At the top of the social scale is a regionless accent which reflects merely the speaker's social status and not his or her geographical origins; this accent is known as Received Pronunciation (almost always referred to as 'RP'). 'Received' is used in the Victorian sense of 'accepted', which perhaps indicates the social confidence of speakers of RP.

The situation with regard to dialect is rather different in some important respects. In relation to accent, RP is really quite uncommon: 'It has been estimated that only about three per cent of the English population speak RP' (Hughes and Trudgill, 1987, p. 3). However, far more people speak and write in standard English; one recent study of children's speech in four widely separated parts of England found that about one-third of the sample used no non-standard dialect features at all (Hudson and Holmes,

1995). At some time in our lives all of us at least attempt to use standard English (if only in writing) and many of us use it all the time. This is not true of RP.

A second important feature of English dialects is that they share so much in common.

> **Quotation 2** Yes, classes influence language, introduce into the language their own specific words and expressions and sometimes understand one and the same word or expression differently . . . [But] such specific words and expressions, as well as cases of difference in semantics, are so few in language that they hardly make up even one per cent of the entire linguistic material. Consequently, all the remaining overwhelming mass of words and expressions, as well as their semantics, are *common* to all classes of society.
>
> Joseph Stalin

Now, Stalin probably had his own agenda in this debate and we needn't perhaps take Soviet statistics of the period very seriously but the point made is a very important one. We tend to think of dialects as being entirely separate entities, each separated from the others. This is not at all the case, in two senses. First of all, words and grammatical constructions have their own patterns of geographical distribution which sometimes cut across dialect boundaries. For example, the word *bairn*, meaning a child, is used all over Scotland and the North East of England whereas *wean*, meaning the same, is restricted to a relatively small part of Scotland only. On the other hand, one major national study of non-standard dialects found that 97.5 per cent of schools surveyed reported the use of *them* as a demonstrative adjective in constructions like 'Look at them big spiders' (Cheshire et al., 1993, p. 65).

Now we come to a very important point: the tendency for all dialects to share words and constructions applies also to standard English because standard English is a dialect by our definition. If we look at the example above, 'Look at them big spiders', we can note that the words 'look', 'at', 'big' and 'spiders' are all used with exactly the same meaning as they would have in standard English. Grammatically there are shared features too, including the use of the imperative 'look' and the adjective 'big' pre-modifying the noun 'spiders'.

Standard English has been mentioned several times now and it is perhaps time to try to define it.

> **Quotation 3** Any standard language is no more than a dialect with an army and a navy.
> Cited in Carter, 1995, p. 149

Carter's somewhat jocular reference highlights the point that standard English is in many ways a dialect which carries with it a particular power and prestige. Standard English is, in fact, a notoriously difficult term to define but one helpful way is to think about the uses to which it is put. Trudgill (1983, p. 17) suggests:

> Standard English is that variety of English which is usually used in print, and which is normally taught in schools and to non-native speakers learning the language. It is also the variety which is normally spoken by educated people and used in news broadcasts and other similar situations.

This should be illuminating for anyone with a good knowledge of the use of English in this country although it does leave the specifics of the grammar and vocabulary unmentioned. Wardhaugh (1992, p. 30) offers another way of thinking about the issue:

> *Standardization* refers to the process by which a language has been codified in some way. That process usually involves the development of such things as grammars, spelling books, and dictionaries, and possibly a literature . . . Standardization also requires that a measure of agreement be achieved about what is in the language and what is not.

It may be helpful, then, to think of standard English as being that dialect of the language whose grammatical features, spelling and vocabulary can be verified in authoritative sources such as those mentioned. However, it should be noted that there is a danger of circularity here. What is standard English? It's what you find in grammars and dictionaries. What gets put into grammars and dictionaries? Standard English. Good grammarians and lexicographers (dictionary-makers) try to avoid this difficulty by basing their work on studies of what people actually say and write. Of course, the 'measure of agreement' that Wardhaugh mentions probably covers the vast majority of features of standard English (which as we have seen are shared by all British English dialects) but we should be aware that the boundaries of standard English are not clear-cut, for several reasons. One of these is illustrated by Activity 1.

Activity 1   Which, if any, of the following sentences are not examples of standard English?

1 Between you and I there's nothing wrong with these sentences.
2 I don't know why people have to constantly look for mistakes.
3 None of the mistakes here are serious.
4 It's different to speaking in a foreign language.
5 Hopefully, we will be more tolerant in the future.

Well, the answer is, it depends on who you are talking to. (Or should I say 'to whom you are talking'?) Many people would regard all of these as perfectly normal examples of standard English but many would object to them; in fact the sentences are based on a list of common complaints to the BBC about non-standard language. (You can find the grounds for some people's objections at the end of this chapter.) There are, to sum up, cases of divided usage where people disagree about what precisely constitutes standard English.

Secondly, standard English has no clearly definable boundaries because it is always changing. All language changes through time and we must adapt our views of what constitutes standard English to accommodate this phenomenon. For example, there is no entry for *microchip* in the 1964 edition of *The Concise Oxford Dictionary* but there is in the 1995 edition.

Finally, different parts of the world have different varieties of standard English. Even Scottish standard English differs from the English version, with words like *ashet* (a serving dish) and constructions like 'My hair needs washed' as opposed to 'My hair needs washing'.

Attitudes towards accent and dialect

We saw at the start of this chapter that many people have powerful feelings about the languages spoken in their country. This is also true of the accents and dialects which people use.

Quotation 4	The accent of one's birthplace lingers in the mind and in the heart as it does in one's speech.
	Rochefoucauld

Quotation 4 highlights the way in which one's native speech can be an important part of one's sense of identity and of belonging to particular groups within society. The way a child speaks when he or she comes into school is something shared with parents, brothers and sisters, aunts and uncles and probably just about everyone he or she knows personally. The language forms of a community are an important aspect of that community's sense of itself.

Unfortunately, a less positive feature of dialect variation in England is that many of us have strong antipathies to the language of groups we do not ourselves belong to.

Quotation 5	It is impossible for an Englishman to open his mouth without making some other Englishman despise him.
	George Bernard Shaw

Shaw, not uncharacteristically, overstates his case somewhat but there is no doubt that there are strong prejudices within society which are largely based on social class divisions and which operate both upwards and downwards on the social scale. Many working-class communities with non-standard dialects have terms for middle-class speech forms which they regard as affected. There are many opprobrious epithets applied to middle-class speakers and, often, to members of one's own community whose speech forms are changing as they advance through the educational system: you may be familiar with terms like 'talking posh', 'talking with a marble in your mouth', 'talking pan loaf' (a Scottish reference to the more genteel of the two kinds of sliced bread to be found in that country) and 'talking lah di dah' (some of you may remember 'Mr lah di dah gunner Graham' from the TV series *It Ain't Half Hot Mum*).

However, middle-class prejudices towards working-class forms of language are far more important because of the power relationships within our society. A child who does not use standard English in school may be seriously disadvantaged and application letters for many kinds of jobs may be frowned upon if not written in standard English.

Quotation 6	Dialect words – those terrible marks of the beast to the truly genteel.
	Thomas Hardy

Many erroneous attitudes to non-standard dialects have persisted in the century or so since Hardy wrote. Sometimes non-standard dialect users will be said to 'have no grammar'. This is wrong on two counts: first, as we have seen, non-standard dialects share most of the grammatical features of standard English; secondly, where they vary from standard English it is not that they have no grammar but simply that they have different grammatical rules. Non-standard dialects are not a free for all in which you can say anything; like all language they have rules which determine what is acceptable but they differ from those of standard English. For example, in standard English we form the past tense of 'come' by changing it to 'came'. So we have 'I came home yesterday'. In many non-standard dialects this verb is treated differently and people will say 'I come home yesterday'. This does not mean that there is no grammar but simply that the grammar of these dialects differs from standard English in respect of how the past tense of *come* is formed. Notice, too, that there is a rule – you have to say 'I come home yesterday' not 'I comed home yesterday' or 'I camed home' or any other possibility.

Non-standard dialects are not 'wrong' in any meaningful sense – they are simply different from standard English. All dialects are full language systems with coherent grammatical and lexical (vocabulary) systems; all can be adapted to any use, even if by convention some situations tend to be associated with standard English. Trudgill (1975, p. 27) nicely illustrates this by translating a passage from an anthropology textbook into a non-standard West of England dialect:

> Social anthropology be a title used in England to designate a department of the larger subject of anthropology. On the continent a different terminology prevails. There when people speaks of anthropology, what to us is the entire study of man, they has in mind only what us calls physical anthropology, the biological study of man.

Notice again how much is shared between standard English and the non-standard dialect but above all notice that it is possible to discuss such subjects perfectly comprehensibly in a non-standard dialect. It's just not very common to do so.

Standard English and the National Curriculum

It should be clear by now that there is a real tension between accepting non-standard dialects which can be very important to children and helping them acquire standard English which may open many doors for them in life. The Cox Report, which provided the underpinnings of the first version of the pupils' National Curriculum for English, argues (DES, 1989, Section 4.10) that

> It is . . . important, in considering Standard English, to bear in mind the particular functions that it serves: for example, in the education system and in professional life, in public and formal uses, and in writing and particularly in print. *It is precisely because Standard English serves as a language of wider communication for such an extensive and important range of purposes that children must learn to use it competently.* (Original emphasis.)

The same report also notes, however, 'Standard English has to be treated very sensitively in schools, since dialect is so closely related to pupils' individual identity' (Section 4.33).

Although the curriculum which was derived from the Cox Report is now relegated to the mists of time, I think it is worth dwelling on it because it got the balance between standard English and non-standard English just about right. What the Cox Report did was to distinguish between speaking and writing in non-standard dialect:

> *The development of pupils' ability to understand written and spoken Standard English and to produce written Standard English is unquestionably a responsibility of the English curriculum.* Standard English is the variety used in the vast majority of printed and published English texts although non-standard English is, of course, used in some imaginative literature.
>
> (DES, 1989, Section 4.34, original emphasis)

This was translated into the original National Curriculum in the following terms: with regard to the Speaking and Listening component, pupils at level 5 (from the age of about 11 onward) should be able to 'recognise variations in vocabulary between different regional or social groups, and relate this knowledge where appropriate to personal experience' (DES, 1990, p. 4); at level 6 (secondary level) they should be able to 'Show in discussion an awareness of grammatical differences between spoken Standard English and a non-standard variety' (DES, 1990, p. 5). Writing is treated rather differently: at level 4 (that of a 'typical' 11-year-old) pupils should be able to 'begin to use the structures of written standard English . . .' (DES, 1990, p. 13); at level 5, they should 'demonstrate increased effectiveness in the use of Standard English (except in contexts where non-standard forms are needed for literary purposes) . . .' (DES, 1990, p. 13); at all subsequent levels up to the age of 16 pupils are required simply to be able to use standard English in writing with the caveat that literary purposes may be served by using non-standard dialect.

The different treatment of speaking and writing was right, in my opinion, for several reasons. In the first place, it is spoken language rather than written which carries with it the associations of home and community which we discussed earlier. Writing is very much a feature of the school and does not carry with it the affective loading of speech. Inappropriate intervention in the way children talk can lead to resentment or even inhibit pupils from talking. Imagine how you would feel about contributing to seminars if you were expected to speak in, say, a Scottish dialect and with a Scottish accent (if you are Scottish, imagine another dialect!).

Next, speech is complex, spontaneous and yet under control. When we speak we are organising sounds into significant patterns, creating complex grammatical structures and selecting appropriate words as well as considering such factors as the impact we want to create and the effect we are having on our listeners. We do all of this, and more, instantaneously. Try pausing for even ten seconds while you are speaking and you will see that it seems like an eternity and yet ten seconds is not long to make decisions about whether or not what you are about to say conforms to a dialect which differs from your own in ways which might seem arbitrary and confusing. In writing we can take our time and no one will ever know from the written product how long we took to wonder about an item, or look it up in a dictionary or ask for advice. There is an old story about Oscar Wilde to the effect that he was asked at dinner one night what he had done that morning. 'This morning, I put in a comma', he replied. 'And what did you do this afternoon?' 'This afternoon I took it out again.'

Another argument in favour of teachers not trying to change the way in which children speak is that they are not very good at it. If teachers could eradicate non-standard forms then they would probably have done so a very long time ago.

Furthermore, people tend to change their own speech forms when they perceive it as desirable to do so. There are many speakers of English in this country who are bi-dialectal, who can speak both in the dialect of their home and in standard English. It seems to be forgotten in National Curriculum documents that children today are exposed to standard English to a very wide extent. Nearly all that they read will be in standard English (another justification for treating standard English as the language of literacy), most of what they watch on television, in the cinema and so on will also be in standard English. We are all at least passive users of standard English as listeners and readers.

The relative liberalism of the first National Curriculum for English is in stark contrast to the current version where at Key Stage 1 'Pupils should be introduced to some of the main features of spoken standard English and taught to use them' (DfEE, 1999, p. 17). Is it really important – or even sensible – to be trying to change the verb usages of working-class 5- and 6-year-olds?

STANDARD ENGLISH AND CONTEXT

To a great extent the tension mentioned at the start of the preceding section between accepting non-standard dialects and equipping pupils with standard English can be countered through the notion of appropriacy. It is more appropriate to use standard English in formal situations, and in most written contexts. We have already seen that pupils have access to standard English; part of the work of the English teacher is, as a document aimed at teacher trainees in the late 1990s (DfEE, 1998, p. 92) stated, to ensure that 'pupils [are] taught about the oral conventions that are appropriate in different situations and for different audiences, including the use of standard English'. We all talk differently in different situations: the language we use when discussing education in the pub with our friends is not the same as that we use in a seminar. This is a question of the vocabulary we use and of the linguistic structures we employ – exactly the features which we have already established define dialects. Such variation is something children learn from an early stage in their schooling and can be extended to cover issues of dialect using approaches such as role play (although sensitivity is always going to be required).

RECENT RESEARCH ON PUPILS' USE OF NON-STANDARD DIALECT

Our understanding of the use of non-standard dialect by British schoolchildren has been extended by three recent studies one of which, Cheshire, Edwards and Whittle (1993), was based on evidence derived from a questionnaire while the others (Hudson and Holmes, 1995; Williamson and Hardman, 1997a and 1997b) were based on studies of children's actual usage.

Hudson and Holmes examined the use of non-standard dialect in speech using material gathered for the Assessment of Performance Unit (APU) in 1988 (Gorman et al., 1989). There were several reasons for using this corpus, one of the most important being that it just predated the inauguration of the National Curriculum and so could be used to give a baseline representation of the situation before any changes which might be brought about by the National Curriculum and could also, therefore, be used to compare findings from later studies of the impact of the National Curriculum (none of which have yet been carried out). Also, the APU tapes were part of a national survey which allowed for the study of speech from different parts of the country. Hudson and Holmes chose four widely dispersed regions – Merseyside, Tyneside, London and the south-west – and examined the speech of 11-year-olds and 15-year-olds.

One of the important findings which Hudson and Holmes report (1995, p. 9) is that 32 per cent of their sample of 350 children used nothing but standard English. Hudson and Holmes (1995, p. 9) make the point that the figure of 62 per cent using at least one non-standard form should be taken as a minimum because of the relative formality of the test situation and because if a longer sample of speech had been provided some of the 32 per cent might have used a non-standard form. Be that as it may, it is important to note that nearly one-third of the pupils studied were capable of speaking exclusively in standard English when the need arose. Further, of those who used non-standard dialect, 85 (24 per cent of the total sample) used only one non-standard form and only 7 per cent used more than four different non-standard forms. The sample as a whole produced a mean of 1.7 non-standard forms (Hudson and Holmes, 1995, p. 23). This suggests that even in speech, usage of non-standard dialect is quite restricted.

Williamson and Hardman (1997a) replicated Hudson and Holmes's study using the *written* texts from the 1988 APU survey, with a sample of 362 children from the same regions and age ranges as the previous work. As might be expected, the incidence of non-standard dialect usage is less in writing than in speech.

Taken overall, just over one-third of the written sample used non-standard dialect forms although there was a range from about a quarter to a half of each of the sub-groups identified in Table 8.1 using non-standard forms. This may seem quite high but the overall figures should also be seen in the light of an analysis of the frequency with which non-standard forms were used.

Table 8.1 Percentage of scripts showing non-standard dialect features in spoken (Hudson and Holmes, 1995) and written English

Region	Age	Written English	Spoken English
Merseyside	11	23	62*
	15	33	83
Tyneside	11	48	56
	15	48	72
South-west	11	26	59
	15	45	73
London	11	37	87*
	15	26	80*

Note: Figures from Hudson and Holmes's study marked with an asterisk are to be 'treated especially carefully' because of small sample size (Hudson and Holmes, 1995, p. 6).

It will be seen that no sub-group averages as many as two forms per script and it should be remembered that Table 8.2 includes only those pupils who used non-standard forms. 'Of the 127 children who used non-standard dialect 89 (70 per cent) did so on only one occasion and only 9 (7 per cent) used more than two *different* dialect features' (Williamson and Hardman, 1997a, p. 293). To set this in a wider context, Williamson and Hardman (1997a, p. 293) note that there were on average seven spelling errors per script whereas only three children out of 362 had as many as five non-standard dialect forms. In addition,

> The incidence of non-standard dialect per word of text decreased markedly between the ages of 11 and 15 [one occurrence every 381 words for the 11-year-olds, one every 569 for the 15-year-olds]. This would suggest that even before the National Curriculum introduced an element of compulsion into the business of teaching pupils to write in standard English there was a progressive decrease in the incidence of non-standard dialect features as pupils matured.
>
> (Williamson and Hardman, 1997a, p. 298)

Table 8.2 Mean number of non-standard forms for each written script containing non-standard forms

Region	Age	Forms per script
Merseyside	11 15	1.2 1.6
Tyneside	11 15	1.8 1.3
South-west	11 15	1.8 1.5
London	11 15	1.9 1.7

Table 8.3 Common non-standard features used by pupils in their writing

		South-west	London	Merseyside	Tyneside
1	Irregular past tense forms	I come	they seen	he give	we done
2	Plural subject with singular verb	squirrels eats	these whiskers tells	we was	they stops
3	there is/was	there is boats	there was other comics	there is others	there is some good stories
4	Adjectives used as adverbs	catch your breath as easy as before	fell asleep very quick	it went very slow	can grip very good
5	Singular subject with plural verb	it get damp			
6	Irregular past participle	[it] will have ran out	I have just came	eggs are took	Louise had drank it
7	'More' plus comparative adjective	more easier	more heavier	more safer	more worse
8	Use of prepositions	down our local school	to put it off of my mind	out the telly	buy what we wanted off them
9	'Me' with subject noun phrase	me and my mum	me and Lisa	me and my family	me and John Bell

Table 8.3 (continued)

	South-west	London	Merseyside	Tyneside
10 No plural marker on nouns of measurement, or quantity	seven foot		in 12 year	I was 19 month
11 'What' as relative	the jacket what is different	a small furry animal what lives	every thing what happened	the size what you want
12 'This' as first mention	this doctor			this single cell
13 'Should of' (etc.)		he must of been	should of	
14 'Which' with human antecedent		there are 70 per cent of under sixteens which . . .		they were only boys which
15 'Me' for 'my'			me dad	me friend
16 Periphrastic 'do'	I do get on with them			
17 'Them' as subject				them are
18 'Them' as determiner				from them diseases
19 Give it me		give me it		
20 'Sat/stood'		we saw three policemen stood		
21 Double negative		they don't know nothing		

This study very definitely suggests that, in spite of the weight given to standard English in the pupils' National Curriculum, there are more important considerations for teachers who wish to further their students' writing development.

Another important finding from both the studies we have been discussing is the extent to which non-standard forms seem to occur across all the regions. Table 8.3 is taken from Williamson and Hardman's data and besides showing how widely spread some forms are, it also provides an idea of some of the commonest non-standard features.

It is noticeable that, of the ten commonest features all bar one appear in all four regions. In fact, if sample sizes were larger, we would probably find some of the blanks filled in; for example, neither Hudson and Holmes nor Williamson and Hardman found examples like 'seven foot' in London but this feature does appear in that area generally.

Activity 2	When you are in school, or any other appropriate setting, listen to children talking or look at their written language to identify examples of non-standard dialect. How many appear on the list in Table 8.3? Are there any specific to the part of the country you are in? For example, Scots have a pronoun 'a'body' which equates to standard English 'everyone'.

Standard English and the 'Standards'

Standard English appears at two points in *Qualifying to Teach*: in terms of entry requirements for teacher training courses, all candidates must 'be able to communicate clearly and accurately in spoken and written Standard English' (TTA, 2002, p. 16). For most people, this is not a major issue because only a few non-standard features are likely to have persisted in their dialect through the years of education but there may still be points on which you have to work – particularly in terms of verbs and of some regional usages; remember that none of this relates to your accent – as long as your grammar and vocabulary are standard you can use any form of pronunciation with which you feel comfortable. Remember, though, that your Head Teacher may not be as liberal in this connection as we are!

The other relevance of this topic to the Standards comes through Section 2.1b of *Qualifying to Teach* which required knowledge and understanding of the National Curriculum for Key Stage 1 and/or 2. As we have seen, the National Curriculum places considerable weight on the development of standard English in all pupils.

OTHER ASPECTS OF LANGUAGE STUDY

Language variety

Teaching effectively to the National Curriculum requires an awareness of some of the ways in which language varies; these include changes over time, the distinctive forms of language used in different situations, differences between speech and writing and differences which reflect the multi-ethnic nature of our society and of the range of languages spoken by English people today.

Speech and writing

The National Curriculum places, naturally enough, great emphasis on speaking and on writing but very much takes for granted the complex relationship between the written and spoken varieties of language. It is important for your work on the development of children's writing skills that you are aware that writing is not simply a direct recording in visual form of the spoken language but that, in important ways, these two modes of language differ from one another. Much of the difference arises from the spontaneous nature of spoken language where we produce (and as listeners, decode) speech instantaneously with, typically, little time to focus on patterns of organisation at different levels whereas writing is a slower, more control-lable form of language use where we can take time to shape and organise our ideas and where, as readers, we can take as long as we need to reflect on what is being said. Other differences arise because speech usually takes place within a face-to-face situation where meanings can, if necessary, be clarified and expanded whereas writing (in out-of-school contexts) is generally produced when one is not in direct contact with the addressee (if we *were* in contact we would speak to someone rather than writing).

One of the main differences is what is sometimes referred to as the 'normal non-fluency' of speech. Precisely because we are engaged in such a complex process when we speak, our spoken language is full of hesitations, false starts and errors. Consider the following short extract from a TV discussion:

> [I] think it's very unfortunate that we make it a lot worst by being so rigid in our attitude to alternative or complementary medicines. We . . . in . . . the . . . because of Newton's opposite and . . . equal and opposite reactions, you naturally get another castle . . . another . . . another entire [interruption] enclosed castle arising . . . without which . . . it builds an entirely different system and I think this is very dangerous and very unhelpful to patients.
>
> (LINC, undated, p. 194)

We see here several of the features of spontaneous talk. There is a grammatical error – 'we make it a lot worst' rather than 'a lot worse'. There are false starts, which happen when we start out on a structure and then find it does not fit what we are going to say: 'We . . . in . . . the . . . because of Newton's'; and 'enclosed castle . . . without which . . . it builds an entirely different system'. The last example also exemplifies an apparent lack of logic – she means the opposite of 'without which' – which charac-terises this type of talk.

Later in the transcript the same speaker continues:

> erm . . . I . . . find this very worrying . . . er . . . er . . . Debra who seems a delightful person has already fallen . . . got into the other camp so to speak . . . rather than um.

Here, in addition to repeating some of the features already mentioned, the speaker uses hesitation phenomena like 'erm' and 'um', which we use when we want to say something but haven't quite got it formalised in our heads, and silence fillers – the two instances of 'er' – which we use to retain hold of our right to speak while again we work out what to say next.

It would be very easy to think that the GP who is speaking is very inarticulate, perhaps because of nerves, but it is *very* important to realise that she is just doing what we all do when we speak spontaneously. We only notice the apparent oddity of the language because we are focusing on it, in a transcribed form. This is important because, unless you are aware of the nature of this normal non-fluency, you may misjudge the speech competence of your pupils, especially when they are trying to express complex ideas.

Other differences between speech and writing are centred on the distinction between the resources available to us as either speaker/listeners or reader/writers. In speech we have a range of features such as stress and intonation which enable us to make fine distinctions of meaning: '*He* wasn't very late' (which implies someone else was) is quite different from 'He wasn't *very* late' (which aims at minimising the degree of his lateness) even though both utterances contain the same words. Very often, a shared knowledge of the situation, in conjunction with how an utterance is delivered, can enable us to mean (and be understood as meaning) the exact opposite of what the words themselves seem to suggest; how often have you heard someone who has just made a hash of something being told 'That was clever'? Reinforcing features of stress and intonation are features of gesture, body language and facial expression. All of these can come together to make a major impact on what we are saying in ways that have no real equivalent in writing. The pupil sitting at the back of your class, slumped down in his (it's usually, though not always, his) chair with a scowl on his face, playing with his biro is communicating to you without even saying a word.

Partly because of what we have just been discussing, and partly because the face-to-face context of speech enables breakdown in communication to be easily repaired, there is a tendency for writing to express its meanings much more explicitly than speech, which tends to leave unsaid that which it can be reasonably assumed the listener will understand. So, discussions like the following are not at all unusual:

Speaker A:	Did you go?
Speaker B:	Yeah!
Speaker A:	What was it like?
Speaker B:	Great.
Speaker A:	Were they good?
Speaker B:	Brilliant.

Such an interchange is perfectly comprehensible if you realise that speakers A and B both know that B was planning to go to a concert the previous evening. There is simply no *need* for A to say 'Did you go to the concert which we were discussing the last time that we met', and so on. In fact, continually giving information in speech which is shared with your interlocutor is a pretty good way of being stigmatised as a bore! Vagueness is tolerated in speech whereas in writing we tend to feel a need to identify what we are discussing much more clearly.

Another major difference between speaking and writing is centred on the features described in the section 'Beyond the Sentence' of Chapter 7 of this book. Writing is generally much more carefully structured than speech in terms of the organisation of the discourse as a whole. Typically, conversation is random in its subject matter and wanders from topic to topic apparently haphazardly, sometimes returning to themes which have been aired minutes earlier. There are exceptions to this – lectures, for example, would normally be expected to be coherently structured (and very informal letters would be an example of writing which can be very loosely structured) – but on the whole, learning to shape and link together a text is a skill which pupils have to acquire in relation to writing and it will be part of your responsibilities to help them do this.

To sum up, item 6c of En 1 for Key Stage of National Curriculum (DfEE, 1999, p. 23) requires that you can ensure that pupils know the differences between speech and writing and it has been suggested here that the main differences are: speech is typically spontaneous whereas writing can be a more deliberate activity and so speech is likely to be replete with the features of normal non-fluency; that speech is supported by features of the voice and non-linguistic communication which play a part in the conveying of meaning that the written equivalent, punctuation, can not fully replicate; that speech usually takes place when there is direct contact between the participants and so is more tolerant of assumptions of shared knowledge than writing, where breakdowns of communication are much more difficult to resolve; the organisation of speech into a coherent overall structure is rare although this is a feature of much writing.

MULTILINGUALISM

Introduction

England is no longer a monolingual country (Scotland and Wales never were); at a conference in 1996, data from the Schools Curriculum and Assessment Authority suggested that over 200 different languages were spoken in the United Kingdom and that about 10 per cent of pupils were bilingual. These pupils present both a challenge and an opportunity for teachers of English in the Primary phase and this section seeks to introduce some of the major issues of which you should be aware.

It is important to start by pointing out that bilingualism is not unusual, even though it may seem so to English people who have been brought up in certain parts of this country. Crystal (1994, p. 360) notes:

> Multilingualism is the natural way of life for hundreds of millions all over the world. There are no official statistics, but with around 5,000 languages co-existing in fewer than 200 countries it is obvious that an enormous amount of language contact is taking place; and the inevitable result of languages in contact is *multilingualism*, which is most commonly found in an individual speaker as *bilingualism*.

The term 'bilingual' is one which has a variety of definitions; in everyday speech it is sometimes used to refer to someone who has a complete mastery of two languages. In practice, this applies to very few people, if only because one language tends to be used in some situations and the other in different contexts. For example, a Bengali-speaking pupil in this country may use Bengali at home and when talking to other members of his or her community, use English at school and when speaking to friends or even siblings and use Arabic in religious contexts. Throughout this section when we talk of 'bilinguals' we will be referring to people who use two or more languages in their everyday lives; there is no implication that they have a perfect command of both languages or that they have the same range of competence in both. In current educational jargon, bilingual children are often referred to as 'children with English as an additional language'; the term 'bilingual' is preferred in this section partly because it is more concise but more importantly because it implies a holistic and positive view of the child.

Racism and culture

It is impossible, with respect to the majority of bilingual pupils in this country, to ignore issues of race and culture.

Racism is a problem at all levels in our society and we can not entirely separate the educational system from the broader environment in which it functions. Racism ranges from relatively minor instances of insensitivity or ignorance to extremes of violence, including arson and murder. It can create both personal and psychological problems for its victims and it is important for you to be on guard at all times. Any school in which you work should have a policy on racial incidents and it is important that you find out what machinery exists in your school (and its Local Education Authority) to deal with such events. At one level, pupils can suffer abuse or violence from their peers and you can make a valuable contribution through your work in English towards developing a culture of tolerance and acceptance of differences. Goody (1992) provides a helpful list of materials. At another level, school as institutions can be racist – make sure, for example, that pupils are not being stereotyped and doomed to failure through self-fulfilling prophecies.

It is also important to be aware of cultural differences which can be particularly important for subjects like English and history which often rely on the shared experience of the white community. Texts may rely on background knowledge which is not shared by all your pupils and it may be necessary to undertake pre-reading activities which will ensure all the class know the starting point for the text. It is essential to bear in mind that cultural differences can also be an enriching asset in your classroom. You may have pupils who can broaden the horizons of others whose view of the world is fundamentally Eurocentric or even Anglocentric. Activities which draw on experiences and understandings that bilingual pupils are willing to share can add a great deal to your pupils' understanding of the world in which they live and of our multicultural, multi-ethnic society.

Mother tongue

There is now widespread acceptance of the view that 'It is crucial for the child who speaks a minority language to see that the minority language is given status and importance outside the home' (Baker and Prys Jones, 1998, p. 491).

This is important, first, because, as we have seen with non-standard dialects, language is an important aspect of one's sense of community and of an individual's sense of self. Wherever possible, interest in and study of works in community languages should be encouraged. Work on a poem in Gujerati for example, if you have a Gujerati speaker in your class, could lead to investigations of the sound system, spelling and grammar as well as consideration of the themes of the text. This can be a valuable extension of language work which would be of value to all pupils as well as having the benefit of casting the Gujerati-speaking child in the role of expert.

Next, use of the mother tongue may be important as a cognitive tool for the bilingual child; language is a tool for thinking and if pupils feel they can best come to terms with complex new material in their first language, then encourage them to do so, either on their own or, if relevant, with peers who speak the same language. There is no need to insist on English being used all the time if to do so would lead to a double handicap of difficult material combined with difficulties in the second language. Why shouldn't the child we imagined above make rough notes in Gujerati if that helps him or her to develop an understanding of the topic in question?

Contexts

There is a great deal of variety in the situations you may encounter with bilingual pupils. First, you must always remember that all the ranges of individual variation which apply to monolingual students also apply to bilinguals. There are very able bilingual children and some who have special needs. There are bilingual pupils with rich, supportive homes and others who suffer from multiple deprivation. There are bilingual pupils whose parents see education as of vital importance and others whose parents do not. As with any pupil, you should never make assumptions until you know the pupils well.

Next, bilingual pupils will vary considerably in terms of their command of English, which is often related to the amount of time they have spent in the English education system. The great majority of bilingual pupils in primary schools have been born in this country, have progressed through the primary phase and may come to you with a command of English which enables them to function perfectly well in your class (although be aware of the BICS/CALP distinction discussed below). Others may have come to this country at a later stage in their childhood, often as refugees, and will have different needs from the first group.

Contexts also vary in respect of the catchment area of the school in which you are teaching. Some schools have a very high proportion of bilingual pupils whereas in others there may be only one or two in each class or even in the whole school. Specialist provision varies across the country and it is difficult to generalise but in many ways the teacher in the first kind of school has certain advantages over those in the second group. In the first place, there is more likely to be substantial specialist support, including hopefully bilingual teachers who can support the child in his or her mother tongue. Next, you are likely to have more access to community members who can help with matters like translating notes from the school to parents who may not be literate in English. You are also more likely to have groups of speakers of the same language in your class and can structure work so that they can support each other in their mother tongue. Finally, the ethos of the school is likely to be more supportive of work with bilingual pupils, this being manifested in terms of, for example: more multilingual displays in the school; providing a community room where parents can come and meet and feel a part of the school community; more encouragement and support for you to undertake further training in working with bilingual pupils.

Withdrawal of pupils to give them extra English work is now relatively rare except in the case of new arrivals to this country; it should always be of a limited duration and lead to a phased introduction to mainstream teaching because withdrawal is racially and socially divisive, cuts pupils off from the mainstream curriculum and reduces contact with English-speaking peers, which is a crucial element in second language learning. The norm is to give support to bilingual pupils who need it in the mainstream classroom. This works best when certain conditions prevail: there should be team work between the mainstream and support teacher with regard to the syllabus, with the support teacher being consulted well in advance of each lesson so that appropriate activities and materials can be prepared; teaching methods must be organised in such a way that the support teacher has an opportunity to participate – a lesson of whole-class work with the mainstream teacher leading from the front may give the support teacher no opening to make a contribution; the support teacher must have appropriate status within the classroom and a clearly understood role as an equal partner in the work of the class – one support teacher reports that mainstream teachers treated her 'like a radiator at the back of the room' (Williamson, 1989, p. 325).

Some key concepts in second language acquisition

One central component of a second language acquisition is the provision of *comprehensible input*. This means making the language your pupils are exposed to as easy to understand as possible. We make sense of language and of the world in tandem and this is much easier when the language is rooted in real experience of the context to which the language refers so that the context supports the attempt to acquire language. This is much easier in 'practical' subjects than in English – for example, in the context of a science lesson, pupils will be able to use a pipette at the same time as learning its name. In English, preparatory work may be valuable before beginning the reading of a text. This can involve activities such as brainstorming, the use of photographs and video, and drama activities such as role-play. It is helpful if you try as much as possible to identify in advance concepts, vocabulary and structures which might create difficulties and try to deal with them before they arise. In other words, follow normal good practice for English teaching.

Next, we need to engage learners in natural communication activities; what bilingual pupils need is exposure to real English used for real purposes, not drills or exercises which do little to further the acquisition and development of communication skills. Formal language teaching is very complex; consider the following as an example: there is a variation in some English verbs in terms of whether a following verb should be in the infinitive form ('to talk') or present participle form ('talking'); some take one, some the other and some can take either:

> I want to talk *but not* I want talking
> I enjoy talking *but not* I enjoy to talk
> I like talking *and* I like to talk

Now, unless you've studied linguistics you have probably never been aware of this little corner of English grammar – you acquired the appropriate structures through exposure to other people using these verbs and learned how to use them yourself. It *would* be possible for students to learn a list of the appropriate uses but it is far easier for them to acquire the usages through experience of hearing them used appropriately, internalising them and then producing them in the way that a first language learner would, in appropriate, meaningful contexts. If you spot a linguistic need, devise an activity which will meet that need through *using* language rather than talking *about* it. For example, if a pupil is having difficulties with some of the question forms in English, rather than trying to explicitly teach these in the abstract, structure a group activity in which a questionnaire is to be devised so that question forms arise naturally and purposefully.

Another important aspect of working with bilingual pupils which is part of normal good practice is the provision of an encouraging, supportive environment in which pupils feel comfortable about using English. Creating a positive attitude to the use of English, strong motivation and self-confidence while reducing anxiety will have a beneficial effect on second language learners (Baker and Prys Jones, 1998, p. 649).

BICS and CALP

It has long been recognised (see, for example, Skutnabb-Kangas (1981) and Cummins (1984)) that there is a distinction between Basic Interpersonal Communication Skills (BICS) and Cognitive/Academic Language Proficiency (CALP). BICS refers to one's use of language in everyday communicative situations, talking to peers, relaxing with friends, discussing the events of the day and so on. This level of language competence is often quickly acquired by bilingual learners who catch up with their monolingual peers quite rapidly. This use of language is typically rooted in a supportive context of shared meanings and understandings. CALP, on the other hand, is typically a context-reduced form of language which is more abstract and less grounded in the here-and-now of everyday conversation. This is much slower to develop in bilingual (and many monolingual children). The great danger which arises from the distinction between BICS and CALP is that erroneous judgements can easily be made. You may have a child in your class who talks to you with native speaker-like proficiency; he or she can tell you about hobbies, interests, how they get to school and so on; they may well talk with a local accent. It is easy to assume, if such a child is having difficulties with the curriculum, that the problem is not one of language but rather lies in a poor attitude to work or a lack of ability. However, it may simply be that 'The child may not have the vocabulary, more advanced grammatical constructions, nor an understanding of the subtleties of meaning to grasp what is being taught' (Baker and Prys Jones, 1998, p. 93).

Summary: some pointers for English teachers

- You must bear in mind the cultural dimension discussed above – remember that reading depends on a knowledge of the world as well as of the language of the text; how do you follow *Cinderella* if you don't know what a pumpkin is? Try to recognise sticking-points in advance and prepare for them to avoid the pupils failing.
- Even if a child appears to have a good command of English, there may be gaps, particularly in vocabulary. If you are going to read the Harry Potter novels, you need to be sure that the children understand the word 'dormitory'; if you go on to *Hard Times* you may need to be sure that they understand the difference between the French Revolution and the Industrial Revolution. Again, think these out in advance and prepare the pupils for them.
- Oral and collaborative work is vitally important because children acquire a great deal of their English from interacting with their peers; if you think of a one-hour period in school with 30 pupils in a class, each child can have only two minutes speaking with the teacher (even assuming all the time is spent in individual interaction, which it never is) so it follows that if a pupil is going to have the chance to *use* English much of the work has to come in peer group interaction. If you have a beginning bilingual in your class, you should be aware of the 'silent period'; in the early stages of acquiring a second language pupils often go for a long time (it can be months) without speaking. You should be aware of this and accept it; the child is busy internalising features of the language which will be turned into speech when he or she is ready.
- Writing may not reflect oral proficiency, for reasons which have much to do with the difference between speech and writing dealt with above. Try to focus on specific points which seem important for further development and work on these one at a time; don't expect everything to be corrected at one go – there will always be another occasion to work on the next point of importance.

- Think about language functions and styles: are there gaps in what the children can use English *for*; can they undertake explanatory writing, persuasive writing and so on? Structure activities which will lead to the acquisition of a range of language uses. This, again, is normal good practice, and is part of the National Curriculum requirements at both Key Stage 1 and Key Stage 2 (DfEE, 1999, pp. 21 and 23).
- Do there seem to be particular grammatical difficulties for your pupils? This may range from relatively simple things like problems with English articles ('the' and 'a') to the more complex structures they may encounter in their reading: for example, 'He is nothing if not cheerful' may be taken to mean 'he is not cheerful' rather than the opposite. When you do identify problem issues devise an activity which will engage the pupils in using the problematic feature.
- As discussed above, make some of the texts you study relate to, and value, the culture and experience of life beyond our often insular, Anglocentric framework. This again is a National Curriculum requirement (DfEE, 1995, p. 19) and is of such value to *all* pupils that you should do this even if there are no ethnic minority children in your class.

A final note on multilingualism

We can only give you the briefest introduction here to working with bilingual children but you should find it amongst the most satisfying and productive areas of your teaching. Remember the following points, above all, and you will have the foundations for success:

- Bilingual children constitute a resource which opens up a whole range of avenues of work on language and literature not otherwise accessible to you and the rest of your pupils.
- In many ways, following normal good practice will lead to success with *all* pupils, bilingual and monolingual.
- Give the bilingual pupils the opportunity to use their English in discussion with their peers so that they can experiment and try it out.
- Respect and value the language and culture which the bilingual pupils bring to your class.
- Try to identify the demands which will be made on bilingual pupils by the lesson you are about to teach and prepare accordingly.

SOUND SYSTEM AND SPELLING SYSTEM

All languages have a sound system and all those with a written form have a spelling system. By 'system' here we mean that the sounds or letters are organised into meaningful patterns.

In relation to the sound system this involves, first of all, selection from the vast range of noises which human beings can make with their mouths; for example, in English we do not make use of the nasal vowels which can be found in French or the clicks which form part of some African languages. Next we organise the sounds which are to be used into contrastive units known as phonemes. A phoneme consists of a set of related sounds which function as a single unit within the sound system; speakers of any given language find it easy to distinguish between sounds which belong to different phonemes but often find it difficult to distinguish between sounds which belong to the same phoneme because the latter differences are not significant in their language and do not differentiate between one word and another. Some examples will make this clearer:

Say the words 'keep' and 'call' out loud; is the initial 'k' sound the same in both words (ignore the difference in spelling, we will return to that later)? If you answer 'yes', say them again and try to feel where your tongue is when you pronounce each 'k' sound. You will find that 'k' in 'keep' is made with the tongue further forward in the mouth than it is for 'call'; this is because the following vowels are made in different parts of the mouth and when we pronounce the initial 'k' we are anticipating where the tongue is going to move to next. Try to start with the 'k' you would use for 'keep' but say 'call' instead – doesn't it feel awkward? You may find it hard to hear, but the different articulation of the two 'k' sounds leads to a difference in the sounds produced. The two 'k' sounds belong to the same phoneme in English; they never differentiate between words but are merely different variants (the technical term is allophones) of the phoneme /k/ (phonemes are cited between slashes) which are used in different phonetic contexts.

Now consider the pair 'keep' and 'peep'; the initial sounds again differ from each other but this time they appear in the same phonetic context and mark the distinction between two different words. What we have here is two different phonemes – /k/ and /p/ – which differentiate between a series of pairs like 'pill, kill'; 'peel, keel'; 'pick, kick' and 'cat, pat'.

Spelling

There are about 44 phonemes in English (we cannot be precise because the number of phonemes varies from accent to accent); problems with spelling arise in large measure because we have only 26 letters in the spelling system. This partly accounts for the fact that the same phoneme can be spelt in a variety of ways: the phoneme /i/ for example can be spelt as in 'feel', 'leaf', 'chief', 'people', 'Crete', 'police', 'be' and 'seize'. Other spelling difficulties arise because the spoken language has changed more than the written version: for example the 'gh' in 'knight' was pronounced at one time (like the final sound in Scots 'loch'); the pronunciation changed but spelling did not change with it. Smith (1978, p. 54) cites a total of over 300 sound-spelling correspondences. LINC (undated, p. 143) notes that 'Less than half the words that most commonly occur in English have a regular sound-symbol correspondence. So, a strategy that is based solely on a phonetic approach is inevitably limited and ultimately misleading.' Accurate spelling is normally rooted in a sense of the shape which a word should take.

It follows from this that there is great value in emphasising to pupils the *visual* aspect of spelling. One technique commonly used to help pupils develop their visual memory is the 'look – cover – remember – write – check' system (LINC undated, p. 144). In this, the pupil looks at the word, covers it up, commits it to memory, then writes it and checks it with the original. The strength of this method lies in its emphasis on the visual form of the word. Other techniques can also be employed: one is to look for root words within the word to be learned and use them as a basis for correct spelling – for example, if you can spell 'road' and 'worthy' it should be easy to spell 'roadworthy'. It is also worth looking at *recurring* patterns of error in individual pupils' work: for example, do they regularly make errors with doubled letters, or with dropping a final 'e' before a present participle ('bake' and 'baking')? If you are about to introduce pupils to a new word with an unusual or irregular spelling, it is worth explicitly drawing their attention to its spelling (DfEE, 1998, p. 95). A knowledge of the spelling of common prefixes and suffixes can also help pupils with long words which they might otherwise feel reluctant to attempt: for example, knowing that the suffix '-ful' is spelt with one 'l' will be helpful in a whole range of words like 'cheerful', 'joyful', 'helpful' and so on.

Punctuation

Like spelling, punctuation is a system which exists only in relation to written language and as such pupils often have difficulty with it. It is assumed here that you, as a student teacher of English, know how to use punctuation in English (if this is not the case, there are many sources you can turn to, among which are: Greenbaum, 1996, pp. 503–55, Wray and Medwell, 1997, pp. 18–20 and 39–42, and websites such as http://cite.telecampus.com/GED/punct.html).

The teaching of punctuation is a relatively little researched area of English teaching; Beard (undated, p. 50) notes, 'Punctuation has rarely been discussed at length in literacy education publications . . . Recent investigations by Nigel Hall and Anne Robinson (1996) have highlighted how little is known about how punctuation is taught and learned.'

As a teacher of English in the Primary phase, pupils should come to you with a substantial command of the major features of punctuation: the National Curriculum for Key Stage 2 specifies that 'In punctuation, pupils should be taught to use punctuation marks correctly in their writing, including full stops, question and exclamation marks, commas, inverted commas, and apostrophes to mark possession' (DfEE, 1995, p. 15). You may find that this is a counsel of perfection and that there is need for revision of these elements; if so, the key is to start from the pupils' own work rather than focusing on decontextualised exercises, which tend not to be generalised into the pupils' own writing. It is very easy to have pupils do exercises on, say, inverted commas with a very high level of success only to find they are not used when the pupils come to write. Exploring children's writing with them and showing them the ambiguity and loss of clarity which arises when punctuation is not used appropriately is a much more direct way of getting to the heart of the matter, which is the incorporation of punctuation marks into the work which the children produce. Likewise, the more 'advanced' punctuation marks not mentioned in the Key Stage 2 Programmes of Study cited above – the colon and semi-colon – can be introduced in relation to children's own writing by showing them the value of these features as a means of clarifying the structure of what they have written. As Beard (undated, p. 50) suggests, knowledge of punctuation 'is likely to be best learned in a context which stresses authentic reading and writing activities'.

Answers to Activity 1

These sentences were based on a list of frequent complaints made to the BBC concerning the use of non-standard grammar. The notes below refer to Fowler (1965) and Treble and Vallins (1961), two of the major texts on prescriptive grammar, that is to say grammar which tells you how you ought to speak rather than providing a description of how people actually speak.

Purists would object to these sentences on the following grounds:

1. 'Between you and I . . .' should be 'Between you and me . . .'. This 'rule' arises from the influence of Latin on early thinkers about correctness in English; Fowler (1965, p. 258) notes, *'Between you and I is a piece of false grammar which, though often heard is not sanctioned.'* Typically of writers on this subject, Fowler omits to say by whom any given usage could or should be sanctioned. (The latest edition of Fowler's book (1998, p. 106) make the point no less strongly.)

2. 'I don't know why people have to constantly look for mistakes.' Purists would argue that an infinitive (the form of a verb which consists of 'to' plus the stem of the verb – 'to know, to see, to comprehend' and so on) should not be interrupted (in this case by the adverb 'constantly'). Fowler, almost unbelievably, devotes two and a half pages to this issue (pp. 579–82).

3. 'None of the mistakes here are serious': Treble and Vallins (1961, p. 123) argue, 'Since *none* = "not one" logical grammar would fix it as a singular.' So, it would be argued, we should have 'None of the mistakes here is serious.'

4. Even Fowler doesn't maintain that 'It's different to speaking in a foreign language' has to be used instead of 'It's different from speaking in a foreign language', asserting that 'the principle on which [different to] is rejected (you do not say *differ to*; therefore you cannot say *different to*) involves a hasty and ill-defined generalisation'. However, some would disagree.

5. 'Hopefully, we will be more tolerant in the future'; many people object to this use of 'hopefully' as a sentence adverbial, qualifying the whole sentence, and feel it should only be used of people who are full of hope as in 'We travelled hopefully.'

REFERENCES/SUGGESTIONS FOR FURTHER READING

Baker, C. and Prys Jones, S. (1998) *Encyclopedia of Bilingualism and Bilingual Education*, Clevedon: Multilingual Matters

Beard, R. (undated) *National Literacy Strategy: Review of Research and other Related Evidence*, London: DfEE

Carter, R. (1995) *Keywords in Language and Literacy*, London: Routledge

Cheshire, J., Edwards, V. and Whittle, P. (1993) 'Non-standard English and dialect levelling,' in J. Milroy and L. Milroy, *Real English: The Grammar of English Dialects in the British Isles*, London: Longman, pp. 53–96

Crystal, D. (1994) *The Cambridge Encyclopedia of Language*, Cambridge: CUP

Cummins, J. (1984) *Bilingualism and Special Education: Issues in Assessment and Pedagogy*, Clevedon: Multilingual Matters

DES (1989) *English for Ages 5 to 16* (The Cox Report), London: HMSO

DES (1990) *English in the National Curriculum*, London: HMSO

DfEE (1995) *English in the National Curriculum*, London: HMSO

DfEE (1998) Teaching: *High Status, High Standards* (Circular 4/98) *Requirements for Courses of Initial Teacher Training*, London: HMSO

DfEE (1999) *English in the National Curriculum*, London: HMSO.

Fowler, H.W. (1965) *A Dictionary of Modern English Usage*, 2nd edn (revised by E. Gowers), Oxford: OUP

Fowler, H.W. (1998) *The New Fowler's Modern English Usage*, 3rd edn, edited by R.W. Burchfield, Oxford: Clarendon

Goody, J. (ed.) (1992) *Multicultural Perspectives in the English Curriculum*, Sheffield: NATE

Gorman, T., White, J., Brooks, G. and English, F. (1989) *Language for Learning. A Summary Report on the 1988 APU Surveys of Language Performance*, London: SEAC

Greenbaum, S. (1996) *The Oxford English Grammar*, Oxford: OUP

Hall, N. and Robinson, A. (eds) (1996) *Learning about Punctuation*, Clevedon: Multilingual Matters

Hudson, R. and Holmes, J. (1995) *Children's Use of Spoken English*, London: SCAA

Hughes, A. and Trudgill, P. (1987) *English Accents and Dialects*, 2nd edn, London: Edward Arnold

LINC (Language in the National Curriculum) (undated) *Materials for Professional Development*, no publisher

Skutnabb-Kangas, T. (1981) *Bilingualism or Not: The Education of Minorities*, Clevedon: Multilingual Matters

Smith, F. (1978) *Reading*, Cambridge: CUP

Treble, H.A. and Vallins, G.H. (1961) *An ABC of English Usage*, Oxford: OUP

Trudgill, P. (1975) *Accent, Dialect and the School*, London: Edward Arnold

Trudgill, P. (1983) *Sociolinguistics: An Introduction to Language and Society*, Harmondsworth: Penguin

TTA (2002) *Qualifying to Teach: Professional Standards for Qualified Teacher Status and Requirements for Initial Teacher Training*, London: Teacher Training Agency

Wardhaugh, R. (1992) *An Introduction to Sociolinguistics*, 2nd edn, Oxford: Blackwell

Williamson, J. (1989) 'An Extra Radiator? Teachers' Views of Support Teaching and Withdrawal in Developing the English of Bilingual Pupils', *Educational Studies*, 15, 3, pp. 315–26

Williamson, J. and Hardman, F. (1997a) 'To Purify the Dialect of the Tribe: Children's Use of Non-standard Dialect Grammar in Writing', *Educational Studies*, 23, 2, pp. 157–68

Williamson, J. and Hardman, F. (1997b) 'Those Terrible Marks of the Beast: Non-standard Dialect and Children's Writing', *Language and Education*, 11, 4, pp. 287–99

Wray, D. and Medwell, J. (1997) *English for Primary Teachers: An Audit and Self-Study Guide*, London: Letts Educational

9 What Do We Mean by Teaching Drama?

JAMES CRINSON

TEACHING DRAMA

This chapter will give you a flavour of how drama can be taught in the primary school. First I describe a couple of projects to give you an idea of the range of activities which drama can encompass. Then I consider the special factors involved in teaching drama to different age groups. Finally I consider key factors such as protection and tension, as well as looking at a range of activities which you could use. Where technical drama terms are italicised they are described more fully in the glossary.

AN EXAMPLE

Imagine a classroom with the usual equipment: board, desk, chairs. The challenge is to turn this into a world of magic. Using drama, this is easy.

I usually start with any group of children emphasising the importance of make believe. I clear away the desks and chairs to the outside of the classroom, and create a circle in the middle of the room. We sit in a circle, and discuss how human beings (uniquely among animals as far as we know) can pretend. We discuss their own pretending games in the playground, being aeroplanes, for example. We discuss if people have gone mad pretending to be aeroplanes. Everyone laughs, and we agree that it's pretending. I say that drama is about pretending. We have a circle, so we can pretend there's something there which isn't really there. I ask the children to suggest something they can pretend. Usually this is not a problem, and often the first suggestion is an animal. I then ask a brave person (depending on the kind of animal) to stroke it, touch its ears, or walk round it in a fearful way. To gauge how many of the group are getting hold of the idea, once the child has done this, I ask everyone else to point to its tail, head. I congratulate someone for pointing at the right height.

The next stage is to get the children to suggest something else. If I don't intervene at this point we will have a succession of animals. So I usually suggest something inanimate. We may then get a door. I invite someone to open it. I then ask the child to step through and say what they see. If they are unsure, I invite someone else to help, and I will often rephrase/enrich the language they use:

Teacher:	Is it an old room?
Pupil:	Yes.
Teacher:	Can you see any furniture?
Pupil:	Chairs.
Teacher:	Right. Old, worn out chairs. They're all different, and stood round an old table. In the middle of the table is a great pot full of food.

I might then invite the child to taste the food, offer it to the group.

The purpose of this is not to begin a drama, although you can do this if you like thinking on your feet. The purpose is simply to begin to open up the pupils' imaginations: the ideas are there, but need opening up.

As part of the preliminary activities I might also invite the pupils to pretend the room could be somewhere else (a doctor's waiting room, a space ship) and to pretend that they are someone else (patients, police officers waiting for a briefing, archaeologists looking at a hole in the ground). All of this will help the pupils develop the idea of role, which is crucial to all drama.

I will now describe a project I carried out over two mornings with Y3 children. The idea here is to give you an idea how a drama project might unfold. You could try this one out, or use other frameworks available in, for example, Crinson and Leak (1993). But the aim here is to give you a flavour of the range of activities available in drama.

We began by finding out some things about Guy Fawkes, using an article which gave the pupils information. They had to find out a fact, and then write it onto a slip of paper. The slips of paper were stuck onto a life size cut-out of Guy Fawkes, which I had previously put on the wall. The facts were such things as that Guy Fawkes had started school at six o'clock, and that he lived in York, that he was a soldier, and that he was put to death. They also liked the idea that he had beer for breakfast aged eight.

I read out the facts, and began to establish some ideas in the children's minds about Guy's life. I then asked the pupils (who were used to drama) to do a *freeze frame* of a moment in Guy's life. They did these in fours or fives. There was a breakfast scene, an army scene, a scene in the Houses of Parliament, and an execution. The children captioned the scenes, and they took turns to view each other's picture.

We then started these scenes and I asked them to move them forward as if it was a video, but a video with the sound off. Once they had done this, I asked them to retrace the action (again in silence) and have another go. Finally we did the same thing with speech, having reminded them that they were in role, and were not pupils at their school any more. We could have shown these little scenes, but it is important not to make performance the goal of every drama.

The next stage was to change role. As *teacher in role* as the King, I invited the children to become my detectives. I told them that if they could read (in role) a particular letter (an original from someone warning his brother not to go to the Houses of Parliament), I would make them King's Investigators. They surprised themselves by being able to work out that the letter was a warning. I then asked them to 'find' (i.e. make) some evidence for or against the guilt of Guy, who was in my prison. The children very much enjoyed making the evidence, which consisted of weapons, fingerprints and so on.

Then, in role as Guy, I listened to their accusations and attempted to challenge their evidence. Note that here the pupils had the dominant talk role: they asked the questions, and I had to reply (*hotseating*).

Finally I asked them to write briefly saying what they thought Guy had done, and why.

The second project is an early years project done with a reception class in the summer term.

I started with a circle session on pretending, as above. After a retelling (rather than a picture book) of Jack and the Beanstalk, the children were encouraged to imagine the giant's palace. I asked them to look round the classroom and see if they could imagine large versions of everyday objects. We created together a mental image of the palace, with its kitchen, dining room, garden, garage, bedrooms and so on. I challenged the children to imagine large versions of everything they had mentioned.

I then suggested that they might take the role of the palace servants. I reminded them of how we had dedicated every area of the classroom as a part of the palace, and asked the children to go and find a part of the palace to work in. They went off readily and began dramatic playing, making beds, cooking food, feeding horses, digging the garden. I went round trying to deepen the activity by reminding them of the size of everything in the palace, and getting them to feel the weight of the things they were carrying. I then encouraged a few of the children to demonstrate their activity, while the others guessed what they were doing. I emphasised the credibility of the movement as a way of raising the status of what we were doing.

I could at this point, if I had wanted to calm the children down, have asked them to draw the object they used most while working in the palace. There is a range of building belief activities, which drama teachers need to use until they feel the children are ready for more active roles.

I sent the children back to their dramatic playing, but I told them that the chief palace servant would be coming soon, and he was very bossy. I didn't prepare them for the fact that it would be me, because I knew these children, and I thought they would work it out. If I had not known the children I might have prepared them for teacher in role by indicating that I would become someone else when I took my jacket off, wore a scarf, hat, or some other symbol.

I went round telling the children to work harder, be tidier, and that the giant was in a bad mood because someone had been in and had stolen his magic guitar. The children were outraged to hear this, especially as it had put the giant in a bad mood. Eventually we agreed that the children would meet the giant, and would help him.

I sat the children in front of a flip chart, and then told them that I would be the chief servant, but that I wanted someone to be the giant. I told the volunteer simply to look sad, and that I would do all the talking.

After finding out why the giant was sad, we agreed to write a letter to the stealer of the guitar (Jack). I told the children that the giant and I could not write, so they would have to write for him. The children wrote a letter asking Jack for the guitar to be returned, because it did not belong to him, but to the giant.

After a break, I said that the children would be meeting Jack soon, and could read their letter to him. But before they got back into role, I encouraged the children to reflect out of role about Jack and his thieving. The children agreed that he had done wrong, even if the giant did want to eat him, and that he should be persuaded to give the guitar back. We considered briefly how the story makes you think it is all right to steal things.

I played Jack very sulkily, while the children read me their letter. After much persuading I agreed to give the giant his guitar back. I thanked the children for helping me do the right thing.

You will notice that the two projects relate to history and literature. These are very common starting points for drama. Obviously dramas can be original (as in the suggestion about the table above) or can relate to children's literature. The impetus for drama can equally come from history, for example, or science, music, poetry. The list is endless.

DRAMA IN THE PRIMARY SCHOOL

Early years

In the early years drama is a natural part of the provision for young children, indoors and out. Early years teachers have always provided opportunities for role activities: Wendy houses, home corners etc. Usually nowadays you will find in any early years setting a 'role-play area'. Here you will find opportunities for interacting in role. Recent examples from my school include a travel agent, a gingerbread house, and a café. These play environments will reflect the kinds of talk the teacher is wishing to promote at this point in the child's development. Typically children will choose to play in this environment. It is worth finding an early years setting and watching this kind of play in action. Children naturally play *in role* in these areas. It can be useful to structure this sometimes, by having an adult participate in the environment and operating in role. While this will restrict what the children might otherwise have done, it can also give the children new and exciting possibilities. For example, if you intervene in role in a home environment, instead of asking for a cup of tea, you might ask the children if they have seen a little pig going past carrying some straw. Children will immediately get the idea. This kind of intervention can give rise to games which then go on independently of the adult for weeks. However, you should also observe the behaviour in the environment without your intervention, to check that the environment is equipped to give the high-quality interaction you are seeking, and modify the equipment if it is not.

Other activities can also be used with early years children. Hotseating, for example, could be the children asking you (or another adult) questions with you in role as the giant. Freeze frame can be used with young children in the same way as it was used in the Guy Fawkes project, as a way of structuring narrative, or of thinking about individual situations or dilemmas.

> **Activity 1** Look at the document for the Foundation Stage (Curriculum Guidance for the Foundation Stage (DfEE/QCA, 2000)) and try to locate where the opportunities for using drama might be.

Key Stage 1

Many Key Stage 1 teachers provide a role-play area, which may be related to topics, literature, or subject areas.

As well as this, it is possible to operate a full drama project with this age group. See the glossary. These techniques are linked together by the story you are telling, providing opportunities for children to have a range of different activities. With the Jack and the Beanstalk activity, for example, a drawing/writing activity would be followed by some dramatic playing getting ready to go on a journey.

Generally with this age group it is important to build belief carefully, and to leave a good deal of time for dramatic play: in the Jack and the Beanstalk example the children will very much enjoy being able to play at being the giant's servants sweeping the floor, planting flowers, cooking food. Teacher in role is a very powerful device with this age group.

At this age it is also possible to use scripted drama or other sorts of performance. Typically these performance opportunities will include class assemblies, Christmas or other shows, and the use within the classroom of playscript-type texts (for example as part of some reading schemes). Young children can enjoy such performance opportunities provided they are properly structured and not threatening. Instead of using scripted drama materials it is possible to use a kind of structured *improvisation*. You might give the children a situation (e.g. the innkeeper apologising for not having a bed for Mary and Joseph in the Christmas Story), but allow the children to find their own words. Subsequently you would rehearse this so that the children could repeat what they had decided to say. This gets over the problem that most young children find it difficult not to speak other people's words without sounding a bit stilted.

It is worth pointing out that the use of the activities suggested in the glossary are excellent activities also to develop and deepen activities in other subjects. For example, teacher in role or dramatic playing can be an excellent way of getting children to write with more imaginative depth than they achieve with other kinds of stimulus.

Key Stage 2

Drama can be a major part of teaching and learning at Key Stage 2. Unfortunately it is often neglected. Children in Early Years and Key Stage 1 will often have a designated drama area in the classroom. This is unlikely at Key Stage 2. Drama will need to be taught as an adjunct to English or other subjects such as history. Some teachers realise how useful drama can be, and will use, say, *still image* or *forum theatre* to create a more imaginative backdrop for creative writing. Drama can be used in history, say in creating a village just before the plague occurred, or a ship of pilgrim fathers going to America. These simple techniques (*dramatic playing*, freeze frame) will immediately switch pupils onto history (or science, RE and many other curriculum areas). Teachers often fear losing control, or that they won't know what to do next. The next section addresses these issues.

This is really the age when almost all of the techniques described below can be used. Pupils are able to do short improvisations, use writing as a part of their drama work, and sustain a story over a day or over several lessons. However, pupils of this age (especially if they are used to working in role) still have the unself-consciousness and spontaneity to fall naturally into dramatic playing, or to carry out mimes, freeze frames or dance activities.

Equally, scripted drama can be used, and pupils will very much enjoy reading plays and performing them. Obviously the opportunity to polish and memorise lines can be a boost to reluctant readers, and texts are available in many reading schemes and other children's literature which provide parts for pupils with better developed and less developed reading skills. These are available on the web also for those preparing the dreaded class assembly. On this subject, class assemblies and other 'performance-type' drama activity (e.g. Christmas shows) are important opportunities for pupils to speak to larger groups (a part of the Speaking and Listening programme of study). Here again it is worth taking scenarios either from websites, from literature or from your own ideas and getting children to improvise the scene within given parameters, as mentioned above in KS1. This will enable children to find their words, and they will memorise their own language much more easily. This is not to say that there is not also merit in using other people's language, including somewhat archaic language, which again is something which must be covered at some point for the programmes of study.

Nevertheless, the most valuable learning will take place in classroom drama activities, where the pupils operate in role, develop the narrative themselves, and are challenged by teacher in role or other devices to deepen their drama, as in the projects above, which both resulted in some powerful learning and some excellent written work, amongst other things. The following section deals with some practical issues which are important to get right if the first few attempts at drama are to be pleasurable for teacher and pupils.

| Activity 2 | Look at the National Curriculum for English and highlight the drama sections, and those which could be addressed through drama. Consider also as an example the Curriculum Document for history, and consider where drama might play a part here also. |

PRACTICAL ISSUES

Where?

Many teachers think that drama, like dance, should take place in a hall. My advice would be to start in the classroom. To a primary school child a hall sends messages of PE and dance. The children will be disappointed when they find they are not rushing around very often, and may even be asked to write or draw. Also halls can be uncomfortable places to sit around, whereas most primary classrooms offer an opportunity to sit on the floor. As I said above, I start with a circle, either of chairs or sitting on the floor, and the desks are put round the outside of the room. The chairs will probably become key props in freeze frame and dramatic playing, and the tables need to be available for writing and drawing if required.

You may wish to go into the hall at the end for some kind of celebration or performance, but even this should not be the automatic aim at the end of a project. Another advantage of the classroom is that they are often fascinating places in their own right, and the objects the children see in the classroom can easily be transformed into items in the drama. For example a radiator can become a fire, a bookcase becomes a mirror. One practical point here is to ban all use of real props. My approach here is always to say that we can pretend a spade or indeed a horse. Otherwise we tend to get children being horses (no real learning) and rulers becoming spades. You can even get children who have disagreements about props on the lines of 'I got it first'. Emphasise how clever they are to be able to pretend.

Who?

Drama will work in any grouping from individual to whole-class. I find that whole-class mixed with individual and pair work is best for the initial stages. When children are more confident in using drama as a learning medium groups of four or five can be used, and the best place to start with this is to use freeze frame, where all they have to decide is who is going to stand where. Children can easily learn to do small improvisations of scenes which they have previously explored during dramatic play. They will wish to perform these, and there can be merit in working a scene through a couple of times for performance. However, it is important that these scenes do not become the only goal of drama activity. The children should see the drama that they make as the story they have made, and the activities as episodes within it.

What?

It is important to vary the activities within any one session, and throughout sessions. As I have implied, there is a movement from simple activities such as freeze frame and dramatic play towards more complex material such as improvisation. An experienced teacher who has decided to come off timetable and to run a day of drama (which would be very much encouraged under the new advice from the government – *Excellence and Enjoyment* (DfES, 2003)) might include elements of the following:

- Talk – in a variety of groupings: teacher to class, pupil to pupil, small groups, small group to class. It is worth pointing out that drama is the only area of the curriculum which can access classroom talk which is not subject to the normal rules of classroom discourse (i.e. the teacher will tend to control the allocation of turns, and will generally evaluate the pupil's contribution). In drama pupils can and will take on the expert role or the challenger role, where in a protected way they can practise being the one who knows, or the one who asks questions.
- Freeze frame – pupils freeze on a prearranged signal. Other pupils can then go and see the pictures, which can be captioned, or have 'speech bubbles' or 'thinks balloons' added. The frames can be rolled on, or the action can restart. Dialogue can be introduced, or the teacher can read out words or dialogue to go with each one.
- Thought tracking is where you develop the thoughts behind a scene, often a still image. Not what they say, but what they're thinking.
- Dramatic playing: where children play as in the school yard, but in the context of your drama, for example: 'It is morning in the village: go about your daily tasks.'
- Class discussion – in role and out of role: hotseating is a version of this, where you or a pupil are asked questions in role in front of the class.
- Writing – in role and out of role.
- Drawing – pupils can draw their most precious possession, a useful tool, or the contents of their suitcase for holiday.
- Modelling/design technology – pupils can make a religious artefact, or a machine. This will then be used symbolically in the drama: 'Our machine will help us escape . . .'
- Found objects: you can also use found objects, say a pair of glasses or a map, of which you claim to know nothing. This again can stimulate curiosity, or have a symbolic role in the drama.
- Presentation – as mentioned above, pupils can see each other's freeze frames, hear the *thought tracking*, or watch and appreciate others' improvisation.
- Listening/responding – to teacher reading or narrating; to each other.
- Mantle of the expert: where the children behave as if they were the ones with the knowledge: see above – the King's Investigators.
- Forum theatre – where the class direct volunteers in a playscene, building a setting and an approach to the story.
- Ritual – using mime, dance, music to create depth and possibly 'awe and wonder' if you're lucky!

The point is to provide a range of classroom activities which allow the children opportunities to be quiet, to be active, to write, draw and make things just like any other school day. This kind of thing can be done as a day, as suggested above.

However, beginners would be better advised to try one or two activities from time to time, and then reflect on how it has gone. It is a good idea to have a common narrative. Children will remember what you did the previous day/week. Indeed, they often remember drama sessions for years.

Having an aim

It is essential in teaching drama to have a learning outcome in mind. This will enable you to choose activities to help you move the children towards this outcome. The learning outcome should be communicated to the children, while emphasising that we will be making a drama together. You might say 'Our story will help us understand how stories can be seen from more than one viewpoint' (Jack and the Beanstalk). If we get it right, children should have new understandings arising from a drama: not just having fun.

Protection

Drama can pose a threat to self-esteem if handled wrongly. Therefore with younger children and with less experienced children it is important to give them less exposed activities initially, until they are confident in and serious about the role. Writing, drawing, freeze frame, talking out of role are all ways of developing protection.

Choice of role

A crucial decision is finding the right role for the children. The right role will take you quickly to your goal of full involvement and enhanced understanding. I often later introduce a new role (a camera crew, or old people reminiscing) as a way of getting a new view on events. As in protection above, it is important initially to pick roles which are not too challenging. If you wanted to look at war, for example, you would be wise not to go straight into being front-line soldiers. A village preparing to welcome soldiers back might be better.

Equally, you need to think about your own role: you may start with a high-status role (e.g. a king), then move towards an intermediate role (a chief servant) and finally to a 'needing help' role, where you enable the children to speak with care and authority.

Building belief

It is important to give the role time to bed down, so that the children feel at home in it. All actors have to build belief in a role. Activities such as drawing a precious possession, putting their house on a map, building a bedroom, writing a letter home (writing in role) and dramatic playing are all ways of building belief in the world you are attempting to create before you then introduce the element of tension which all stories require.

Tension

Tension needs to be established to get a story to have a forward motion. Causes of tension do not need to be a major disaster or a massive conflict. They are simply the elements of complication needed by any good story. Can the girl spin all the straw into gold before morning? There is a strange message on the boy's wall. What do the psychic researchers make of it?

CONCLUSION

Drama fits perfectly with the new understanding we now have about how children learn. It naturally uses all the normal learning channels of visual, auditory and kinaesthetic. However, it is very unusual in making its learning mode mostly kinaesthetic. Mostly in drama you are doing things with your body. Meaning is made as much through movement, position and gesture as through words, and indeed the normal thrust of a drama session is from movement to words. This process engages all learners. Research suggests that a majority of boys are kinaesthetic learners, and that they are often failed in our schools. Drama teachers are not surprised to hear that drama will engage boys where other modes of learning do not.

Drama need not be difficult to teach and will undoubtedly be rewarding. Teaching any subject using drama will enable you to bring ideas to life. And, as a primary teacher, you can always move onto something else, and come back to drama when you have worked out the next activity. You can be sure the children will welcome drama whenever you choose to do it.

GLOSSARY

Dramatic playing: a development of the children's own play.

Forum theatre: the whole class takes on the role of director.

Freeze frame: sometimes called **tableau**, **photograph** or **still image**: the children are asked to create a still image either on their own or in small groups, usually to capture a moment in time. For example, a particular point in a story might be depicted.

Games: often used as warm-up activities or enhanced in a drama context. For example, the game 'keeper of the keys' can easily be turned into a dramatisation of a pirate story where an evil pirate is guarding treasure.

Hotseating: where an individual (teacher or pupil) in role answers questions as if he/she were a character in the drama. Questions can address the motivation of characters as well as issues relating to plot.

Improvisation: all examples of drama where pupils work without a script.

Teacher in role: where the teacher takes on the role of a specific character. This character can be 'in charge' of a situation or act in a more subsidiary role, e.g. 'I've just been told that we have to organise a summer fair for next week.'

Thought tracking: where you develop the thoughts behind a scene, often a still image. Not what they say, but what they're thinking.

REFERENCES/SUGGESTIONS FOR FURTHER READING

Brecht, B. (1974) *Brecht on Theatre*, London: Methuen
Crinson, J. and Leak, L. (eds) (1993) *Move Back the Desks*, Sheffield: NATE
DfEE/QCA (2000) *Curriculum Guidance for the Foundation Stage*, London: HMSO
DfES (2003) *Excellence and Enjoyment*, London: HMSO
Fleming, M. (1994) *The Art of Drama Teaching*, London: David Fulton
Heathcote, D. and Bolton, G. (1995) *Drama for Learning*, Portsmouth, NH: Heinemann
Stanislavsky, K. (1967) *Stanislavsky and the Art of the Stage,* London: Faber
Winston, J. and Tandy, M. (2001) *Beginning Drama 4–11*, 2nd edn, London: David Fulton

10 ICT for Literacy

STEVE HIGGINS AND NICK PACKARD

ICT (Information and Communication Technology) has the potential to support effective teaching and learning in the teaching of English. Since most schools teach English overtly through the Literacy Strategy, this section focuses on the use of ICT in the strategy. It is essential, however, to ensure that when ICT is to be used in support of teaching and learning in literacy, it is the literacy learning objective that remains the prime focus of the lesson. In this chapter we will look at how ICT can be used to support the teacher in preparing and delivering effective literacy lessons and how ICT can be used to help pupils develop their literacy skills, knowledge and understanding.

One of the most important contributions that ICT can make in supporting learning in literacy is in helping teachers provide pupils with resources that allow them to focus on the learning objective and avoid getting bogged down in other issues. A typical example would be using a word processing package that includes a Word Bank tool. A Word Bank usually provides pupils with a simple way of getting prepared vocabulary into their written work without worrying about how to spell, or for that matter write, each word. Many such packages would also include what is called a text-to-speech facility, which 'reads' the text back to the pupil, helping them focus on the meaning of the writing without constant rereading. Literacy work done this way may help pupils concentrate on the flow of text and its meaning and reduce the relevance of issues relating to handwriting, spelling, editing and rereading.

ICT IN WHOLE-CLASS TEACHING IN LITERACY

When considering the use of ICT in the teaching of literacy and the Literacy Strategy there is a range of opportunities to consider. Given the access to the right kit, using ICT in the whole-class teaching elements of the strategy can be very powerful. If you are lucky enough to have access to a digital projector in the classroom where you teach literacy this can dramatically enhance the opportunities you have for whole-class teaching. With a digital projector, sharing texts, activities and presentations is not only possible, it's a real boon.

Presenting raw texts on a projector screen for shared text work is possible, though using extended texts involves a huge amount of scrolling up and down pages or flicking through slides, which can be something of a distraction. The real power lies in being able to interact with the text in different ways. With text presented in a word processor, such as Microsoft Word, it is possible to discuss features of text and highlight those features as necessary, perhaps by changing the colour of the section of text or perhaps by using the purpose-made editing features built into the application. A simple search for the adjectives in a piece of text is now a very visual and engaging whole-class task. It provides pupils with strong visual clues that help them develop their understanding of the concept being discussed. This not only helps pupils engage with the concept but also provides a degree of support when offering suggestions of their own. They can use the evidence of other people's answers to help them work out whether the answer they want to offer seems to fit. A degree of comfort about the accuracy or appropriateness of your answer tends to make you much more willing to contribute to the discussion!

A digital projector will also enable you to demonstrate how to use worksheets or other prepared resources if they were originally developed on a computer. If you create a worksheet or activity on a computer then you can use the original file to show pupils how they should use the paper-based version of the resource. Even more powerful is the ability to use this file again in the plenary session where it is possible to discuss pupils' ideas and answers and share those ideas instantly with the whole class.

A digital projector also gives you the opportunity to use presentation software, such as Microsoft Powerpoint or Textease Presenter, to present ideas and concepts in more engaging ways. This type of software allows teachers to build presentations that incorporate animations, sound effects and transitions and add time delays and so on. Recent research suggests that these features, well used, can help pupils follow and recall the main features more effectively. It is also possible that a presentation used within a whole-class session could also be used by pupils in small-group or individual work sessions. This provides a good introduction to the task but also provides an excellent platform for pupils to present their work and their ideas. All they have to do is run the presentation from the PC connected to the projector, and describe what they have done.

Whole-class presentation technology also gives you easy ways to bring stimulating materials into the class; you could project current news items from the World Wide Web as a way of discussing report genre or idioms; you could show short video clips or play real news radio footage to discuss features of spoken news reporting; you could study the features of scripts for radio plays or adverts; you could use live web pages to look for information about specific topics or different points of view when discussing arguments; you could conduct searches of CD ROMs to find text relevant to the subjects you are discussing and so on. It would even be possible to have a piece of text and a video clip from the same story to play side by side to discuss the changes and differences between the two formats. None of these ideas requires the use of an

Interactive Whiteboard, but consideration of the opportunities that that might offer should be made.

Not all schools have digital projectors and fewer have them available for use in classrooms, though this picture is changing rapidly.

Case study

The following describes how a teacher might use ICT in whole-class teaching within the Literacy Strategy.

> The teacher of a Year 3 class has access to the ICT suite twice a week. Usually she uses the suite once for delivery of the ICT Curriculum and once for using ICT within the curriculum. This lesson is a literacy lesson. The suite is set up with 16 computers on benches around the suite and has some tables set up in the middle of the room for work away from the computers. There is a digital projector and screen at the front of the classroom.
>
> The teacher has brought photocopies of a play script to use as the shared text. The script was printed using a word processor having been downloaded from the internet and the original file is projected onto the main screen for all to see. At first, the teacher reads the script, using different voices for each character in the play. The class discuss the structure of the script and the clues to characterisation within it. The teacher uses the highlight function in the word processor to show the bits of text that the children think give clues to the nature of each character in turn. The class make some decisions about the nature of each character and the teacher makes notes on the whiteboard to the side of the projector screen. The teacher then shares out the roles to some of the class and they reread the script, trying to use some of the ideas modelled and discussed previously.
>
> The annotated script is left projected on the screen in the ICT room as the pupils move onto the individual and group-level work.

Activity 1	**Using ICT in whole-class teaching**

Find out if there is a digital projector available at your next or current school placement and, if it is not sited in a teaching area you have access to, find out what the procedures for booking and using it are.

Using the ideas above as a starting point, design a whole-class activity that fits with your literacy planning and try this out with the class. If you need to build your confidence, try the idea in a group work session instead. This could be done around a single monitor instead of using a digital projector and could be a good way of trying the idea out if you are working in a school that does not have projection facilities.

ICT IN GROUP OR INDIVIDUAL WORK IN LITERACY

ICT can also provide valuable opportunities for pupil learning through group or individual work. Many teachers will use ICT to assist in the preparation of worksheets and learning resources for use within the classroom. This section, however, covers the use of activities that are designed to be carried out on a computer. Some of the ideas and activities are applicable for use with group activities, in which case it may be possible to use a single PC or laptop in the classroom; others really require individual access for pupils. Some schools have access to several computers in classrooms, especially where access to a suite of wireless laptops has been provided. It is more likely that you will have access to a computer suite and it should be possible that a literacy lesson can be delivered in this setting, or that groups can access the suite during the lesson.

Access to resources and activities on the computer can provide pupils with similar supports outlined in the previous section at an individual level, too. Working with raw or prepared texts on a computer can help pupils focus on specific objectives and identify relevant features, record observations and ideas and amend relevant sections quickly and easily. Identifying parts of text for further work/discussion or analysis can be done simply by highlighting text and changing its colour or emboldening it to make it stand out. Some word processors also provide specific highlight functions. Once relevant features have been identified, they can easily be reworked, without the need for laborious rewriting.

Many word processors also provide pupils with access to 'writing tools', which might help them review or refine their work. Access to spell checkers can obviously help pupils to identify and correct spelling or typing errors, though whether this is beneficial in improving a child's ability to spell accurately is debatable. Spell checking tools can be used proactively, however, by getting pupils to keep a record of spelling errors that are regularly identified by the checker. These words can be entered (copied and pasted?) into spelling logs or word webs which can then be used as devices to focus on developing more effective spelling strategies later. Many word processors also have grammar checkers, which can be used to help pupils focus on the sense and structure of their writing. Both these services can also be turned off if they interfere with the process (sometimes it can be appropriate to turn writing tools off so that little red wiggly lines don't distract pupils from the actual writing process, or interrupt the flow. Tools can be turned back on during the editing and reviewing stages of the writing process).

There is a great deal of evidence that one of the things primary age pupils find most frustrating about the editing process is the rewriting of the text that it often involves. Editing on-screen can help tackle some of these issues. Indeed, it also makes breaking the editing process into single-step processes easier. (Editing involves several steps: checking for meaning, grammar, punctuation, good use of language and finally presenting the text. These can all be tackled separately and individually on a PC.) It may also provide wider opportunities for developing and working with texts. Since electronic versions of texts are easy to distribute to several people (printed copies or emailed attachments or use of ICT networks), texts may be shared for use in 'peer review' sessions. This is especially effective if you are using a word processor that can 'track changes'. ICT can also provide authors with an audience. Through email or use of the web, children can start to write for real and varied audiences and purposes.

Individual work can be effectively supported through use of specialist software, such as the word banks and speech feedback facilities mentioned earlier. Such facilities can be very effective in providing full access to learning opportunities for less able pupils and, indeed, even more specialised equipment can also help provide great access to a mainstream curriculum for pupils with even severe and complex special educational needs.

It is the flexible nature of ICT resources that is the most important factor here. First, there is the opportunity for effective differentiation that ICT provides. If a teacher sets up a specific activity for higher achieving pupils, say a prepared text for studying idiomatic language, then it can be a simple process to adapt that resource for others within the class. Here, high-achieving pupils may be asked to identify and explain the idioms within the text; others may have the idioms highlighted for them and all they have to do is explain what they mean. Others might be given explanations and they have to identify the idioms from those explanations; some might even have a text-to-speech function enabled so that they can 'read along' with the computer to help them follow the meaning of the text.

Flexibility is also provided through the range of sources of information pupils may have access to. Access to the internet may provide pupils with opportunities to explore sources of information, especially up-to-date information, that can be hard to provide through other media. The internet can also provide a wide range of opportunities for studying differing points of view by looking at differences in reported information from different organisations. This can provide an amazing insight into the importance of taking everything you read on the internet with an enormous pinch of salt and is extremely important in helping children to become 'critical users' of the internet – indeed, critical users of any source of information.

Work at any level can be provided using software for different purposes. For instance, a computer-based activity at word level, identifying and sorting verbs perhaps, using software that is really designed for desktop publishing, can be very effective. Desktop publishing software (you may come across packages such as Microsoft Publisher or Textease Studio in schools) is designed to make manipulation and placing of separate elements easy. In the above activity, the words are the separate elements and being able simply to drag them around the screen makes for a simple sorting device. The page would be set up with elements such as instructions and spaces into which words can be sorted first. These elements can often be 'locked' in place so that only the words to be sorted, which are added later, can be moved. Sorting in this way allows for review and a change of mind in ways that cut-and-stick or transcribing words from a given list don't!

On the other hand, providing prepared texts for pupils to use in a presentation package such as Microsoft Powerpoint can offer access to the same range of writing tools that you might find in a good word processor, but has the advantage of having presentation features built in. Work done with presentation software is ready to present back to the class at the end of the activity. Not only will this provide effective material for use in the plenary to a lesson but also provides opportunities for pupils to develop speaking and listening skills as well as allowing children to reflect upon their performance and their understanding. An example may be a prepared file with a sequence of instructions for a simple task. In Microsoft Powerpoint, with the instructions presented in the wrong order, each instruction can be 'dragged' into the right place to construct the correct sequence. This can be especially effective if the sequence is potentially ambiguous: does it matter if you fill the kettle first or wash your hands first when making a cup-a-soup? This opens up debate and encourages children to justify their ideas.

It may also be worth considering using different software tools for different stages in the writing process. For instance, mind-mapping software could be very useful in the planning stages of the writing process. Mind mapping software is designed to help children clarify their thinking by allowing them to discuss and reflect upon the relevant issues in a task. Everything you know about making a model in technology could be written down as separate elements in the software and then sorted, categorised and linked together to provide a 'map' of your ideas.

It is important that the software tools you choose to use with pupils are appropriate for their skill level, of course. It is also essential that they are familiar with the use of these pieces of software before you use them in a literacy lesson to ensure learning is specifically focused on the Literacy Learning Objective.

Case study

Following on from the whole-class work described in the section above, the class go on to further work on characterisation, some working at PCs, using word bank software, which they have used many times before, to help them describe illustrated characters on the screen. Others working at tables in small groups are highlighting clues to characterisation in another piece of script and are illustrating what they think the characters would look like. Pupils working at the computers save their work onto the shared drive on the school's network so that it can be retrieved later.

In the plenary, the teacher shows a couple of examples of descriptions of characters done at the computer and discusses with the class the choices made. The work done at the computers is printed out and used in a group discussion in the next literacy lesson. The teacher intends to review work with the group and see if everyone agrees about the descriptions of the characters the pupils were given. The children will be encouraged to make changes to their descriptions if they have changed their minds about the characters after the discussion. Others will be encouraged to 'polish' their language and try to find more effective adjectives to use within their writing. Children will return to the computer suite to make these changes in the following lesson. The final versions of the printed text will be used in a 'Rogues Gallery' display in the classroom.

Activity 2	**Using ICT in group or individual work**

Before trying to use any of the ideas above with the class, learn how to protect the files you prepare. On most computers this involves 'write protecting' the file by right-clicking on the file, selecting 'properties' from the menu and making sure the 'read only' box towards the bottom of the Properties window is checked. This has two effects. First, it means that the file can be shared by several computers at once (essential if you are going to use shared work areas) but secondly and more importantly it means that any changes made by the pupils will not change your original file. When they come to save their work they will be asked to give the file a name as if it was a brand new piece of work and they won't be able to overwrite your original file.

It is also essential that you know how to access shared areas on the computer network. Ask the schools ICT coordinator or technical support person to show you how to use the network.

ICT IN PLANNING AND PREPARATION FOR TEACHING LITERACY

ICT offers teachers many ways in which to handle their professional responsibilities in terms of planning, preparing and delivering effective lessons as well as in managing their classrooms and their pupils. Many teachers use word processors or databases to compile termly or yearly reports, to keep work records and pupil profiles up to date and so on. When it comes to the teaching of literacy, ICT is especially useful in terms of preparation and delivery of learning opportunities as discussed above. ICT also provides teachers with access to resources that help them manage this process.

The government is keen to promote the use of ICT, and particularly communications technologies, to help teachers develop their professional practice and for this reason the DfES put a great deal of effort into its online strategy. All planning documentation used in schools, including the National Curriculum for English and the Literacy Strategy, are available online through the Standards site. To back up this planning the Literacy Strategy also publish a significant amount of support material, from lists of recommended texts to support for the use of the Literacy Strategy for pupils with special needs. Through the NCAction website (www.ncaction.org.uk), the DfES are also providing materials to help teachers assess their pupils' work and government-sponsored sites such as Teacher Net (www.teachernet.org) or Gridclub (www.gridclub.org) have materials that directly support teaching in literacy. Through the e-Learning Credits scheme (together with Curriculum Online) the government are effectively sponsoring the adoption of e-learning materials in British schools.

Individual schools also have access to specific learning materials, possibly purchased through government schemes and delivered through ICT – banks of interactive learning materials including video clips that act as stimulus for lessons or interactive activities that are designed to help pupils consolidate basic skills. It is worth finding out what is available in schools you may work in that is specific to that school.

As mentioned earlier, many teachers prepare resources for their lessons using computers. A digital version of a worksheet is easy to adapt and therefore provides opportunities for effective differentiation. Preparing and storing work on a PC provides starting points for new work. Many teachers that use ICT regularly to develop teaching resources and classroom aids will tell you that they never open an empty file and start work; they almost always open an existing file that is similar and work over the top of that. This approach is usually much quicker as there is less formatting and planning to be done.

If you try preparing resources that pupils will use on computers (as discussed in the section above) then an awareness of the level of support and control the pupils get when using the resource is important. For instance, checking a piece of text (perhaps originally written by the pupil) for spelling errors is extremely valuable. There is a reasonable amount of evidence that suggests that pupils find it easier to spot errors in printed or on-screen text because it is more clearly presented. However, leaving the spell-check function in a word processor switched on may undermine the benefits somewhat. Finding out how to switch writing tools on and off can be extremely useful. In a similar vein, knowing how to add or remove tool palettes in different pieces of software can be useful. If you want pupils to use text formatting menus that allow them to select fonts, styles and sizes easily then these tools need to be present before you start. On the other hand, having tools that allow them to turn text into data-entry forms may be a distraction, so removing them before you start might be useful, too. Again, find out how you do this with the software you are using with your pupils. In many cases it is simply a matter of looking under the 'View' menu and selecting 'toolbars'.

When preparing files for use on the computer, it is also worth considering whether the format is appropriate for your pupils. Clearly, selecting the right sorts of fonts (probably those that match the school's handwriting policy as closely as possible) is important, but it is also important to consider whether they are an appropriate size. Are they clearly legible? Does the presentation (style, colour etc.) help to clarify meaning or does it make it difficult to read? Can the page be set up to support specific needs? (For visually impaired pupils, increasing font size may work, but it might make little difference; children with conditions such as dysphasia may find that changing the background colour of the page from white to, say, blue, enhances their ability to read text and so on.) Is the presentation supporting independent work? (The idea of locking parts of a page down so that they can't be moved is discussed in the previous section but also consideration of instructions and prompts on screen might be helpful. If you have a talking word processor, these instructions could even be 'read' by the computer!)

Preparing a series of templates for pupils to use for written work might be appropriate. These templates could contain standard structures to help organise text and the idea of writing frames works extremely well on computers. However, simply setting a blank template with the font and size of text already selected so that the pupils simply get on with the task of producing the writing can be very useful, too.

It is also worth considering how the resources you create will be distributed. If you have access to a networked suite, it is likely that there will be a 'shared' storage area on a server. Storing files here gives access to anyone with appropriate network access rights. Storing files here could give every pupil access to the work you want them to use without the need to copy the files to each machine (see the task above before trying this!).

Case study

In a follow-up lesson to the one on characterisation described above, the teacher prepares a piece of text describing a character from a book the class shared recently. The character was fairly peripheral to the story so the class's ideas about the character are fairly limited. The shared text for the lesson is a passage from the book where the character is involved and the class discuss the clues as to the character's motivation and appearance. The prepared text is shared with the class and it is noted that the descriptive language does not help bring the character to life.

As an individual task, pupils are asked to consider how this description of the character could be improved and consider whether the new description is compatible with what they already know about him from the book. The teacher has planned three different tasks around the same idea. More able pupils get a printed version of the text and, in pairs, are identifying sections of the text that they think could be improved, making notes about their ideas and using thesauruses to find better descriptive words. For the pupils of average ability, the text is presented on computer screen and in pairs pupils are reworking the text, including using the online thesaurus built into the word processor (they have used this several times before). The least able pupils have a version of the text that uses 'drop-down forms'. Here, pupils click on a descriptive word or section and select a 'better' word or phrase from the list that appears.

In the plenary, the teacher shares a couple of examples of how the text has been adapted and can compare work from across the ability range without having to deal with huge discrepancies in the outward quality of the work.

Activity 3 **Using ICT for preparing resources**

The main point of this section is that ICT provides teachers with access to useful resources and the ability to adapt and share those resources easily.

Use ICT to develop an appropriate activity for use in teaching literacy for your next placement. Using this activity, create two further activities, one providing a greater challenge, the other additional support. These activities can be for use on or off screen, depending on your confidence and the access to ICT within the school.

Try out the activity with your class and keep a careful eye on how effective the differentiation of the activities was.

REFERENCES/SUGGESTIONS FOR FURTHER READING

Devon Curriculum Service (2000) *Making Connections: Using ICT in the Literacy Hour*, Exeter: Devon Curriculum Services

Higgins, S. and Moseley, D. (2002) 'Raising Achievement in Literacy through ICT' in Monteith, M. (ed.) *Teaching Primary Literacy with ICT*, Buckingham: Open University Press

11 Whole-class and Group-based Teaching and Learning in the National Literacy Strategy

FRANK HARDMAN

The aim of this chapter is to review recent research into whole-class and group-based teaching in the National Literacy Strategy (NLS) and to consider the pedagogical implications of the research for your professional development as a teacher.

WHOLE-CLASS TEACHING

In the NLS Framework, successful whole-class teaching is described as 'discursive, characterised by high-quality oral work' and 'interactive, encouraging, expecting and extending pupils' contributions' (DfEE, 1998, p. 8). Consequently, 'whole-class interactive teaching' has been adopted as a means to raise standards of literacy in state-maintained primary schools and there has been an emphasis on the use of direct, interactive teaching focusing on higher order questioning and discussion. Such an approach is seen as a move away from a traditional 'lecturing and drill' approach in which pupils remain passive by encouraging an 'active teaching' model promoting a two-way process.

In order to promote interactive whole-class teaching, training materials (DfEE, 1999a, b, c) were produced and distributed to schools suggesting that teachers could use a range of discourse strategies in addition to teacher questions to encourage more sustained pupil contributions. These included asking for clarification of a pupil answer, encouraging pupils to elaborate on their answers and giving them time to gather their thoughts before answering a teacher's question. However, recent research (Alexander, 2000; Mroz et al., 2000; English et al., 2002; Fisher, 2002; Hardman et al., 2003; Moyles et al., 2003; Smith et al., 2004) suggests that despite official endorsements of interactive whole-class teaching, teachers continue to use traditional forms of teacher-led recitation as reported in earlier studies of the primary English classroom (Galton et al., 1980, 1999; Mortimore et al., 1988; Pollard et al., 1994; Alexander et al., 1996). Since the introduction of the NLS, teachers are more directive in their teaching, thereby closing down opportunities for pupils to explore and elaborate on their ideas.

In its prototypical form, teacher-led recitation consists of three moves known as Initiation, Response and Feedback, or IRF. The *initiation* is usually in the form of a teacher question, the *response* is usually where a pupil attempts to answer a question, and the *follow-up* move is where the teacher provides some form of feedback (very often in the form of an evaluation) to the pupil's response. Far from encouraging and extending pupil contributions to promote higher levels of interaction and cognitive engagement, research suggests the majority of the time teachers' questions are closed and often require convergent factual answers and pupil display of (presumably) known information. This style of teacher questioning therefore seeks predictable correct answers and only rarely are teachers' questions used to assist pupils to more complete or elaborated ideas.

The figure below shows the typical *teacher-initiated* discourse profile for a literacy hour (Hardman et al., 2003; Smith et al., 2004). The data show the averages per hour, thus taking into account the length of each teacher's lesson.

Figure 11.1 Discourse profile for a typical literacy hour

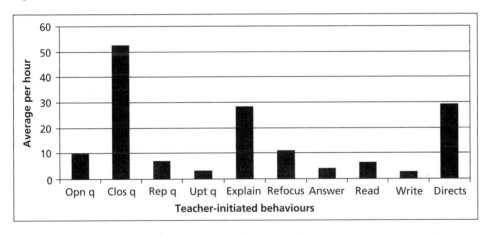

(Key: Opn q = open question, Clos q = closed question, Rep q = repeat question, Upt q = uptake question, Explain = teacher explanation, Refocus = teacher refocuses the class/pupil, Answer = teacher answers question, Read = teacher reads, Write = teacher writes, Directs = teacher directs class)

This graph shows that closed questions were the most frequent form of discourse behaviour (on average 52 closed questions were asked per literacy hour). The teachers in the national sample of 105 teachers directed the pupils 29 times and explained 28 times per literacy hour. It is clear that teacher-presentation and teacher-directed question and answer dominated most of the classroom discourse in all 105 lessons.

Less frequent teacher-initiated behaviours included *uptake* questions – where a teacher builds in a pupil answer into a subsequent question (three per literacy hour), writing – where the teacher would be writing on a board (three per literacy hour), and answering a pupil's questions (four per literacy hour).

When we look at the most common forms of discourse shown by the pupils in the table below, we see that when pupils spoke it was to answer a question (86 per cent of the time) using three words or less for 90 per cent of the time. Reading was the next most common activity (10 per cent). Pupils therefore rarely asked questions or offered information.

Table 11.1 Discourse profile for all pupils during whole-class teaching

Behaviour	Frequency	Percentage
Open question	17	0.3
Closed question	53	1.0
Explain	75	1.4
Answer	4468	85.7
Read	534	10.2
Write	65	1.2
Total	5212	100

The following extract, taken from a Year 5 class in an urban primary school, is typical of the discourse style used by teachers when interacting with pupils. The transcript has been coded using a framework adapted from Sinclair and Coulthard (1975) who first identified the IRF teaching exchange. Sinclair and Coulthard identify ten categories of teaching exchanges with specific functions and unique structures. The four main functions of exchanges are: informing, directing, eliciting and checking. The *teacher inform* exchange is used for passing on facts, opinions, ideas and new information to the pupils and usually there is no verbal response to the initiation. The *teacher direct* is designed to get the pupils to do but not say something, whereas the *teacher elicit* is designed to get a verbal contribution from the pupil. The elicit exchange which occurs inside the classroom has a different function from most occurring outside it because the teacher usually knows the answer to the question which is being asked. This accounts for the *feedback* move being an essential element in an eliciting exchange inside the classroom because the pupils, having given their answer, want to know if it was correct.

In the extract from the lesson, the teacher is exploring various grammatical features in a newspaper report (the *moves*, Initiation, Response, Feedback, make up the three-part teaching exchange which in turn are made up of *acts*: cl = clue; com = comment; e = evaluation; el = elicitation; i = inform; n = nominate; rep = reply; s = starter):

Exchanges			Moves	Acts
Teaching	T	looking at the text now I want you please to tell me what tense the first paragraph is in what tense the first paragraph is in	I	s
				el
2	P	the past tense	R	rep
3	T	yes it's in the past tense	F	e
4	T	how do you know it's in the past tense	I	el
5	P	because it says August 1990	R	rep
6	T	you know by the date it's in the past tense	F	e
7	T	but you know by something else you know you know by the doing words in the text that change what's a doing word what do we call a doing word David	I	s
				el
				n
8	P	a verb	R	rep
9	T	a verb good	F	e
10	T	will you give me one verb please out of this first paragraph find one verb in this paragraph Stephen	I	s
				el
				n
11	P	rescued	R	rep
12	T	rescued excellent excellent and that's in the past tense	F	e
				com
13	T	does the tense change when it comes to the next paragraph remember it's the verb that will tell you skim find the verbs that was the past that happened before this is now it's happening now does the verb change Julie	I	s
				cl
				i
				n/el
14	P	it's the present	R	rep
15	T	it's the present tense of the verb	F	e
16	T	can anybody find me one verb in there in the present tense skim down see if you can find a verb in the tense Lucy	I	s
				el
				n
17	P	catch	R	rep
18	T	catch right	F	e

This section illustrates clearly the teacher's pervasive use of the three-part exchange which is nearly always being played out as teacher–pupil–teacher and the elaborate nature of many of her sequences of questions which are chained together to form a lengthy transaction. The extract also illustrates how the teacher often uses *starter* acts

(Turns 1, 7, 10, 13, 16) as a matter of routine in opening moves. These are similar in function to what Edwards and Mercer (1987) call 'cued elicitations', where she provides advance warning that a question is imminent and provides some clues as to how to answer it. Most of the questions are 'closed' (i.e. calling for a single response or offering facts) rather than 'open' (i.e. defined in terms of the teacher's reaction to the answer: only if the teacher accepted more than one answer to the question would it be judged as open). We also see her 'reformulate' a question (Turn 7) in the sequence in an attempt to arrive at the answer she desires, by simplifying and building into its restatement some of the information needed for the acceptable answer and where the ingredients of an appropriate answer might lie. It shows the way in which teacher-directed talk of this kind creates the impression of knowledge and understanding being elicited from the pupils rather than being imposed by the teacher. The extract also reveals the rapid pace of the teacher's questioning and the lack of time for reflection on the topic. The pupils' responses, which are often brief and mainly recall of information, are evaluated and commented on by the teacher who has the right to determine what is relevant within her pedagogic agenda.

Like Skidmore et al. (2003), we also found teachers showed little variation in their discourse styles when working with groups of children during the twenty-minute guided reading and writing activities. Contrary to expectation, teachers exercised a more directing influence over the talk when working with a group of pupils. It was assumed that by working with a smaller number of pupils, teachers would relax their directing influence over the talk, thereby providing more opportunities for pupils to initiate ideas, ask questions and elaborate on their answers. However, teachers tended to use lower cognitive interactions, with fewer challenging questions and sustained interactions with pupils. We also found differences across key stages: Key Stage 1 teachers were more directive in their teaching than Key Stage 2 teachers and they asked twice the number of closed questions and had fewer sustained interactions suggesting a lower level of cognitive engagement with pupils. Teacher-presentation and teacher-directed question and answer therefore dominated most of the classroom discourse whether it was with the whole class or when the teacher was working with a group.

Such an emphasis on directive forms of teaching in the NLS goes against the widely accepted social constructivist theory of learning (Mercer, 1995) which suggests that classroom discourse is not effective unless pupils play an active part in their learning. According to this theory, our most important learning does not take place when we relate new information, new experiences, new ways of understanding to our existing understanding of the matter in hand. One of the most important ways of working on this understanding is through talk, particularly where pupils are given the opportunity to assume greater control over their own learning by initiating ideas and responses which consequently promote articulate thinking. If the pupil is allowed to contribute to the shaping of the verbal agenda in this way, the discourse is more effective in developing the pupil's own cognitive framework. However, the research findings suggest pupils are mainly expected to be passive and to recall, when asked, what they have learned and to report other people's thinking. It therefore questions the value of the linguistic and cognitive demands made on pupils within the traditional teacher-led whole-class and group-based format and suggests there may be benefits from pupils being given wider communicative options. This is supported by research into reciprocal forms of teaching which shows significant gains in learning were achieved when pupils were able to talk about their understanding in their own ways which acted as an important aid to increasing knowledge and improving understanding (Johnson and Johnson, 1990).

ALTERNATIVES TO TEACHER-LED RECITATION

Despite the dominance of teacher-led recitation, we did find some individual variation suggesting that the 'Initiation–Response–Feedback' (IRF) structure could take a variety of forms and functions leading to different levels of pupil participation and engagement, particularly through the use that is made of the follow-up move. Nassaji and Wells (2000) suggest that through feedback which goes beyond evaluation of the pupil's answer, the teacher can extend the answer to draw out its significance so as to create a greater equality of participation for the pupils. Similarly, Nystrand et al. (1997) advocate that teachers pay more attention to the way in which they evaluate pupil responses so that there is more 'high-level evaluation', whereby teachers incorporate pupil answers into subsequent questions. In this process, which they term *uptake*, they suggest that teacher questions should be shaped by what immediately precedes them so that they are genuine questions. This is in contrast to recitation where there is usually a prepared list of *test* questions with prespecified answers from a list of 'essential' information against which a pupil's knowledge can be checked. Another helping behaviour is 'probing' (Borich, 1996). Probing refers to teacher questions and statements that encourage pupils to elaborate upon an answer, either their own or another pupil's. Probing can elicit clarification of an answer, solicit additional information about a response, or redirect a pupil's response in a more fruitful direction.

Our review of the research suggests the following list of alternatives to teacher questions can lead to very different levels of pupil participation and engagement as they make different use of the *feedback* move. Through feedback which gets beyond evaluation of the pupil's answer, the teacher can extend the response to draw out its significance, or to make connections with other parts of the pupil's life experience so as to create a greater equality of participation. Instead of asking frequent questions teachers can give their own thought and ideas in the form of statements in which they speculate, surmise, interpret, illustrate, or simply listen and acknowledge what pupils have to say. These alternatives to teacher questions which include telling, suggesting, negotiating and listening are designed to free pupils to give their own views, to reveal their knowledge and areas of uncertainty, and to seek information and explanation through questions of their own. Once the pupils have helped to shape the verbal agenda, teacher questions are more likely to promote discussion in which there is an exploration of a topic, an interchange of ideas and questioning by pupils, with pupils and the teacher following up on each other's statements.

Alternatives to teacher questions include:

- *Statements of*:
  referral, i.e. state the relationship between what the pupil has just said and what a previous speaker has said, referring one speaker to another;
  thought, i.e. state the thought that occurs to you as a result of what the pupil has just said;
  reflection, i.e. state your understanding of what the pupil has just said;
  interest, i.e. state what it is you are interested in hearing further about.
- *Teacher speculation* (encourages pupils to speculate and explore ideas).
- *Personal contribution*: teachers making a personal contribution from their own experiences by telling the class something (encourages pupils to offer contributions of their own, discuss the teacher's contribution or to ask the teacher a question).
- *Incorporating pupils' answers into subsequent questions*: questions are shaped by pupil's contribution.
- *Deliberate silence*: maintain a deliberate, appreciative silence for three to five seconds until the original speaker resumes or another speaker enters in silence.
- *Signals*: signal your reception of what the pupil is saying, without yourself taking the floor, e.g. verbal encouragers, quiet exclamations, passing the turn by gesture or word.
- *Pupil questions*: invite pupils to ask questions about classmates' contributions.
- *Invite elaboration*: invite pupil to elaborate on what has just been said ('I'd like to know more of your views on that . . .').
- *Restate the spoken word* (signals importance of careful listening and encourages elaboration, e.g. 'Then I guess you think . . .').
- *Indirect question* (describes your state of mind, e.g. 'I was just thinking whether that made any difference?').

COLLABORATIVE SMALL-GROUP WORK

Because of the difficulties of managing the turn-taking of large numbers of pupils, many teachers and researchers (e.g. Edwards and Mercer, 1987; Norman, 1992; Edwards and Westgate, 1994, Barnes and Todd, 1995; Corden, 2000) have advocated the use of collaborative group work as a way of 'decentralising' classroom communication so as to encourage greater pupil participation. Collaborative group work has also drawn a lot of theoretical justification from the social constructivist view of learning discussed earlier because it allows more space for pupil initiatives or elaboration of ideas by regularly involving them in problem-solving activities and sustained discussions of their own ideas. Therefore learning and teaching are seen as collaborative and involving the social and cultural perceptions of all participants; and talk is central to this process as it is the primary medium of interaction which enables learners to make explicit what they know, understand and can do.

In discussing the features of group work where pupils are encouraged to explore meanings collaboratively, Edwards and Westgate (1994) and Barnes and Todd (1995) point out the clear differences in discourse structure between this and whole-class instruction. Because the absence of the teacher means there is no authoritative figure to dominate the discourse, there are no clearly marked asymmetrical relationships and the consequent lack of preallocated rights makes it necessary for the pupils to negotiate the terms of their interaction as they go along. Turn-taking is managed locally and interactionally in such group discussion and it sets up different expectations and patterns of working because speakers potentially have equal rights and joint ownership of the interaction. The patterns of interaction are therefore strikingly different from the kinds of discourse associated with the whole-class model of teaching discussed above. There are frequent overlaps and a lack of pauses as it is usually not clear until the moment of decision who will enter and who will control the up-coming turn. Each pupil's contribution is also closely contingent on the contributions of others and necessitates close listening to what has gone before. The absence of an authoritative figure in the conversation also means that there is no one to evaluate responses so pupils have to pool their responses to draw their own conclusions or refine their responses. It also allows for an interplay of alternative frames and relevance, and because power is distributed amongst the pupils they have a greater opportunity to initiate questions, to evaluate each other's responses, and to control the discourse for their own purposes. In this way, as Edwards and Mercer (1987) suggest, pupils can share in and practise forms of academic discourse of the classroom normally dominated by the teacher: that is, sharing, comparing, contrasting and arguing from different perspectives, providing opportunities for shared construction or negotiation of meaning. Therefore pupils are given more opportunities to develop linguistically and cognitively in the discourse structure of collaborative group work.

While research points to the effectiveness of group work, it concludes that genuine collaborative work is rarely found in the primary classroom. Two major weaknesses have been found: the fact that children are often seated in groups but working on individual tasks, and that teachers assume children have the skills and attitudes upon which successful collaborative work depends. Bennett and Dunne (1992) and Galton and Williamson (1992) found that the most problematic area for teachers was the planning of tasks which were both collaborative and productive of worthwhile learning. When discussing cognitive demands, both pairs of authors agree that collaborative tasks should be 'problem-solving' in a wide sense with tasks that could include, for example, responses to a poem or short story. They also suggested that careful attention be paid to appropriate groupings and they favoured flexible, mixed ability groupings.

In addition to the task and grouping, Galton and Williamson (1992) point to the importance of children's perceptions and attitudes towards collaborative group work being considered as part of the planning. They suggest that the crucial factors affecting success in group work are pupil self-concept and teacher behaviour. Because children are motivated to maintain self-esteem and minimise risk, they often see group work as a high-risk area: they are not sure why they are doing it, how they are meant to behave, what will count as success, how the teacher will react and who owns the process. The teacher's role, therefore, is to establish a climate in which risk-taking is valued by establishing and reinforcing group work skills, explaining the learning purpose of an activity, valuing and explaining the importance of the collaborative process, allowing groups to take responsibility and establish ownership, and modelling appropriate group behaviour.

Similarly, Bennett and Dunne (1992) argue that successful group work only occurs when pupils are made aware of the purpose of the task, and the skills and behaviours that are essential for its effective operation. They strongly advocate training in group work skills: for example, this might entail knowledge of how to listen, to question or challenge within a group discussion. They also emphasise the need for teachers to make their expectations explicit through clear 'ground rules' so that the pupils realise the importance teachers attach to such behaviours. By emphasising and encouraging such cooperative effort, and by providing feedback about the gains, Bennett and Dunne (1992) suggest children will perceive the value and benefits of talking and cooperative group work. An important aspect of their work was the need for monitoring and self-evaluation. This would need to be a regular part of group activities if children are to move beyond learned behaviours and develop the attitudes and skills necessary for effective group work.

In order to illustrate the importance of training children in group work skills, an extract has been taken from a case study of an inner city primary school (Hardman and Beverton, 1995). The teacher had been working with the Year 6 class for two terms to develop their collaborative group work skills and attitudes. Prior to her taking over the class, they had been perceived as a difficult class to handle in terms of their behaviour and willingness to work together. Therefore she had started off the year with a discussion of what makes for good group discussion and from this negotiated a list of 'ground rules' for group work which were permanently displayed in the classroom; these were constantly referred to when setting up and evaluating group work. When organising group work, the teacher would always explain the purpose of the work and talk through the benefits of group talk, emphasising the need for shared ideas and stressing the importance of helping each other and ensuring that everyone contributed by asking questions and listening carefully to each other. She would also remind groups of the importance of sitting in friendly formation to ensure eye contact and convey interest. In this way she got them to value the support of peers in their learning, to work effectively with each other and tackle tasks collaboratively, and to take collective responsibilty for the functioning of the group. She also favoured mixed ability and gender groups and operated regrouping strategies such as 'jigsawing', 'envoys' and 'snowballing' (see Johnson, 1991) which allow for an equitable allocation of roles and responsibilities.

Once discussion was underway, rather than fading into the background and allowing the groups to sustain themselves, the teacher would model a range of roles such as responding as a working group member which went beyond the familiar role of the teacher as expert and evaluator (see Corden, 2000). In this way she modelled different speaker and listener acts (e.g. turn-taking, supporting and building on the comments of others, showing respect for the other's views) for pupils to experience and incorporate into their own repertoires.

The group of pupils featured in the following extract, from a discussion that lasted twenty-five minutes, are discussing their perceptions of Cairo having watched a video which aimed to dispel myths about Egypt as a developing country. The group was selected to ensure a mix of abilities and gender and was made up of three boys and two girls. Using Sinclair and Coulthard's (1975) coding categories, the pupils' initiations are made up of pupil informs or statements:

Exchanges			*Moves*	*Acts*
1	Ben	I was totally shocked at how poor it was and how many homeless there were whereas in Newcastle there's only about twenty homeless.	I	i
2	Gary	yeah I was shocked I didn't know it was like that. I thought it was much nicer I thought that it would be nice for the poor but it was horrible.	I	i
3	John	I was surprised at all the people there The kids playing on the streets and that.	I	i
4	Rachel	I thought it would be all desert with palm trees and that but it wasn't.	I	i
5	Claire	I thought the same as Ben I was quite shocked really I thought that people would have had more homes than in Cairo if they did have homes they were not that nice.	I	i
6	Ben	the Dead City [. . .] the tombs of their ancestors . . . that's about the best the cleanest place for them to live in.	I	i
7	Gary	I thought it'd be really old-fashioned without TVs and videos and old-fashioned clothes [. . .].	I	i
8	John	they had cars and that.	I	i
9	Claire	I didn't think it'd be that big and the same as John I didn't think they'd have cars and that.	I	i
10	Rachel	I didn't think they'd have cars either	I	i
11	Ben	[. . .] I didn't think they'd have any computerised stuff or cars, buses . . .	I	i
12	Gary	some bits are similar to Newcastle it's got a lot of traffic [. . .] but in Cairo there's a bit more traffic.	I	i

The whole of the discussion featured in this extract is characterised by what Bennett and Dunne (1992) call 'abstract collaborative talk'. We see a high level of group interaction and cooperation with the pupils showing a knowledge of the 'rules' of turn-taking which they are doing in a sensitive and intelligent manner. Throughout the discussion the group are speculating, reasoning and responding to each other's ideas and supporting and building on the previous contributions to shape and refine the topic which they are making their own. For example Ben, who has been given the role of chair, readily introduces his reaction to the poverty of Cairo (Turn 1) which is picked up and developed in the next four turns, helping to dispel the holiday brochure image of 'deserts with palm trees' which Rachel raises (Turn 4). Similarly in Turn 6 Ben introduces a new perspective or viewpoint by contrasting the Dead City with Cairo. This is picked up and developed by Gary who was surprised to see modern technology in an ancient place, thereby moving the group on to consider how their antiquated views of Egypt has been dispelled by the television programme (Turns 7–11). Gary then goes on to introduce the comparison with Newcastle (Turn 12). All the way through the group are keen to play a positive role by showing interest and respect, and listening for and negotiating meaning, to arrive at a shared understanding of present-day Egypt. The success of the group work reflects the experience the pupils have of working in this way and their raised level of awareness as to the importance of group work in their learning.

The pattern of interaction is strikingly different from the kinds of discourse associated with whole-class teaching: as we have seen, the teacher controls the turn-taking, and the duration of the turns, by presenting closed questions to pupils and deciding who will answer and how, thereby providing little opportunity for pupil-initiated discussion.

In summary, research into collaborative group work suggests that:

- group work needs to be carefully planned, well structured and appropriate to the learning task;
- pupils need to develop and to understand the ground rules for small group learning;
- pupils need to be clear about what is expected of them in terms of both working practices and expected outcomes;
- appropriate and effective teacher intervention is essential;
- there is a potential repertoire of roles for the teacher to adopt;
- an important feature in the planning of group work which needs to be addressed is the pupils' perceptions and attitudes which they bring to such work. Making pupils explicitly aware of the features of collaborative talk and the part it will play in their learning will develop the skills and attitudes necessary for effective collaborative group work;
- collaborative tasks should be 'problem-solving' in a wide sense with tasks that could include, for example, responses to a poem or short story;
- careful attention should be paid to appropriate groupings;
- the teacher's role is to establish a climate in which risk-taking is valued by establishing and reinforcing group work skills, explaining the learning purpose of an activity, valuing and explaining the importance of the collaborative process, allowing groups to take responsibility and establish ownership, and modelling appropriate group behaviour;
- teachers should stress the need for cooperation and emphasise the value of sharing ideas;

- pupils need to be made aware of the purpose of the task, and the skills and behaviours that are essential for its effective operation. Teachers therefore need to make their expectations explicit through clear 'ground rules' so that the pupils realise the importance teachers attach to such behaviours. For example, this might entail knowledge of how to listen, to question or challenge within a group discussion;
- by emphasising and encouraging such cooperative effort, and by providing feedback about the gains, children will perceive the value and benefits of talking and cooperative group work. Monitoring and self-evaluation need to be a regular part of group activities if children are to move beyond learned behaviours and develop the awareness necessary for effective group work.

BECOMING A REFLECTIVE PRACTITIONER

Overall, the research reviewed above suggests 'top-down' curriculum initiatives like the NLS, while bringing about a scenario of change in curriculum planning, assessment and record keeping, often leave deeper levels of pedagogy untouched. In other words, they will not easily replace existing practices as there is a process of adaptation of top-down initiatives which leaves discourse styles and patterns of interaction largely untouched. Obviously, teaching involves a sense of timing, sequencing and pacing that cannot be conveyed by any list of behaviours. It is the thinking that connects these behaviours together that is important to the effective teacher, giving each its proper emphasis in the context of the classroom. It is the combination of curriculum, learning objectives, instructional materials and learners that provides the decision-making context for the reflective practitioner. It also points to the need for coaching and feedback to go hand-in-hand with teachers' professional development (Joyce, 1992; Joyce and Showers, 1995). Observation schedules to record teacher–pupil interactions can provide a useful tool for professional development as they allow for sympathetic discussion by groups of teachers of data derived from their own classrooms.

Our review of the research into whole-class and group-based teaching suggests the need for the exploration of alternative teaching and learning strategies in order to raise the quality of teachers' interactions with their pupils in whole-class and group-based teaching. If the IRF structure is to take a variety of forms and functions, leading to different levels of pupil participation and engagement, teachers will need to pay attention to their use of questions and introduce alternative conversational tactics to teacher-led recitation of the kind discussed above. If teachers are going to use alternative discourse strategies to teacher-led recitation, monitoring and self-evaluation will need to become a regular part of in-service training so as to give teachers a degree of ownership of the process of school improvement.

Tharp and Gallimore (1988: 191) suggest that because innovation and change always cost time, anxiety and uncertainty, it is essential that teachers have supportive interactions with peers through modelling and feedback if the 'recitation script' is to be changed to 'new repertoires of complex social behaviour necessary for responsive teaching'. Similarly, Dillon (1994) suggests that coaching and talk-analysis feedback may be useful tools for professional development whereby sympathetic discussion by groups of teachers of data derived from their own classrooms could be an effective starting point. In addition to recordings and transcriptions, systematic observation schedules could prove a very useful means of providing such quality feedback. Research by Moyles et al. (2003) also suggests that if teachers are to modify their practice in order to encourage reciprocal interactive teaching, they need the opportunity to identify and work through their own educational beliefs. Moyles and her colleagues found using video clips of lessons selected by the teacher to be a powerful means of promoting critical reflection on professional practice. They found that their video project, entitled video-stimulated reflective dialogue (VSRD), encouraged teachers to articulate and demonstrate their own understanding of their interactive styles and provided opportunities for monitoring and self-evaluation.

ACTIVITIES FOR OBSERVING CLASSROOM INTERACTIONS

It has been argued in this chapter that in order to change traditional patterns of whole-class and group-based interaction, thereby encouraging higher levels of pupil engagement and thinking, monitoring and self-evaluation need to become a regular part of staff development programmes. Coaching in alternative strategies, followed by lesson observation and feedback, can be a useful tool for professional development whereby data derived from your own classroom is used as a starting point for critical reflection.

The following activities are designed to provide classroom data. They can be used by you or a mentor, tutor or class teacher to provide feedback on a lesson observation:

1   Draw a simple map of the room with the pupils located by symbols, indicating whether they are male or female. During the whole period of the lesson record the number of interactions between the teacher and each pupil, on the map. Distinguish between teacher-initiated and pupil-initiated interactions. After the lesson redraw the map to tidy it and if possible add the names. If possible get some feedback from the class teacher or mentor on your results that might help you with your interpretation. How would you explain the pattern that the activity has shown?

2   Time lines can be used to record how long a particular activity lasted. One way of doing this economically is to draw a line across graph paper with each square representing a unit of time (e.g. a minute) to show the length of time spent on the aspect of the lesson being studied. An observer might, for example, be watching a literacy hour lesson, and wish to know whether the teacher was talking, or a pupil, or no one, in which case the time line might look like this:

Teacher talks _____ _____   _____
Pupil talks _.   __   _____
No one talks   ___

3   A category system, as shown below, can record all interactions that take place in a block of time in whole-class or group-based teaching, e.g. ten minutes. The following example focuses on teacher questions and feedback in the three-part, IRF structure discussed above. You may choose to focus on a more limited number of teacher behaviours and include pupil initiations in the form of questions and statements. Alternatively, you could choose a sub-group and concentrate on these. It could be a group of four, two boys and two girls, chosen from a range of abilities, hoping that these will be representative of the overall patterns observed in the class.

Category system

1	Teacher asks closed question	////////	8
2	Teacher asks open question	//	2
3	Boy answers	/////	5
4	Girl answers	///	3
5	Choral response	///	3
6	Teacher gives praise	////	4
7	Teacher affirms answer	////	4
8	Teacher uses criticism	//	2
9	Teacher probes answer	//	2

It will be important to define what you mean by each of the categories. The following example has been adapted from a system devised by Good and Brophy (1991) based upon the three-part IRF structure:

Behaviour	Definition
TEACHER QUESTIONS	
O = Open question	The question calls for more than one answer
C = Closed question	The question has just one correct response
RESPONDER	
Male	The pupil answering the question is male
Female	The pupil answering the question is female
Choral	The whole class, or group of pupils within class, respond together

TEACHER FEEDBACK REACTION	
Praise	Teacher praises pupil either in words ('fine', 'good', 'wonderful', 'good thinking') or by expressing verbal affirmation in a notably warm, joyous or excited manner
Affirms answer	Teacher simply affirms that the pupil's response is correct (nods, repeats answer, says 'Yes', 'OK', etc.)
Negates answer	Teacher simply indicates that the pupil's response is incorrect (shakes head, says 'No', 'That's not right', 'Hm-mm', etc.)
Criticises answer	Teacher criticises pupil, either in words ('You should know better than that', 'That doesn't make any sense – you'd better pay close attention' etc.) or by expressing verbal negation in a frustrated, angry or disgusted manner
Teacher makes no response	Teacher makes no response whatever to pupil's response – s/he goes on to something else
Teacher asks other pupil	Teacher redirects the question, asking a different pupil to answer it
Other calls out	Another pupil calls out the correct answer and the teacher acknowledges that it is correct
Teacher gives answer	Teacher provides the correct answer for the pupil
Teacher repeats question	Teacher repeats the original question, either in its entirety or with a prompt ('Well?', 'Do you know?', 'What's the answer?')
Probe	Teacher stays with the same pupil and asks further questions
Uptake	Teacher incorporates the pupil's answer into subsequent questions

4   A sign system can be used to break a lesson down into segments of time (e.g. two minutes) and records the main activity within that block of time as set out below:

Sign system
Activity

Teacher explanation	/				
Teacher asking questions		/	/		
Pupils working, teacher monitors					/
Pupils working, teacher not monitoring					
Pupils reading				/	
Pupils writing					
Pupil presenting to class					/

REFERENCES/SUGGESTIONS FOR FURTHER READING

Alexander, R. (2000) *Culture and Pedagogy: International Comparisons in Primary Education*, Oxford: Blackwell

Alexander, R., Willcocks, J. and Nelson, N. (1996) 'Discourse, pedagogy and the National Curriculum: Change and Continuity in Primary Schools', *Research Papers in Education*, 11, 1, pp. 81–120

Barnes, D. and Todd, F. (1995) *Communication and Learning Revisited: Making Meaning Through Talk*, Portsmouth, NH: Heinemann

Bennett, N. and Dunne, E. (1992) *Managing Classroom Groups*, Hemel Hempstead: Simon and Schuster

Borich, G. (1996) *Effective Teaching Methods*, 3rd edn, New York, NY: Macmillan

Corden, R. (2000) *Literacy and Learning through Talk: Strategies for the Primary Classroom*, Buckingham: Open University Press

DfEE (1998) *The National Literacy Strategy Framework for Teaching*, London: DfEE

DfEE (1999a) *The National Literacy Strategy Training Modules 1: Teaching and Learning Strategies*, London: DfEE

DfEE (1999b) *Talking in Class*, London: DfEE

DfEE (1999c) *Engaging All Pupils*, London: DfEE

Dillon, J. (1994) *Using Classroom Discussion*, Milton Keynes: Open University Press

Edwards, A.D. and Westgate, D. (1994) *Investigating Classroom Talk*, London: Falmer Press

Edwards, D. and Mercer, N. (1987) *Common Knowledge: The Development of Understanding in the Classroom*, London: Methuen

English, E., Hargreaves, L. and Hislam, J. (2002) 'Pedagogical Dilemmas in the National Literacy Strategy: Primary Teachers' Perceptions, Reflections and Classroom Behaviour', *Cambridge Journal of Education*, 32, 1, pp. 9–26

Fisher, R. (2002) *Inside the Literacy Hour*, London: Routledge

Galton, M. and Williamson, J. (1992) *Group Work in the Primary Classroom*, London: Routledge and Kegan Paul

Galton, M., Simon, B. and Croll, P. (1980) *Inside the Primary Classroom*, London: Routledge

Galton, M., Hargreaves, L., Comber, C., Wall, D. and Pell, A. (1999) *Inside the Primary Classroom: 20 Years On*, London: Routledge

Good, T. and Brophy, J. (1991) *Looking in Classrooms*, 5th edn, New York, NY: Harper and Row

Hardman, F. and Beverton, S. (1995) 'Developing Collaborative Group Work in the Primary School: The Importance of Metacognition, *Reading*, 29, 2, pp. 11–15

Hardman, F., Smith, F. and Wall, K. (2003) 'Interactive Whole Class Teaching' in the National Literacy Strategy, *Cambridge Journal of Education*, 33, 2, pp. 197–215

Johnson, J. (1991) 'Classroom Strategies', in *Teaching and Learning 5–16: An In-service Pack on Oracy for Teachers*, Milton Keynes: Open University Press

Johnson, D.W. and Johnson, R.T. (1990) 'Co-operative Learning and Achievement', in S. Sharan (ed.) *Co-operative Learning: Theory and Research*, New York, NY: Praeger

Joyce, B. (1992) 'Cooperative Learning and Staff Development: Teaching the Method with the Method', *Cooperative Learning*, 12, 2, pp. 10–13

Joyce, B. and Showers, B. (1995) *Student Achievement Through Staff Development: Fundamentals of School Renewal (2E)*, New York, NY: Longman

Mercer, N. (1995) *The Guided Construction of Knowledge: Talk among Teachers and Learners*, Clevedon: Multilingual Matters

Mortimore, P., Sammons, P., Stoll, L., Lewis, D. and Ecob, R. (1988) *School Matters*, Wells: Open Books

Moyles, J., Hargreaves, L., Merry, R., Paterson, F. and Esarte-Sarries, V. (2003) *Interactive Teaching in the Primary School: Digging Deeper into Meanings*, Berkshire: Open University Press

Mroz, M., Smith, F. and Hardman, F. (2000) 'The Discourse of the Literacy Hour', *Cambridge Journal of Education*, 30, 3, pp. 379–90

Nassaji, H. and Wells, G. (2000) 'What's the Use of "Triadic Dialogue"? An Investigation of Teacher-Student Interaction', *Applied Linguistics*, 21, 3, pp. 376–406

Norman, K. (1992) (ed.) *Thinking Voices: The Work of the National Oracy Project*, London: Hodder and Stoughton

Nystrand, M., Gamoran, A., Kachur, R. and Prendergast, C. (1997) *Opening Dialogue: Understanding the Dynamics of Language and Learning in the English Classroom*, New York, NY: Teacher College Press

Pollard, A., Broadfoot, P., Croll, P., Osborn, N. and Abbot, D. (1994) *Changing English Primary Schools?* London: Cassell

Sinclair, J. and Coulthard, M. (1975) *Towards an Analysis of Discourse: The English Used by Teachers and Pupils*, London: Oxford University Press

Skidmore, D., Perez-Parent, M. and Arnfield, S. (2003) 'Teacher–Pupil Dialogue in the Guided Reading Session, *Reading*, 37, 2, pp. 47–53

Smith, F., Hardman, F., and Wall, K. (2004) 'Interactive Class Teaching in the National Literacy and Numeracy Strategies', *British Education Research Journal*, 30, 3, pp. 403–19

Tharp, R.G. and Gallimore, R. (1988) *Rousing Minds to Life: Teaching, Learning, and Schooling in Social Context*, Cambridge: Cambridge University Press

12 Planning and Assessment

EVE ENGLISH

Planning and assessment are dealt with in this chapter as part of a cyclical process. Each informs the other and both are at the heart of effective teaching. (This is reflected in the requirements of the Professional Standards for the award of QTS: 3.1 and 3.2 (Teacher Training Agency, 2002).) The generic requirements of trainee teachers in terms of planning are as follows:

Those awarded Qualified Teacher Status must demonstrate all of the following:

3.1.1   They set challenging teaching and learning objectives which are relevant to all pupils in their classes. They base them on their knowledge of:

- the pupils;
- evidence of their past and current achievement;
- the expected standards for pupils of the relevant age range;
- the range and content of work relevant to pupils in that age range.

3.1.2   They use these teaching and learning objectives to plan lessons, and sequences of lessons, showing how they will assess pupils' learning. They take account of and support pupils' varying needs so that girls and boys, from all ethnic groups, can make good progress.

3.1.3   They select and prepare resources, and plan for their safe and effective organisation, taking account of pupils' interests and their language and cultural backgrounds, with the help of support staff where appropriate.

3.1.4   They take part in, and contribute to, teaching teams, as appropriate to the school. Where applicable, they plan for the deployment of additional adults who support pupils' learning.

3.1.5   As relevant to the age range they are trained to teach, they are able to plan opportunities for pupils to learn in out-of-school contexts, such as school visits, museums, theatres, fieldwork and employment-based settings, with the help of other staff where appropriate.

The standards for monitoring and assessment are as follows:

3.2.1 They make appropriate use of a range of monitoring and assessment strategies to evaluate pupils' progress towards planned learning objectives, and use this information to plan their own planning and teaching.

3.2.2 They monitor and assess as they teach, giving immediate and constructive feedback to support pupils as they learn. They involve pupils in reflecting on, evaluating and improving their own performance.

3.2.3 They are able to assess pupils' progress accurately using, as relevant, the Early Learning Goals, National Curriculum level descriptors, criteria from national qualifications, the requirements of Awarding Bodies, National Curriculum and Foundation Stage assessment frameworks or objectives from the national strategies. They may have guidance from an experienced teacher where appropriate.

3.2.4 They identify and support more able pupils, those who are working below age-related expectations, those who are failing to achieve their potential in learning, and those who experience behavioural, emotional and social difficulties. They may have guidance from an experienced teacher where appropriate.

3.2.5 With the help of an experienced teacher, they can identify the levels of attainment of pupils learning English as an additional language. They begin to analyse the language demands and learning activities in order to provide cognitive challenge as well as language support.

3.2.6 They record pupils' progress and achievements systematically to provide evidence of the range of their work, progress and attainment over time. They use this to help pupils review their own progress and to inform planning.

3.2.7 They are able to use records as a basis for reporting on pupils' attainment and progress orally and in writing, concisely, informatively and accurately for parents, carers, other professionals and pupils.

What a daunting task! But do not forget that you are not reinventing the wheel. Teachers have been planning and assessing in this detailed way now for a number of years and will be only too willing to help. Structures and systems will be set up in school and, while these differ from school to school, all must meet statutory requirements.

PLANNING

Long-term planning for English

Long-term planning for English is a whole-school process usually led by the English coordinator. It should:

- address statutory requirements in terms of the National Curriculum;
- reflect recommended curricula such as the National Literacy Strategy;
- ensure that the curriculum is broad and balanced;
- ensure continuity and progression;
- address issues of equal opportunity.

As a trainee teacher you should make yourself familiar with long-term planning so that you understand the full context and are not planning in isolation.

Medium-term planning for English

Once the long-term planning is in place teachers can then look at the next level of planning. Medium-term planning is usually the job of the class teacher or teachers if there is more than one class in a year group. This planning is more detailed than long-term planning and usually addresses the main learning objectives for a particular year group. It is usually organised on a termly or half-termly basis. Medium-term planning should:

- be informed by the long-term planning for English;
- address all the English work to be undertaken by a group of children in a class or year group over a period of time such as a term or half-term;
- identify the relevant parts of the Programmes of Study and Attainment Targets of the National Curriculum Order for English to be covered;
- identify formal assessment opportunities.

Please note that the National Literacy Strategy does not explicitly cover the Speaking and Listening (En. 1) requirements of the National Curriculum so if you are using the NLS objectives for medium-term planning then you must, in addition, plan for Speaking and Listening. The NLS Framework for Teaching includes objectives for each term. These correspond to, but are more detailed than, the NC for English En. 2 (Reading) and En. 3 (Writing). The Framework recommends that, for each half term, medium-term planning identifies continuous work and then 'blocked work', i.e. work to be carried out in specific weeks. You will find a NLS planner in the Framework. This, however, might be a good place to make you aware of the fact that, while this 'minimalist' medium-term planning might be acceptable for experienced teachers, your planning will need to be more detailed both for your sanity and for QTS requirements. Table 12.1 sets out a proforma for medium-term planning that you might find useful.

Short-term planning for English

Activity 1 Choose a learning objective from the NLS Framework as a basis for a lesson. Without describing the detail make a list of the headings that you think should be on a planning sheet to enable you to teach that lesson effectively.

Table 12.1 Medium-term planning for literacy

Week	Phonics, spelling and vocabulary	Grammar and punctuation	Comprehension and composition	Texts	Resources	Assessment opportunities
	Continuous work	Continuous work	Continuous work			
	Learning objectives and brief details of activities	Learning objectives and brief details of activities	Learning objectives and brief details of activities			
Week 1						
Week 2						
Week 3						
Week 4						
Week 5						
Week 6						
Week 7						
Week 8						

Look at the list below and see how your list compares.

Short-term planning for English should:

- evolve directly from the medium-term planning for English;
- address all the English work to be undertaken by the children in a class or year group over a short-term period like a day or a week;
- use the results of prior assessment to address the needs of the individual children in the class;
- describe the English activities to be undertaken, including:

  1 prior assessment outcomes that will inform planning;
  2 timing (date, time, approximate length of the lesson/activity);
  3 pacing (approximate length of each part of the lesson/activity);
  4 class organisation (whole-class, group or individual work);
  5 teacher focus (teaching whole-class, group or individual work);
  6 resources needed (what, when, where);
  7 how the work addresses the NC Programmes of Study;
  8 main learning objectives;
  9 organisation for differentiation;
  10 main assessment targets.

- allow for evaluation and reflection to inform future planning;
- ensure that over the long term the balance of the activities matches those identified in the long-term planning for English.

Once again, the NLS Framework provides an example of a short-term (in this case, weekly) planning sheet. Here, the learning objectives that you identified in your medium-term planning need to be expanded upon and you also have to organise the teaching of those objectives into shared, guided, independent and plenary work. Your school will probably require you to complete a weekly planning sheet but, once again, to support your teaching you will need to plan in much more detail. Table 12.2 sets out a proforma for a weekly planning sheet that is more detailed than that provided by the NLS while Table 12.3 is a lesson plan for reading and writing that can be used in the planning of shared whole-class or guided group work. Ideally the use of both these planning sheets will help you identify the key elements for your teaching. (Planning for speaking and listening will be addressed at the end of this section.)

Planning for speaking and listening

Because the NLS does not explicitly describe opportunities for teaching the objectives of the NC programme of study for Speaking and Listening (En. 1) you will need to plan separately for this. This does not mean that a lot of speaking and listening does not go on in the literacy hour but you must plan those opportunities.

Table 12.2 Short-term weekly planning sheet for reading and writing

Week beginning: . . . . **Year group:** . . . . **Class:** . . . .

	Whole-class shared reading and writing	Whole-class phonics, spelling, vocabulary and grammar		Group	Tasks		Plenary
Monday	Text . . . . L.O.	L.O. A.	L.O. A	L.O. A	L.O. A	L.O. A	L.O. A	
Tuesday	Text . . . . L.O.	L.O. A.	L.O. A	L.O. A	L.O. A	L.O. A	L.O. A	
Wednesday	Text . . . . L.O.	L.O. A.	L.O. A	L.O. A	L.O. A	L.O. A	L.O. A	
Thursday	Text . . . . L.O.	L.O. A.	L.O. A	L.O. A	L.O. A	L.O. A	L.O. A	
Friday	Text . . . . L.O.	L.O. A.	L.O. A	L.O. A	L.O. A	L.O. A	L.O. A	

Table 12. 2 (continued)

Resources:	Additional Activities:	Implications for ICT:

Table 12.3 Short-term planning sheet for shared whole-class or guided group work

Date:	Time:	Class:
Shared Text, Word or Sentence Level Work or Guided Work		
Learning Objective:		
Implications from prior assessment:		
Activity		

Introduction: (mins) Key Questions: Development: (mins) Conclusion:	Teacher's Role:

Activity 2 Consider the criteria above for effective short-term planning and devise a short-term (daily) planning sheet that will help you plan for the teaching of speaking and listening. Remember that these skills can be taught outside English lessons so you will need to identify the subject lesson that is being taught. Is just one example of a proforma that could be useful in your planning. How does it compare with yours?

Table 12.4 Daily lesson plan for speaking and listening

Date:	Time:	Class:

Learning Objective:

Subject Area:

Activity:

Implications from prior assessment:

Introduction: (mins)	Teacher's Role:
Key Questions:	
Development: (mins)	
Conclusion:	

Assessment Opportunities:

ASSESSMENT

Assessment has to be an integral part of the teaching process. By considering planning and assessment together in this chapter you will, hopefully, realise that the two should not be separated. Medium- and short-term planning requirements should be informed by assessment as we saw above. There is no doubt, however, that assessment has become a very emotive issue. Teachers would have very little problem with assessment if its only purpose was to ensure that they knew exactly what their pupils had learned so that they could build upon this. Unfortunately, there is now such an emphasis on external assessment leading to league tables of schools' performances in tests that the aim of improving learning seems to have been sidelined. External assessment (through Standard Assessment Tasks (SATs)) has led to union action, accusations of cheating and, even, the imprisonment of one headteacher. Having thoroughly panicked you I now want to convince you of the value of assessment.

Different types of assessment

Activity 3	As a class teacher, what would you like to know about your class's understanding of a lesson you have taught? How could you get this information?

Your response to the first question will probably have been a simple statement that you need to know whether the pupils have understood what you have taught, that the planned learning objective has been achieved. This is *formative* assessment and there are a number of ways in which you can elicit this information. Compare your list with that compiled by a group of PGCE students:

- individual discussion with the teacher;
- answers to questions in class (open and closed comprehension questions);
- discussion with parents;
- interview about a pupil's reading habits;
- drawings and diagrams;
- group discussions;
- pupil presentations;
- homework;
- drafts of writing;
- notes;
- reading aloud to teacher;
- reading aloud in class;
- finished writing products;
- miscue analysis;
- diagnostic tests;
- brainstorming;
- class discussion;

- video of oral work;
- drama presentations;
- responses to other pupils' writing;
- pupils' own comments on their work.

(Fleming, 2001)

However you decide to get the information you need it is important that you have this knowledge before you plan your next lesson. You will have seen in the planning section above that short-term planning includes some reference to earlier assessment. If, for example, on Monday you planned and taught a lesson on the function of adjectives and found, through questioning, that the pupils did not understand then there would be little point in progressing, on Tuesday, with 'experimenting with the impact of different adjectives through shared writing' (DfEE, 1998, NLS, Framework for Teaching, 1998, Year 3 Term 2, Sentence Level Planning).

Table 12.5 (Formative assessment) is a proforma that you might find useful in the planning of your assessment opportunities.

Marking written work

You will now realise that there are at your disposal many alternatives to the marking of written work as a means of assessing children's understanding. However, there will still be occasions when marking is the most appropriate form of assessment. Many schools have marking policies and you will need to make sure that you are aware of the requirements. Traditionally, work has been marked with minimal comment such as 'good' or 'well done' with, perhaps, spelling mistakes underlined. Written work is now usually marked, however, in a more focused way. This may relate to a pupil's own writing development and his/her own individual target or may be focused on the learning objective covered. Pupils tend to have more ownership of their targets now and should be clear about what they are aiming for. A Year 1 pupil might have, as one target, 'adding question marks to questions' and the teacher would mark work with this in mind. The activity below asks you to consider a piece of writing in terms of marking.

| Activity 4 | Mark the following piece of writing, focusing on the learning objective for the work which is 'to experiment with the impact of different adjectives'. |

The writing followed shared reading and writing work on 'strengthening adjectives'.

It was a very hot day and I went for a walk. I went to the park and it looked nice. The swings looked good and there was no one about so I decided to go on them. Then a nice girl came along with a very nice dog and we threw a ball for it to catch. Then it started to rain so we ran for shelter. We found an old hut and went inside. It was an awful hut and we were frightened so we thought we'd be better off in the rain.

The first comment that you make should be positive, for example, 'What a good idea to get out of that hut.' Then you can go on to comment on the use of adjectives. 'Can you think carefully about what the park looked like? What about the dog?

Table 12.5 Formative assessment

Name: . . . .   **Subject:** . . . .   **Term:** . . . .

Date	Learning objective	Assessment strategy	Source of evidence	Attainment	Comments/Follow-up

Describe that dog exactly. Why was the hut awful? Can you think of any other adjectives that might describe exactly how awful it was? Think about what we discussed in lesson.' Obviously, the marking process would be much more meaningful if you could talk through the work and the comments with the pupil. This is not always possible but the issues could inform your future planning.

Activity 5   As a class teacher, what information would you need about your pupils at the beginning of a school year from their previous class teacher? How would this information have been gathered?

The information you require will be based on *summative* assessment and will often ascribe an attainment level to a pupil's work. This level may be the result of teacher assessment or SATs. Summative assessments are carried out at the end of a period of teaching. This may be the end of a term or year but can also be at the end of a particular topic. It can be used to pass on to the next class teacher as described in the activity above or by a class teacher to sum up a pupil's progress at the end of a term, often drawing together information gained from formative assessment. Summative assessment will form the basis of the information provided for parents at open evenings or in end of term reports.

Activity 6   If a child is having difficulty with an aspect of English what would you, as a class teacher, like to know about the child's strengths and weaknesses in that particular area and how would you go about getting this information?

This question brings you in to the area of *diagnostic* assessment. This assessment is detailed and can help identify problems that a pupil may be experiencing. Formal diagnostic assessment tests can be used, or more informal assessments such as reading running records or miscue analyses. Running records are now very familiar to Year 2 teachers who use them as part of Key Stage 1 SATs. They are also, however, a very useful tool in determining which strategies a pupil is, or is not, using, in his or her reading. The teacher makes notes while a pupil reads a passage of text, recording the pupil's miscues (errors) with a note of the strategy that he or she seems to have used (often no more than a P if the child uses a phonic strategy, an S if the child has been aware of syntax or a C if the child has made use of context). At a very simple level a child might read the following sentence: 'The brown and white cow was asleep in the barn' as: 'The brown and white cow was asleep in the shed.'

Clearly, the word 'shed' is a miscue but consider carefully the information this miscue gives you. The child has an awareness of context and meaning because the substituted word makes sense. He or she also has a knowledge (probably implicit) of syntax because the substituted word belongs to the correct word class (it is a noun). However, because the word 'shed' does not even begin with the same sound as 'barn' it would appear on this occasion that phonic strategies are not being used. If many of the child's miscues are of this nature then he or she will need to be assisted in learning how to apply phonic strategies.

Activity 7	Consider the following sentence:

'The brown and white cow was asleep in the barn.'

A pupil reads the sentence as:

'The brown and white cow was asleep in the blue.'

What does the miscue tell you about the strategies this child is using when reading?

Here, the child is using some phonic knowledge in that 'blue' begins with the same letter/sound as 'barn'. However, there is no sense of bringing meaning to the text in that the miscue does not make sense, or of using knowledge of syntax as an adjective has been used instead of a noun.

A miscue analysis is very similar to a running record but can be much more detailed and can require the tape-recording of the child reading a text so that it can be analysed later.

Recording pupils' work

Schools will have policies on the recording of pupils' work and you need to be aware of these. Formative and summative assessment tasks and the results of those tasks will be kept in individual folders for each pupil. These should be relevant and kept up to date. A typical portfolio for English would include:

- notes from reading conferences;
- some interesting or informative pieces of work;
- some significant formative assessment;
- results of summative assessment of reading, writing, speaking and listening (sometimes recorded as an attainment target level);
- examples of summative assessment;
- results of SATs and optional SATs.

One interesting idea that I have come across in a primary school is the inclusion in the pupils' record folders of pieces of writing from the end of each primary year, from Reception to Year 6, all on the same subject ('About Myself' would be a useful topic). The pupils' writing development is clearly shown from the first pictures and simple sentences to the well-constructed pieces of writing produced in Year 6.

Like planning, assessment is a vital part of the education process, each informing the other. Assessment should be relevant, giving you the information you need in terms of a pupil's individual progress but also giving you information about your own teaching and the experiences you have provided for the children. Newton (2000) described a cartoon that appeared in the *Times Educational Supplement* that showed a boy giving his school report to his teacher with the words 'I think you'll find my test results are a good indication of your abilities as a teacher!' The assessment process is one that many trainee teachers find the most difficult part of their work. I hope this chapter has shown you how invaluable a tool it is.

REFERENCES/SUGGESTIONS FOR FURTHER READING

Davis, A. (1998) *The Limits of Educational Assessment*, Oxford: Blackwell

DfEE (1998) *The National Literacy Strategy Framework for Teaching*, London: DfEE

Drifte, C. (2001) *Foundations for the Literacy Hour, A Framework for Planning Literacy in the Reception Year*, Leamington Spa: Step Forward

Fleming, M. (2001) 'Assessment', in J. Williamson, M. Fleming, F. Hardman and D. Stevens (eds) (2001) *Meeting the Standards in Secondary English*, London: Routledge Falmer

Kerry, T. (1999) *Effective Learning Objectives, Task-Setting and Differentiation*, London: Hodder and Stoughton

Newton, L.D. (2000) *Meeting the Standards in Primary Science*, London: Routledge Falmer

TTA (2002) *Qualifying to Teach: Professional Standards for Qualified Teacher Status and Requirements for Initial Teacher Training*, London: Teacher Training Agency

13 The Implications of Transition and Transfer between the Key Stages for Teachers of Primary English

FRANK HARDMAN

The purpose of this chapter is to review the research into the impact of transition and transference across Key Stages 1–3 and to consider the pedagogic implications for the teaching of English in the primary school. Suggestions for practical action on transfer and transition will also be explored.

Research and evidence from Office for Standards in Education (Ofsted) inspections suggests that at certain points in pupils' school careers there can be a decline in progress and in commitment to learning (QCA, 1997, Ofsted, 1998; Galton et al., 1999). These can include transitions within a school, from one year to another, and transfers between schools. After such transitions and transfers, a 'dip' in progress can occur as routine replaces the novelty of a new teacher or school or if pupils become bored with work that they see as unchallenging and repetitive. The dip has been particularly noted during Years 3 and 8 in comparison with the years preceding and following them. A report for the Qualification and Curriculum Authority (QCA) suggested that in Year 4, which is a mid–point in pupils' progress from KS1 to KS2 at which to assess progress, a significant minority of pupils (up to a third) were failing to make as much as a level's progress over the course of the two years (Minnis et al., 1998). On transferring from primary to secondary school it has been found that up to two out of every five pupils fail to make the progress expected during the year immediately following the change of school.

In explaining the causes, the research suggests some pupils feel they are going over work already covered or fail to make the connection between working hard and later achievement or feel they should be viewed as having more maturity as they move up through the school. Others develop negative images of themselves as learners and seek refuge in friendships with the result that powerful anti-work peer groups can develop. Some groups appear to be at greater risk than others: at Key Stage 1, for example, special educational needs pupils, those from certain ethnic groups and boys in inner city areas are of particular concern. At Key Stage 2 there is a group of students, mainly able boys, whose attitudes decline after transfer to secondary school.

Over the last twenty years a great deal of attention has been paid to ensuring that the move from one school to another works smoothly administratively and that pupils' social and personal concerns are dealt with so that transfer is a less stressful experience for pupils. Research (Galton et al., 1999) and inspection (Ofsted, 1999) suggests that schools have been generally successful in meeting these objectives but that discontinuities often exist in teaching approaches across subjects. This results in pupils often being unclear what is expected of them when attempting to achieve new learning outcomes and what guidance is available when they encounter difficulties. Much remains to be done therefore to overcome the more intractable problems to do with curriculum continuity and teaching and learning.

With regard to transfer, Galton et al. (1999) found that the great majority of secondary schools focused their efforts upon managerial, personal and social approaches in ensuring transfer proceeds smoothly. However, less than a quarter of schools engaged in curriculum initiatives and less than five schools in one hundred reported any activity to do with developing closer cooperation in matters of teaching and learning or helping pupils to manage their own learning.

In the case of English, research found that although the National Curriculum had supported continuity across the primary/secondary phases there were differences in emphasis, particularly in writing and speaking and listening, in the different phases. For example, Marshall and Brindley (1998: 125) found that the differences arise because 'secondary teachers put response to literature as their main concern; and writing and talk often arose from reading' while 'their primary colleagues focused more on literary skills'. Therefore in Year 6 the emphasis was more on comprehension than response and Hargreaves and Galton (1999) also found that poor readers found it very difficult to cope with the secondary approach in what were usually mixed ability classes and began to lose interest. While the NLS and Key Stage 3 English Strategy can be expected to reduce differences in approaches to teaching and learning in English, there will remain a need for teachers from each phase to continue attempts to resolve some of the discontinuities in pupils' experiences.

Only recently has the spotlight fallen on problems at Year 3 and, to a lesser extent, Year 4 with a reported dip in motivation and performance (Doddington et al., 1999). In some schools Year 3 is more like a school-to-school transfer than a within-school transfer: pupils move from a separate site infant school to a junior school. Even within a primary school the break between Years 2 and 3 may be made so explicit that pupils find themselves moving from one distinct phase to another with a separate group or teachers and ways of working. This may result in different approaches to literacy so that pupils lose ground as they adjust to the new ways of working.

WHAT CAN BE DONE TO EASE TRANSITIONS AND TRANSFERS?

A report entitled *Building Bridges* by the QCA (1997) drew together examples of good practice in order to suggest a variety of ways in which schools might develop their approaches.

Approaches involving both primary and secondary schools and focusing on Year 6 and 7 pupils included:

- secondary school pupils visiting primary schools and giving talks to Year 6 pupils;
- Year 6 pupils having taster sessions of 'new subjects' or 'new teaching/ learning styles', particularly those they were anxious about (e.g. modern languages);
- summer schools in particular subjects for the whole year group or for pupils finding learning in a particular subject a struggle (e.g. writing, reading, spelling);
- newsletter for Year 6 pupils written by pupils in Year 7 and personal accounts put on the web by new Year 7 pupils for the next Year 6 pupils to read;
- extended induction sessions of one to five days' duration spent by year 6 pupils in the secondary school.

Approaches focusing on teachers of Year 6 and Year 7 included:

- meetings to look at the 5–16 curriculum experience of their pupils, to consider the achievements of Year 6 pupils, to work on assessment levels and to observe each other teach;
- visits by Year 6 teachers to their former pupils in Year 7;
- computer systems between schools allowing for a common system for recording progress;
- secondary Special Educational Needs (SEN) teachers talk with primary heads about pupils who are very able or who find learning difficult.

Approaches in secondary schools that concentrate on Year 7 pupils included:

- study days where Year 7 pupils discuss different forms of learning, their strengths and weaknesses as learners, and their preferred learning styles;
- tracking of the most able pupils (top 10 per cent) in some subjects for the first half term or longer to ensure that they are being stretched;
- early Year 7 parents' evenings after the start of the new school year;
- in-depth, once a week counselling sessions for Year 7 parents to lessen their anxieties and those of their children.

As a trainee teacher, you could become involved in similar initiatives to those listed above if any of them are available in your placement schools.

REFERENCES/SUGGESTIONS FOR FURTHER READING

Doddington, C., Flutter, J. and Ruddock, J. (1999) 'Exploring and Explaining "Dips" in Motivation and Performance in Primary and Secondary Schools', *Research in Education*, 32, 2, pp. 110–29

Galton, M., Gray, J. and Rudduck, J. (1999) *The Impact of School Transitions and Transfers on Pupil Progress and Attainment*, London: DfEE

Hargreaves, L. and Galton, M. (1999) (eds) *Moving from the Primary Classroom: 20 Years On*, London: Routledge

Marshall, B. and Brindley, S. (1998) 'Cross-phase or Just Lack of Communication: Models of English at Key Stages 2 and 3 and their Possible Effects on Pupil Transfer', *Changing English*, 5, 2, pp. 123–33

Minnis, M., Seymour, K. and Schagen, L. (1998) *National Test Results of Years 3, 4 and 5: Optional Tests*, Slough: NFER

Ofsted (1998) *Standards and Quality in Schools 1996/97 (Annual Report of the Chief Inspector of Schools)*, London: HMSO

Ofsted (1999) *Standards and Quality in Schools 1997/98 (Annual Report of the Chief Inspector of Schools)*, London: HMSO

QCA (1997) *Building Bridges*, London: Qualifications and Curriculum Authority

14 Into Your Future

EVE ENGLISH

You will begin to apply for teaching posts around the January or February of your final year. This means that you have to think about your future before you have finished the training programme. It is very easy during the last months of an ITT course to put off thinking about jobs because you have so many other things you have to do: assignments and school placements to name just two. This is obviously not sensible; you need to remember exactly why you have worked so hard and focus on getting the right job. In the first part of this chapter, we will consider what you should think about and expect when you apply for your first teaching post.

APPLYING FOR TEACHING POSTS

Good classroom practitioners who have performed well during their training programme, both professionally and academically, are not necessarily good at 'selling themselves'. Yet that is what the interview game is all about. There are a few basic rules that can help you.

First, in the Autumn begin to think about where you want to teach: do you want to stay where you are training, go back to your home area or go somewhere completely new? Begin scanning various newspapers and publications (like the *Times Educational Supplement* or the National Union of Teachers' *The Teacher*) to get a feel for the way posts are advertised. Because schools now control their own budgets under the Local Management of Schools (LMS) arrangements, appointments are now made directly by the school, although some Local Education Authorities still offer initial screening interviews and you could become part of the LEA pool and schools in the LEA will have access to the recommendations. This, however, will not guarantee you a job.

Activity 1   **Applying for jobs**

Look in a recent issue of an education newspaper like the *Times Educational Supplement* for the posts available in the key stage for which you are training.

Choose one of the posts that attracts you. Draft a letter of application and a *curriculum vitae* (CV) as if you intended to apply for the post.

Show your application to your tutor or mentor for comment and advice on how to improve it.

Once you have spotted the post or the LEA pool you wish to apply for, you should write to the address provided (either the school or the LEA office) for the details and an application form. Take care, even with this preliminary letter, to make a good impression. What exactly is asked of you varies, but usually you are asked to include three things in an application: a *letter of application*, a *curriculum vitae* and names of people who will provide *references*.

A letter of application

Some schools or LEAs will ask you to include a short letter of application. Even if not asked to do so, it is always wise to include one. This should be a short, personal statement about your interest in the post/LEA, your suitability for it (identify two or three strengths that you would bring to the situation) and your potential (again, two or three points). Normally, a letter of application should not run over one, or at the most two, sides. In a way, it is pulling out the key points you want to emphasise from the formal application form or curriculum vitae. Try to put something of yourself in it by showing how much you enjoy teaching. Make sure that your letter makes some reference to the school, rather than producing a 'one size fits all' type of letter.

Sometimes you are asked explicitly to write your letter of application in your own handwriting. It is important to comply with this, as it will be used in the decision-making procedure.

A curriculum vitae (CV) or a completed application form

This usually includes brief biographical details to provide a personal and academic context, qualifications and experience before and during your training programmes and your different and varied experiences teaching in schools. With respect to the latter, remember that if you decide to identify the schools where you have had placements, the headteachers of those schools may be contacted. It is polite to check with them first that they do not mind you identifying the school.

Application forms commonly have an open section that asks you for a personal statement. You can also include such a personal statement with your CV. Link your personal statement to what you know about the school. Write confidently about your experience and expertise, your strengths and developing interests in terms of primary teaching and learning. Finally, indicate how you would fit in with the philosophy of the school and help to meet the needs of the children. This might include reference to a *portfolio* that you would take to the interview, if invited to attend (see below).

Names of at least two, possibly three, people who will provide references

Never give people's names without first contacting them for permission. One referee should be someone from your training course. This person can comment on your academic and professional profile. A second person should be able to comment on you as a person. This may be a tutor, but could also be someone who has known you in other contexts, for example someone associated with voluntary work you have undertaken. Finally, whoever you use, give them some information about the post you are applying for and some brief points about any specific things you would like them to refer to in their reference. This helps them tailor the reference to suit the post.

You should have been sent some general information about the school with the details of the post and the application form. Do your homework. At the very least, look up the school's most recent Ofsted report on the internet. This will give you a feel for the 'official' face of the school. If the school is local, try to visit it one evening or weekend, to get a feel for the area and the environment. If you like what you see then go ahead and apply for the post. If you are invited to go on a visit prior to an interview, try to do so. It not only gives you a chance to look around the school and meet staff and children but also to ask some informal questions. It enables you to go into the interview feeling confident that you like what you see and would like to teach there. It also shows the headteacher that you are taking the application seriously. On very rare occasions, the reverse can happen. You find this is not the right school for you. You can save everyone time and effort by withdrawing before the interview. This really is better than going through an interview and possibly being offered the post, just to turn it down. That creates ill-feeling and if you are applying for other posts in the same area you can put yourself at a disadvantage if it becomes known.

Completing forms and writing letters is a time-consuming, tedious task. Do not underestimate how long it will take. Start early and give yourself plenty of time to do the job well, to gather information, contact referees and prepare the materials you must send. The professional way you do this will show. When shortlisting is being carried out, the quality of the application itself can make the difference between you and someone else with similar experiences and qualifications being called for interview. Information technology has made the task of writing personal statements and letters of application and CVs easier. It is possible to change them and adapt them to school-specific contexts relatively easily, so take advantage of that.

Another advantage you can give yourself is to prepare a *personal portfolio*. Refer to this in your letter of application and/or personal statement and take it along for interview.

Activity 2   **Creating a portfolio**

In order to 'sell yourself' well, you need to be thoroughly prepared for your interview. This includes preparing a personal portfolio to show to the interview panel so they can gain a feel for you in the school and classroom context. It is also a chance to show off your ICT skills.

Use a file with plastic wallets and collect positive, high-quality evidence to show at interview. This could include:

- an attractive front page with brief biographical information, perhaps even a photograph of yourself;
- a brief CV;
- a synopsis of your experiences in schools and with children;
- some examples of your planning which you feel shows your thoroughness, imagination and professionalism;
- examples of workcards or worksheets you created (particularly some showing evidence of differentiation);
- photocopies of good observation reports by your tutors or mentors;
- photocopies of good report forms from previous school placements;
- photographs of displays you created in schools;
- photocopies of children's work, showing the quality you maintained and how you marked it;
- examples of some good lesson evaluations.

There are more things you could include. It is up to you to choose what will show you at your best. Remember to label your samples.

Good personal portfolios take time to prepare. They are not something that can be left to the weekend before the interview. This is something you can begin at the start of your course to show progression in your skills, knowledge and understanding as a teacher as well as your best qualities. Most importantly, make sure you bring it to the attention of the interviewing panel. Offer it to the chairperson when you go in to the interview and suggest you leave it with them and collect it later.

ATTENDING FOR INTERVIEW

Far more people tend to apply for posts than can possibly be interviewed and so a shortlisting panel is set up. In school, this is usually the headteacher and the chair of the governing body and perhaps a local primary adviser. For the LEA pool interview it may be a primary adviser with one or two headteachers. The task is to select from those who are thought suitable a manageable number for interviewing.

If you are called for an interview and you are on school placement, arrange with your class teacher what she or he will do while you are away. Try to plan, prepare and mark so that you are up to date. Allow the night before the interview to concentrate on preparing yourself. This does not mean just reading through what you said in your application and rehearsing your answers to possible questions. You need to plan your route to the school and the times of local transport. Think about your physical appearance, decide what to wear and make sure everything is ready. Remember that outlandish fashion can reflect your personality but could also count against you in a professional context. Try to relax and have a reasonable night's sleep and a decent breakfast. Give yourself plenty of time so that you do not have to rush.

Activity 3   Interviews

At interview you are likely to be asked questions which will help the interview panel make comparisons between you and other candidates. Remember, they want the right person for the post.

In the context of English, how might you answer the following questions? They are in no particular order but are typical of the kinds of questions asked at interviews.

1   How do you feel English contributes to the all-round education of primary school pupils?
2   What methods of organising and managing children and classrooms have you experienced?
3   Use specific examples from your school placements to give us a feel for how you would plan for, teach and assess English.
4   Do you think too much time is given to the teaching of English in primary schools to the detriment of other subjects? Give reasons for your answer.
5   How will you manage the teaching of English with a class of 35 pupils, all with very different needs and abilities?
6   How would you assess children's learning in English?
7   How could you link skills taught in English to other areas of the curriculum?
8   What do you feel is the most serious problem facing you when teaching primary English?
9   Do you feel the National Literacy Strategy covers all areas of primary English? Elaborate on this.
10   What are your main strengths and weaknesses as a teacher of primary English? How will you address the latter?

Which questions would you find difficult? Draft responses to them.

The focus at interview could be on:

- *You as an individual*
  Are you an interesting person? What are your personal interests? What do you do outside school? Will you fit in with the existing team of teachers? Where do you see yourself in five or ten years' time?
- *You as a potential primary teacher*
  What attracts you to teaching as a career? Why do you want to work in that area, school, and with that age range? What is your philosophy of education?

How do you see yourself in the classroom? How would you organise, manage and assess the teaching and learning situation? How would you deal with specific situations (for example, bullying or bad behaviour)? What extra-curricular experiences could you bring to the school?

- *You as a potential subject coordinator*

   If you were asked to lead an area of the curriculum, what would it be? Why? What sorts of things would you need to think about? The role of the English coordinator is looked at more closely later in this chapter. You may also be asked to plan and teach (and sometimes evaluate) a lesson. You should be well used to being observed by this point so be confident. Choose a lesson that will give you a chance to shine and will motivate the children but without taking too many risks as you will be working with pupils you might never have met before. Plan in a detailed way and make sure you have all the necessary resources. You may also like to produce planning for activities that could be used as follow-ups to your lesson.

A final point: do not become disheartened if you do not succeed immediately. This is not unusual and it may take several interviews before you are successful. This reflects the current economic situation in education and the level of competition. Learn from the experience. Take opportunities offered to you to be given feedback on your performance at interview and act on the advice given. It pays to do so.

CAREER ENTRY AND DEVELOPMENT PROFILES AND INDUCTION

Since May 1999 (DfEE, 1999) all newly qualified teachers (NQTs) have been required to complete an induction period of three school terms if they are to work in maintained primary or secondary schools or non-maintained special school in England. This follows and builds upon the award of Qualified Teacher Status (QTS), which is awarded on the satisfactory completion of a programme of initial teacher training (ITT). NQTs who are awarded QTS but who do not satisfactorily complete a statutory induction period will not be eligible for employment as a teacher in a maintained school or non-maintained special school. Circular 5/99 (DfEE, 1999) sets out the arrangements for the induction period and the induction standards against which the NQTs will be assessed. The headteacher will be responsible for the assessment process but if he or she is not your induction tutor then some aspects of that assessment might be delegated to that tutor. You will be assessed against the national standards for completion of induction and will have to demonstrate that you continue to meet the QTS standards. You should have a number of formal review meetings throughout the year. At the final review, the head should tell you whether or not you will be recommended as meeting the standards for successfully completing the induction period. The head will make this recommendation to the appropriate body, usually the LEA, and this body will make the final decision. That is the bad news! But the good news is that the induction period was introduced not only as an additional assessment of NQTs but as a way of ensuring that support was given to new teachers. Career Entry and Development Profiles (CEDPs) provide the bridge between QTS and the induction year and should be the lynch pin of the support NQTs will receive in their first year of teaching.

BENEFITS, SUPPORT AND GUIDANCE

Your school induction tutor will help you build on the strengths and areas for development as identified in your CEDP. Together you should set targets and compile an action plan to help you to consolidate and develop your teaching skills. You will have a 10 per cent reduction in your teaching timetable for planned professional development and preparation. Your teaching will be observed and you should be given feedback on your performance and have opportunities to see experienced teachers at work. Unlike the original Career Entry Profiles (CEPs) the CEDPs look beyond the first year of teaching towards the rest of your career. In this way it is the beginning of your professional development as a reflective practitioner.

> **Activity 4**   Discuss with your tutor the following as a way of preparing for the completion of your CEDPs:
>
> - At this stage, which aspect(s) of teaching do you find most interesting and rewarding?
> - What do you consider to be your main strengths and achievements as a teacher?
> - In which aspects of teaching would you value further experience in the future?
> - As you look ahead to your career in teaching, you may be thinking about your longer term professional aspirations and goals. Do you have any thought at this stage about how you would like to see your career develop?

BECOMING AN ENGLISH COORDINATOR

The term 'English coordinator' will be used throughout even though the alternative 'literacy coordinator' is sometimes used. You should not be asked to be a subject coordinator during your induction year but you may well be preparing for this role from the outset. It is usually the case now in primary schools that all members of staff will have the responsibility for the coordination of at least one subject area.

> **Activity 5**   During your time in school discuss the role of the English coordinator to find out the following:
>
> - the administrative responsibilities, including ordering of resources;
> - the responsibility for the training of staff in new English initiatives;
> - the responsibility for data collection and target setting in English;
> - the monitoring of teachers in the teaching of English;
> - the responsibility for whole-school planning and assessment in English.

English Coordinator – a case study

S has been an English or literacy coordinator for two years in a primary school in the north of England. She finished her teacher training at the end of the 1960s so has seen many changes in the primary curriculum and certainly in the role of subject coordinators. S's specialism was religious education and she had, in the past, coordinated that subject but had had experience of being English coordinator for Key Stage 1 for a while before the introduction of the National Curriculum. She became Literacy coordinator when the previous member of staff with that responsibility left the school. S had been 'shadowing' or deputising for that member of staff. The school has a very useful system of shadowing, where all curriculum subjects have a coordinator but also a 'second-in-charge' who can help and, in the case of S, can step into the role if teachers leave the school. These deputies also, of course, have their own subjects to coordinate. Where possible the coordinators and shadows have experience in different key stages but this is not always logistically possible. S teaches in Key Stage 1. Her shadow is also a Key Stage 1 teacher but has experience of Key Stage 2.

So, how does S see her role? S is responsible for the management of the teaching and learning of all aspects of English across the whole of the primary school. That responsibility extends to the organisation of the library. In consultation with all members of staff she has drawn up long-term plans that address National Curriculum and Foundation Stage requirements. She has also checked teachers' medium-term plans. A relatively new role for coordinators has been the monitoring of teaching. This peer monitoring could have presented difficulties and demands interpersonal skills but appears, in the case of S, to have gone fairly smoothly. S has managed resources through a system of auditing and is responsible for the ordering of resources. Funding for the different curricular areas is related to the targets identified in the school's management plan and a lot of resources have been purchased in the recent past to meet the requirements of the NLS. An area that the school identified as needing further development was that of the children's creative writing. This obviously came under S's remit and she has visited other schools to look at good practice and also taken LEA advice. S has stressed that any developments are whole-school developments and no one individual has the daunting task of working unaided, in isolation.

S is also the school's assessment coordinator and so has taken a leading role in the analysis of assessment data and target setting but as a subject coordinator she would be involved in data analysis in her subject area.

> S has overseen the reorganisation of the Key Stage 2 library and has
> introduced a system of computer borrowing based on the children's
> fingerprints. This has most definitely motivated the upper primary
> children in terms of book borrowing. She also organises the school's
> book fair. She is still relatively new to the role but would expect to take
> over book-related events that have previously been held in schools.
> These might include arranging author visits and book weeks. She also
> has the reorganisation of the Key Stage 1 library to look forward to.

How qualified is S for her role? Certainly, English was not an original specialism but
she acquired experience throughout her years of teaching. It would be fair to say,
however, that it was the needs of the school rather than her own expertise that
resulted in her taking on this particular role. Having said that, she has carried out what
is now a management role with enthusiasm and commitment, has attended courses,
and has asked for LEA advice. Information gained has to be disseminated to staff
through school in-service training.

Research into the role of English coordinator

How typical is S's experience? Wragg et al. (1998) carried out research into the
improvement of literacy in primary schools and considered the role of the English/
literacy coordinator. Interviewees were asked to give a description of their role
(1998, pp. 95–6) and then the researchers categorised the identified responsibilities
in terms of the categories described in the Ofsted publication *Primary Matters*
(Ofsted, 1994). In this publication Her Majesty's Inspectors set out the following
responsibilities:

a)   to develop a clear view of the nature of their subject and its
     contribution to the wider curriculum of the school;
b)   to provide advice and documentation to help teachers to teach the
     subject and interrelate its constituent elements; and
c)   to play a major part in organising the teaching and learning resources
     of the subject so statutory requirements are covered.

(Ofsted, 1994, p. 9)

Wragg et al. found both from interviews and from the national questionnaire that the
coordinators described exactly the responsibilities identified in the Ofsted publication,

> . . . namely monitoring and evaluating teaching, providing advice, leading
> in-service training and helping to formulate and disseminate the school's
> language policy, giving practical advice.

(Wragg et al., 1998, p. 95)

Wragg et al. also found that as well as these core responsibilities there were additional tasks such as the organisation of bookshops and literacy events. Many responses also included the need for enthusiasm for the subject.

Our case study would seem, then, to describe a fairly typical English coordinator whose role has grown radically in recent years and includes many more management tasks. How confident do you feel that you could, with help, begin to carry out this role in your second year of teaching, remembering that, like S in the case study, English might not be your original specialism? So do not stop reading now because you consider yourself to be, perhaps, a science specialist at the moment. Doing this next activity might focus the mind.

Activity 6	For each of the following questions ask yourself how confident you feel in this respect and justify your response:

1 Am I up to date on English and English-related pedagogy?
2 Do I have an understanding of the key issues in English teaching?
3 Have I a broad overview of English in the curriculum as a whole?
4 Am I aware of recent research in English teaching?
5 Have I read the recent, relevant publications from government and other national bodies pertaining to the teaching of English?
6 Do I know what national inspection evidence tells us about different aspects of English teaching?
7 Will I be able to compare the achievement of pupils in my school with national standards in English?
8 Will I have the confidence, with support, to monitor teaching to ensure that the teaching of English is effective?
9 Do I understand how children with different needs learn most effectively in English?
10 Am I committed to providing pupils with experiences that will ensure that they become life-long readers?

Becoming an English coordinator can be one of the most exciting roles in education. Ensuring that all the pupils in your school experience and enjoy fiction and non-fiction books, meet authors, have stories read to them and get involved in book-making and drama activities is extremely rewarding. Enjoy it!

ACKNOWLEDGEMENT

Thanks to staff at Esh Winning Primary School, Esh Winning, Co. Durham for their help in describing the role of the English coordinator.

REFERENCES/SUGGESTIONS FOR FURTHER READING

If you would like to explore further some of the issues touched upon in this chapter, the following books should be of interest to you:

Bubb, S., Heilbron, R., Jones, C., Totterdell, M. and Bailey, M. (2002) *Improving Induction – Research-based Best Practice for Schools*, London: Routledge

DfEE (1999) *The Induction Period for Newly Qualified Teachers* (Circular 5/99), London: DfEE

Merchant, G. and Marsh, J. (1998) *Co-ordinating Primary Language and Literacy*, London: Paul Chapman

Moyles, J. (1995) *Beginning Teaching, Beginning Learning in Primary Education*, Buckingham: Open University Press

Moyles, J., Suschitsky, W. and Chapman, L. (1998) *Teaching Fledglings to Fly . . .* , London: Association of Teachers and Lecturers.

Ofsted (1994) *Primary Matters : A Discussion on Teaching and Learning in Primary Schools*, London: Ofsted Publications

Proctor, A., Entwistle, M., Judge, B. and McKenzie-Murdoch, S. (1995) *Learning to Teach in the Primary Classroom*, London: Routledge

Tyrell, J. and Gill, N. (2000) *Co-ordinating English at Key Stage 1*, London: Falmer Press

Waters, M. and Martin, T. (1999) *Co-ordinating English at Key Stage 2*, London: Falmer Press

Wragg, E., Wragg, C.M., Haynes, G.S. and Chamberlin, R.P. (1998) *Improving Literacy in the Primary School*, London: Routledge

THE *TIMES EDUCATIONAL SUPPLEMENT*

This weekly journal is a useful source of information about teaching posts around England, Wales and Scotland. In addition, occasional special interviews are aimed directly at students applying for their first teaching posts, and focusing on how to apply, what to expect at interview, what to expect in your first year, and so on.

15 Conclusion

JOHN WILLIAMSON

One of the underlying aims of this book has been to encourage you to think for yourself about the issues related to the teaching of English. That seems to be a fairly obvious intention but it is sometimes difficult to keep faith in the importance of independent thought when so much in education is prescribed and controlled. Professional development should never be simply about putting received ideas into practice. It is our view that proper acquisition of the standards cannot take place fully without some understanding of the underlying tensions, theoretical debates and research.

Increasingly, government agencies such as the TTA seek to help you develop into a skilled as well as an experienced teacher through the Professional Development initiatives which are now in place. These are laudable schemes but they depend entirely upon your readiness as a newly qualified teacher to see your professional and intellectual development as your own responsibility. You must be proactive in your approach to your own development in order to ensure a rich and fulfilling career.

This is perhaps the most fitting place to draw this introduction to English teaching to a close; we hope you have benefited from reading this book and from your experience as a PGCE student more generally but we also hope that you will be ready, both as a newly qualified teacher and in your longer term future in education, to continue to develop intellectually and professionally. In doing this, you will not only give more to your pupils but will ensure for yourself a rich and fulfilling career.

Index

Page numbers in *italics* refer to figures and tables.